D0762735
10th Internat … Exhibition
Citie… Architecture and Society

ART CENTER COLLEGE OF DESIGN
3 3220 00247 2038

Cities

Architecture and Society

la Biennale di Venezia

10. Mostra Internazionale di Architettura

Fondazione
La Biennale di Venezia

Friends of La Biennale
Friends of La Biennale is an independent, international, non-party initiative, aimed at public or private companies and associations. The funds collected will be used to support the activities and programmes of La Biennale. Companies and bodies (in the person of their presidents and managing directors) can join the initiative. The invitation is also for individuals, on the bases of their competence in the areas in which La Biennale works and their specific cultural, academic and political interests in Italy and abroad.

Founding members

Assicurazioni Generali
Antoine Bernheim, *president*

Edizione Holding
Gilberto Benetton, *president*

Participating members

Colussi
Angelo Colussi, *president*

Gruppo Coin
Stefano Beraldo, *managing director*

Porsche Italia
Loris Casadei, *general manager*

RaiCinema
Giancarlo Leone, *managing director*

Thanks to Friends of La Biennale for the support to the activities.

10th International Architecture Exhibition
Cities. Architecture and Society

Director
Richard Burdett

Manager
Renato Quaglia

Administrative secretariat
Stefania Guerra
Maria Bruschi

Organizing coordination
Rita Bertoni
Paolo Cimarosti

Participating countries Responsible exhibition venues
Roberto Rosolen

Collateral events, jury and workshop organization
Paolo Scibelli
with Chiara Costa

Public promotion and didactics activity
Martina Flaborea
Arabella Adamo
Fabiana Causin
Lucia De Manincor

Relations with Partner
Micol Saleri

Workshop curator
Guido Martinotti

Coordinator Learning from Cities project
Francesco Garofalo

Exhibition content development
Sarah Ichioka
(coordination)

Spatial data research (London School of Economics/Urban Age)
Bruno Moser
(coordination)
Miguel Kanai
Adegbola Ojo
Andres Tacsir
Jorge Vera-Garcia
Megan Worthington

Film/video project manager
Cassim Shepard
(editing and supervision)
Michael Ichioka
(sound assistant)
Paul Bercovitch
(sound editor)

Installation concept
Cibic & Partners

Project by
Aldo Cibic
Luigi Marchetti

Project managers
Gian Luca Poggi
Roberta Sartori
Luigi Fumagalli

Art direction and exhibition graphic design
FRAGILE
Mario Trimarchi
Andrea Plenter
Pamela Visconti
Alessandro Boscarino
Marco Miglio
Elena Riva
Julia Maquieira
Luisa Vozza
Chiara Poletti
Chiara Banchini

Art direction and communication graphic design
Dario and Fabio Zannier

Rescape
Neutral
Christian Grou
Tapio Snellman
Cristina Liao
Michael Castellana

Mobility studies
Systematica
Fabio Casiroli
Davide Boazzi

Picture research
Mika Burdett
Ji Yoon Moon
Emily Smith
Valentina Vecchio

Film archive
John Smith, BBC Worldwide
Alan Yentob, BBC
Claire Gould and Kate Warner, BBC Motion Gallery
Stella Waltemade and Lluis Ruscalleda, Footage Farm
Daisy Njoku, Human Studies Film Archive—Smithsonian Institution Museum Support Center, Washington D.C.
James Kearney, Film Images, London

Exhibition texts translation
Manuela Crea
Floriana Pagano

Cities of Stone
Section of the 10th International Architecture Exhbition promoted by the project *Sensi Contemporanei*

Curator
Claudio D'Amato Guerrieri

Organizing coordination
Matteo De Vittor

Franco Defilippis
Giuseppe Fallacara
Michele Montemurro

Installation concept
Cerardo Cejas
La Biennale di Venezia Servizi SpA
Enzo Magris
La Biennale di Venezia Servizi SpA

Website editor
Dario Daddabbo
Marco Orsini

Photographic campaign
Guido Petriccioli

Graphic design
Nunzio Perrone

City-Port
Section of the 10th International Architecture Exhbition promoted by the project *Sensi Contemporanei*

Curator
Rinio Bruttomesso

Organizing coordination
Francesca Montorio

General coordination
Marta Moretti

Portus Prize coordination
Paola Pierotti

Installation coordination
Nicola Tonutti

International relations
Maria Giulia da Sacco
Mara Vittori

International section consultant
Alessandra Badami

Relations with italian cities
Oriana Giovinazzi

Portus Prize secretariat
Paola Vitiello

Curator secretariat
Federica Marafante

Secretariat
Cinzia Mauri
Antonella Ruggiero

Installation concept
Davide Testi
La Biennale di Venezia Servizi SpA

Palazzo Forcella De Seta
City-Port. Maps for New Urban Routes
Studio Italo Rota & Partners

Sant'Erasmo
City-Port. Great South
City-Port. Palermo, Mediterraneo
Alessandra Raso,
Luca Poncellini,
Matteo Raso,
Stefano Testa / CLIOSTRAAT

EXPA Galleria di Architettura
City-Port. Portus Architecture Prize
Tiziano Di Cara
and Giuseppe Romano

Portus Prize Website
Mario Caruso
AgoràMed

Italian Pavilion
Commissioner
Pio Baldi

Curator
Franco Purini
with Nicola Marzot
Margherita Petranzan
Livio Sacchi

Installation project
Franco Purini
with Massimiliano De Meo
Carlo Meo Colombo
Franco Puccetti
Valter Tronchin

Organizing coordination
Renato Quaglia

Installation management
Angelo Boscolo

Structures and security management
Enzo Magris

Film
Marta Francocci

Direction
Giorgio De Finis

Scientific advisor
Franco Purini
Livio Sacchi

Le Città Nuove
Franco Purini
Livio Sacchi
Laboratorio di Disegno della Facoltà di Architettura di Pescara
Emiliano Auriemma
Giovanni Caffio
Alessandro Luigini
Massimiliano Mazzetta
Verusca Collicchio
Fabrizio De Rosa
Tatiana Mariani
Francesco Martelli
Roberto Potenza
Fabrizio Susi

Webcam
Marco Brizzi
Furio Barzon

Vema Masterplan
Franco Purini
with
Francesco Menegatti

Model
DIAPREM, Facoltà di Architettura di Ferrara

Logistic technical services
Cristiano Frizzele

Nicola Bon
Lucio Ramelli
Pino Simeoni
Maurizio Urso

Insurance and transport of works
Alessandra Durand de la Penne
Sandra Montagner

Matteo Liguigli

Angela Bianco
Luana Lovisetto
Elena Seghetti

Purchasing
Fabio Pacifico
Marianna Ferrazzuto

La Biennale di Venezia Servizi SpA

Exhibition concept
Manuela Lucà Dazio

Massimiliano Bigarello
Nicola Ragazzini
Silvia Catami

Logistic, facilities and security
Piero Novello
Mascia Pavon

Organizing services
Angelo Boscolo
Maurizio Celoni
Elisabetta Parmesan
Jessica Giassi
Alessandro Mezzalira
Cristiana Scavone

Technology and information sistems
Andrea Bonaldo
Michele Schiavon
Leonardo Viale

Vernissage press room installation concept
Elena Lingeri

Communications
Giovanna Usvardi

Assistant to Communications
Veronica Mozzetti-Monterumici

Communications administrative secretariat
Cristina Lion

Head of press office Architecture
Alessandra Santerini

Assistants to press office and accreditation
Elena Casadoro
Lucia Veronesi

with Sara Chiotto and Giovanni Sgrignuolo

Biennale press office coordination
Paolo Lughi

International press accreditation
Michela Lazzarin

Italian press accreditation
Fiorella Tagliapietra

Website
Giovanni Alberti

Publicity and graphic design office coordination
Eugenia Fiorin

Michela Mason

Lucia Toso

Maddalena Pietragnoli

Graphic realization
Alberta de Grenet
Nicola Monaco

Photographer
Giorgio Zucchiatti

Catalogue

Catalogue content development
Sarah Ichioka

Interviews
Ellis Woodman

Editorial staff
Francesca Del Puglia

Chiara Calciolari
Letizia Gullo
Stefania Ivanovich
Valentina Vecchio

Catalogue graphic design
Dario and Fabio Zannier

Fund management
Gaetano Guerci (ad interim)

Elena Croci

Francesco Di Cesare
Marzia Cervellin
with Glenda Manzetto

Events management
Gaetano Guerci (ad interim)

Elena Croci

Events management administrative secretariat
Cristina Graziussi

Protocol office and events organization
Elisa Ceri

Cristina Cinti
Daniele Maruca
Eleonora Mayerle

Daniela Dagnino Donà dalle Rose

Hospitality
Enrica Zanchetta

Laura Aimone
Zeudi Fiorasi

President and General manager's secretarial office
Daniela Barcaro
Roberta Savoldello

Valentina Baldessari

General manager staff
Sandro Vettor

Legal services
Debora Rossi

Cinzia Bernardi
Alberto Bogoni
Federica Marchiori

Human resources
Debora Rossi

Silvia Bruni
Graziano Carrer
Giovanni Drudi
Cristina Innocenti
Antonella Sfriso
Alessia Viviani

Chief Financial Office
Valentina Borsato

Martina Fiori
Bruna Gabbiato
Manuela Pellicciolli
Cristiano Tanduo
Giorgio Vergombello
Sara Vianello
Leandro Zennaro

Special projects
Pina Maugeri

Jörn Brandmeyer
Davide Ferrante
Arianna Laurenzi

Archivio Storico delle Arti Contemporanee
Giorgio Busetto

Angelo Bacci
Maria Elena Cazzaro
Valentina Da Tos
Erica De Luigi
Lia Durante
Roberta Fontanin
Giuliana Fusco
Michele Mangione
Giovanna Pasini
Antonia Possamai
Adriana Scalise
Michela Stancescu

Catalogne production
Marsilio Editori

Editing and layout
in.pagina srl
Mestre-Venezia

Copy editing and translations
David Graham

Photolithography
Fotolito Veneta
San Martino Buonalbergo, Verona

Press
Offset Print Veneta
Verona

Binding
Legatoria Barizza
Loreggia, Padova

Ca' Giustianian,
San Marco 1364/a
30124 Venezia
www.labiennale .org

isbn 88-317-8956

Distribuited in the UK and Europe
By Windsor Books
The Boundary
Wheatley Road
Garsington, Oxford ox44 9EJ

First edition: september 2006

10th International Architecture Exhibition
Cities

The 2006 edition of the International Architecture Exhibition – the tenth – proposes rather than an exhibition of (models and examples of) architecture, a discourse on the consequences and possibilities of architecture applied to urban and meta-urban systems: the world-city. A discourse on architecture offering interpretations of themes closely related to questions of civil coexistence, the obligation to plan the future and its proposals for changing the way of living in the present.

The Exhibition directed by Richard Burdett is entitled *Cities. Architecture and Society*, and focuses on the key themes currently faced by urban and meta-urban agglomerations with a population of over three or four million (the new global cities). The Exhibition analyses aspects that have become critical today: the interaction between city, architecture and inhabitants; the role of architects and architecture in the creation of democratic and sustainable urban contexts; the politics of intervention, and the actions of governing and developing.

At the Corderie dell'Arsenale the urban experiences of some of the most emblematic cities on four continents are represented: Shanghai, Mumbai and Tokyo in Asia; Caracas, Mexico City, Bogotá, São Paulo, Los Angeles and New York in the Americas; Johannesburg, Cairo and Istanbul in Africa and the Mediterranean area; London, Barcelona, Berlin and Milan-Turin in Europe. In the Padiglione Italia at the Giardini, some international research institutes present models and projects on an urban and meta-urban scale. Some specialized publishers present projects and points of view on contemporary and historical architectural planning. The traditional collateral events will this year be flanked by three partners' initiatives. The historic presence of over 50 countries with their own national pavilions will be accompanied by a workshop with some of the Mayors of major Italian and international cities, providing an opportunity for dialogue and direct contact which La Biennale, together with its partners, intends offering on the level of experiences, models and policies for growth.

The Exhibition will, once it closes, present a "manifesto for twenty-first century cities" to be proposed to those governing or participating in the government of cities and the complex systems regulating their rhythms and development.

With a new project that saw the involvement not only of the Biennale, but also of the Ministero dell'Economia (Dipartimento delle Politiche di Sviluppo e Coesione) and the Ministero dei Beni e delle Attività Culturali - DARC, many contemporary art exhibitions and training, study and promotional activities in 2003 and 2004 were held in seven regions of the South of Italy and their main cities. Following the renewed presentation of the 9th International Architecture Exhibition, "Metamorph" in Reggio Calabria in December 2005, the discussion on architectural consequences and possibilities finds concrete (and often urgent) application opportunities in Italy's southern regions, in redefining urban trading centres (within the relation *City-Port*, the same of the exhibitions curated by Rinio Bruttomesso), as also in the projects for restoring the Italian and Mediterranean coastal landscape (in the *Cities of Stone* exhibitions curated by Claudio d'Amato Guerrieri).

The inauguration of a section of the 10th International Architecture Exhibition in Palermo (the *City-Port* exhibition), assumes a further value tied to the function that La Biennale di Venezia has wished and succeeded in taking on, in recent years, offering all of its own skills and cultural energies to the Country and its strategies for development.

With the new Italian Pavilion (which will be inaugurated this year at the Arsenale in Venice by the Biennale and DARC), and the exhibition project that Franco Purini is dedicating to a future city (possibly to be founded between Verona and Mantua), the presence of an exhibition that is explicitly representative of the Italian architectural culture (this year and in 2008; in 2007 for art) allows to respond to the expectations of the entire national system, now at last on the same level as the opportunities available in other Countries.

Moreover, it makes it possible to complete, with a further and different approach, the subject of the city that this 10th International Architecture Exhibition brings into focus on various levels and scales, and to be able to declare, once more and as in the case of other events in the disciplines covered by the Biennale, that only various viewpoints enable us to start understanding the present.

10th International Architecture Exhibition

la Biennale di Venezia

10. Mostra Internazionale di Architettura

Cities. Architecture and Society

Director
Richard Burdett

Venice
10 September – 19 November 2006

Cities of Stone

Curator
Claudio D'Amato Guerrieri

Venice
10 September – 19 November 2006

Section of the 10th International Architecture Exhibition promoted by

sensi CONTEMPORANEI

la Biennale di Venezia

with

City-Port

Curator
Rinio Bruttomesso

Palermo
15 October 2006 – 14 January 2007

Section of the 10th International Architecture Exhibition promoted by

sensi CONTEMPORANEI

Ministero dell'Economia e delle Finanze MEF

Ministero per i beni e le attività culturali
Dipartimento per i beni culturali e paesaggistici
DARC Direzione generale per l'architettura e l'arte contemporanee

la Biennale di Venezia

with

and with

Italian Pavilion

Curator
Franco Purini

Commissioner
Pio Baldi

Venice
10 September – 19 November 2006

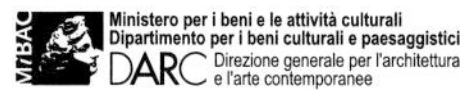

10th International Architecture Exhibition

For the support of 10th International Architecture Exhibition Fondazione La Biennale di Venezia thanks

Main Partner

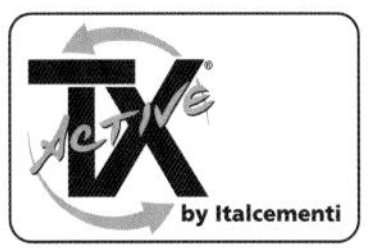

Partner

Sponsor

Technical sponsors

Sponsors Cities of Stone

Sponsors City-Port

Sponsors Italian Pavilion

Introduction

Davide Croff
President of La Biennale di Venezia

Now, in 2006, the third year of activity for the Fondazione that directs the Biennale di Venezia, we can claim that the Architecture Section is the main organizational change, and symbol of the new aims of the Fondazione itself.

The main features of this new Biennale are the responsibility and centrality of its thematic choices, the opening of the Italian Pavilion in the Tese delle Vergini, the two epoch-making exhibition events on the South of Italy, for the first time presented simultaneously in Venice and Palermo, the intense programme of international conferences and workshops and the propositional presence of important private partners. It is a Biennale that intends spending its second century taking new roads, intensifying and radicalising the initiatives undertaken both in and out of Venice rather than simply resting on its past.

It is no mere chance that the emblem of this new direction is the Architecture Section. Despite it concerning one of the oldest artistic disciplines, it is a very young part of the more than a century old Biennale: this is the 10th International Architecture Exhibition in a quarter of a century. But it has mainly been distinguished by its successful provocation, its courageous ability to find new exhibition spaces and new organizational formulas, as is widely the case again this year, gradually earning the international acclaim both of the critics and the public (whose numbers at the last two presentations exceeded the respectable figure of 100,000 over its two month season).

We briefly recall that it was the fundamental exhibition La presenza del passato (The presence of the past), directed by Paolo Portoghesi, that in 1980 inaugurated the new section on contemporary architecture.

Organized at the Arsenale, the exhibition also had the merit of reopening one of the oldest and most interesting spaces of the Serenissima, an architectural heritage subsequently further restored by the Biennale and gradually returned to Venice and the world. Other pioneering initiatives were taken in the '70s along the way, such as the A proposito del Mulino Stucky (About the Mulino Stucky) conference on the possible ways to use this space, which is now finally being restored, and the celebrated and much quoted Teatro del Mondo (World Theatre) presented in winter 1979-1980 by Aldo Rossi at the Punta della Dogana, another place still at the centre of ongoing debates on its possible use.

These are just some of the more significant examples of our history that it is right to recall in presenting this year's news, because it is precisely with the open, innovative spirit of those initiatives and their function as a stimulus that we want to reconnect.

We firstly emphasize the reason for the theme chosen by the Biennale for this 10th Exhibition: *Cities. Architecture and Society*.

The theme is intended to confirm the Biennale's wish to aim for a highly legible, international formula, to study a critical aspect in contemporary society that now directly affects most of the planet's population and that for a decade has engaged town planners: the changes going on in the physical and social morphology of the land and of urban agglomerates.

The Biennale invited one of the leading urbanism experts in the world, the Englishman Richard Burdett, to direct the 10th Exhibition around this theme. We sincerely thank him for the enthusiasm and commitment with which he has directed the exhibition, presenting the urban experiences of 16 major cities on four continents. It will stay in the memory of specialists and the public for its scientific rigour, its great expository clarity and its concrete approach to the new urban centres' problems of governance.

On the logistical innovation and cultural front, the Biennale is for the first time opening an Italian Pavilion. It will this year be devoted to highlighting contemporary

Italian architecture, curated by Franco Purini. The pavilion will then be used for contemporary Italian art during the editions of the International Art Exhibition. This 1000-square-metre space in the first Tesa delle Vergini at the Arsenale, in the extraordinary multipurpose buildings that will house the Biennale of the future, is the result of collaboration between the Biennale and the Ministero per i Beni e le Attività Culturali – DARC. Building on the Biennale's great tradition of research and of finding new talent, it will make a decisive contribution to the international circulation and growth of our architects and artists. The Italian Pavilion thus completes the picture of national participation: 50 at this 10th International Architecture Exhibition, all of whom we want to thank, because since the origins of the Biennale they have represented its absolute originality and an incalculable exhibition and organisational strength.

The other important news is the structure of the exhibition itself. It is being organised in several sections and venues that are intended to be distinct but complementary.

The changes in architecture and town planning in the regions of South Italy are the focus of two exhibition events: one in Venice, at the Artiglierie dell'Arsenale, *Città di Pietra* (*Cities of Stone*), curated by Claudio D'Amato Guerrieri; the other in Palermo, *Città–Porto* (*City-Port*), curated by Rinio Bruttomesso, which will open in October and close in January 2007, thus extending the normal timing and locations of the Architecture Biennale.

These two events reflect the constituent form and aims of Sensi contemporanei, the project promoted since 2003 by the Biennale, the Ministero per i Beni e le Attività Culturali – DARC, and the Ministero dell'Economia e delle Finanze – DPS, for the development of contemporary art and architecture in the Italian South.

Why have the Biennale and the two ministries again joined forces this year to organise two initiatives on the South at the same time as the 10th International Architecture Exhibition?

Firstly as a matter of principle, to find new ways of meeting the Biennale's moral obligation to disseminate its knowledge and initiatives.

We think that with two complex events of original quality arising from the Biennale's experience in the South over these years we can suggest the advisability of new and interesting programming.

Secondly, but this is perhaps a corollary of the first consideration, we show how the cities and regions of Italy can even more unite to achieve common aims, also in terms of cultural development.

The Biennale is trying to go beyond a traditional condition with these initiatives, to take on new roles. In particular, we are sure of the interest that will be aroused by the main exhibition. But having noted the enthusiasm for previous Sensi contemporanei activities, which saw a solid increase in numbers, we trust in the innovation and success of the two exhibitions on the architecture of the South, together illuminated by the Mediterranean light of Venice and Palermo, and therefore ideally drawn together.

This is also because, as Le Corbusier said, architecture must above all be 'forms assembled in light'.

Introduction

Richard Burdett
Director 10th International Architecture Exhibition
La Biennale di Venezia

The second volume of the catalogue of the 10th International Architecture Exhibition *Cities. Architecture and society* celebrates cities at a moment in time when more than half the world's population has moved into urban areas. With contributions of over 50 countries whose work is exhibited in the national pavilions – including the new Italian pavilion featuring the exhibition *Italia-y-2026. Invitation to Vema* curated by Franco Purini - in the Giardini and collateral events across Venice, it provides a truly global perspective of what is happening in cities across the world today, as illustrated on the map (next page).
The focus on Southern Italy and the Mediterranean afforded by the exhibitions *Cities of Stone* at the Arsenale and *City-Port* in Palermo (both part of the 'Sensi contemporanei' initiative at the 10th International Architecture Exhibition) gives even greater depth and precision to the understanding of the contemporary urban condition.

With its multi-faceted, multi-layered and multi-locational initiatives, the 10th International Architecture Exhibition La Biennale di Venezia perhaps more than any previous manifestations - offers the visitor and the reader an opportunity to travel across a range of urban panoramas and experiences unavailable to any single individual in their own lifetime. As such, this Biennale offers not just an overview of how architects and urban designers respond to the challenges of massive urban migration, the energy crisis and social inclusion but also acts as a platform for research and debate that will influence the shape and thinking about cities in the twenty-first century.

I would like to acknowledge the enormous energy and commitment of all the commissioners, curators and collaborators who have worked so hard to respond to the theme of *Cities. Architecture and society* and thank the hundreds of individuals across the world who have contributed to this publication and the realization of the 10th International Architecture Exhibition. In addition, I offer my thanks to the many sponsors who have contributed to the special partners projects and other initiatives which have made this exhibition possible.

Director's acknowledgements

Richard Burdett
September 2006

The *Cities. Architecture and Society* exhibition would not have happened without the involvement of over one hundred people listed overleaf – self-motivated teams in each city who worked incessantly to produce material for the Biennale, driven by a collective passion for cities which we celebrate in Venice. In particular, though, I want to thank three colleagues based at the London School of Economics without whose personal commitment nothing at all would have ever happened at my end: Sarah Ichioka, who tirelessly travelled across the world and helped me every inch of the way to shape the intellectual content and structure of the exhibition and publications, including this catalogue which she co-edited; Bruno Moser, who reinvented himself as a specialist on every possible source of data on cities and generator of sublime images; and Cassim Shepard, whose thoughtful eye has translated human experiences of sixteen cities on screen. I have relied on a 'tribe of urbanists' - Richard Sennett, Saskia Sassen, Richard Rogers, Jerry Frug, Deyan Sudjic, Josep Acebillo, Jacques Herzog, Guido Martinotti, Andy Altman and Norman Foster, amongst others – for their insights on cities. The strong elements of the exhibition come from them, the weaknesses are all mine. The approach of an interdisciplinary analysis of cities, which links urban form to urban society, comes from the pioneering work carried out at the Urban Age project, organised by the LSE with Deutsche Bank's Alfred Herrhausen Society, a programme of conferences and investigations on of six of the cities included in the Venice Biennale. Without Wolfgang Nowak and the AHS support of this ongoing project, much of the material gathered in this exhibition simply would not exist. Guido Martinotti took on the task of exposing the architectural community to profound social thinking by curating the workshops for the Biennale. Other colleagues at the LSE have provided input and support, including Philip Rode and Miguel Kanai (who doubled as co-author and Hispanic-Japanese interpreter) together with a team of researchers led by Bruno Moser. Mika Burdett lived the intensity of the one year journey and contributed in many more ways than advising on the selection of images, supported by researchers Emily Smith and Ji Yoon Moon. Aldo Cibic and Luigi Marchetti and their colleagues at Cibic & Partners held my hand throughout in conceiving the experience of the show, and Mario Trimarchi with his team at Fragile and the Neutral team made me rethink how to communicate to the Biennale's diverse public. John Smith and Alan Yentob allowed us to use archive footage from the BBC archives. Ultimately, I would have been unable to achieve anything without the generous financial contributions from all the sponsors and wish to single out Luigi and Stefania Zunino and the Gruppo Risanamento for their patronage. The large and multi-talented Venice Biennale team, led by Renato Quaglia, with special input from Rita Bertoni and Manuela Lucà Dazio, have been all-too tolerant of my delays and indecisions, and helped steer this large urban tanker to its home in Venice. I am indebted to them all.

Acknowledgments

For the collaboration to the realization of the 10th International Architecture Exhibition
La Fondazione La Biennale di Venezia with Richard Burdett thank

Ministero della Difesa, Marina Militare di Venezia
Ammiraglio Div. Ernesto Muliere, Comandante Istituto Studi Militari e Presidio Marina Militare
Comandante di Vascello Francesco Carlo Bottoni, Istituto Studi Militari e Presidio Marina Militare
Comandante di Vascello Cristiano Patrese, Istituto Studi Militari e Presidio Marina Militare

Ministero delle Finanze, Agenzia del Demanio, sede di Venezia

Ministero delle Finanze, Circoscrizione Doganale Venezia II, Venezia Salute e Venezia Marittima

Soprintendenza per i Beni Ambientali e Architettonici di Venezia

Regione Veneto

Autorità Portuale di Venezia

Capitaneria di Porto

Barcelona
Barcelona Regional
Josep Acebillo
Eva Serra
Joana Llinas

Iñigo Bujedo Aguirre
Gabriele Basilico
Beth Galí
Roger Gual
Manuel Huerga
Jordi Todó/Tavisa

Berlin
Barbara Hoidn
Wilfried Wang

Senatsverwaltung für Stadtentwicklung, Berlin

Jens Bisky
Robert Fenz
Philipp Meuser
Lena Mueller
Markus Rosenthal
Paolo Rosselli
Anja Schlamann
Wendy Taylor
Judith Utz

Bogotá
Por el Pais que Queremos Foundation
Oscar Edmundo Diaz
Enrique Penalosa
Eduardo Plata
Juan Camilo Macias
Carolina Rogelio

Grupo Esperienze Urbane
Simone Grobberio
Guido Robazza

Diana Barco
Claudia Bermudez
Lorenzo Castro
Adriana Cobo Corey
Alvaro Duran
Jose Roberto de Andrade Filho
Felipe González
Alicia Naranjo
José Camilo Santamaría
Armando Silva
Giovanna Silva

Cairo
Seif El Rashidi
Maria Golia

Centre d'Etudes et de Documentation Economiques, Juridiques et Sociales (CEDEJ)
Halla Bayoumi

Contemporary Image Collective
Christian Grou
Magdi Habachi
Linx Productions for the Aga Khan Development Network
Gary Otte
Mohamed El Sawy
Heiner Schmitt
Randa Shaath
Yahia Shawkat
Tapio Snellman
Nick Warner
Dario Zannier

Caracas
Urban Think Tank
Alfredo Brillembourg
Hubert Klumpner
Marcelo Elola
Karolina Stahl

Alcaldía del Distrito Metropolitano de Caracas
Hector Sanchez

Axel Capriles
Sara Muzio
Carlos Armando Planchart
Luisa Ramírez
Art Rothfuss

Istanbul
Bilgi University
Murat Guvenç
Serhan Ada
Ayca Ince
Sevin Yildiz

Human Settlements Association
Korhan Gumus
Elsa Mekki-Berrada

Instanbul Metropolitan Planning and Urban Design Center
Huseyin Kaptan
M. Sinan Özden

Emre Akay
Elif Akcali
Gabriele Basilico
Metin Cavus

Istanbul Metropolitan Municipality
Emrah Engindeniz

Francesco Jodice
Margarete von Lupin
Andy Rice
David Rosenthal
Paolo Rosselli

Johannesburg
Lindsay Bremner

Hlakanaphila Analytics (s21)
Michael O'Donovan

Statistics South Africa
Kevin Parry

Adam Broomberg
Oliver Chanarin
Ismail Farouk
Loanna Hoffmann
Mpethi Morojele
Mabet Van Rensburg
Ilana Ron

London
GLA Architecture & Urbanism Unit
Eleanor Fawcett
Ben Burley
Emily Greeves
Mark Brearley
Richard Rogers
Deborah Mathieson
Alex Bax
Jamie Dean
Paul Harper
Toby Goevert

Transport for London
Isabel Dedring

Matteo Cainer
James Goggin
Jo Murtagh
Luca Paci
Deyan Sudjic
Alexander Weil

Architecture Foundation
Elias Redstone

Newbetter
Cityscape
Hayes Davidson
Richard Bryant
Paolo Rosselli

Los Angeles
University of California, Los Angeles
Ed Soja
Ava Bromberg
Jacqueline Leavitt
Luca Martinazzoli

Jeffrey Inaba

Helen Kolikow Garber
Lars Jan
Young Sun Kim
Richard Koshalek
Thom Mayne
Nicholas Olsberg
Paul Preissner
Bas Princen
Paolo Rosselli
Michael Speaks
Jean Paul Travers
Donald J Waldie
Peter Zellner

Mexico City
Pamela Puchalski
Alejandro Hernandez

Pablo Benlliure
Dante Busquets
José Castillo
Gareth Jones
Francisco (Cisco) Laresgoiti
Armin Linke
Enrique Martin-Moreno
Maria Moreno
Enrique Norten
Iliana Ortega-Alcazar
Scott Peterman
Juan Villoro

Milan and Turin
Stefano Boeri

Università degli Studi di Milano-Bicocca
Guido Martinotti
Marxiano Melotti
Giovanni Oggioni

Gaia Caramellino
Filippo De Pieri

Bruna Biamino
Mario Boffi
Vincenzo Castella
Matteo Cibic
Piero Derossi
dot dot dot productions
Michele d'Ottavio
Marianna Dovidio
Davide Ferrario
Lorenzo Pallotta
Renzo Piano
Fabio Terragni

Mumbai
Urban Design Research Institute
Rahul Mehrotra
Benita Menezes
Pankaj Joshi
Kapil Gupta

Biond Software
Milind Dalvi
Amit Dutta

Shai Heredia
Suketu Mehta
Gagan Palrecha
Sadia Shepard
Vineet Shroff
Dhiren Shukla
Jehangir Sorabjee
Rajesh Vora
Dario Zannier

New York City
Pamela Puchalski

NYC Department of City Planning
Amanda Burden
Jennifer Posner

Princeton University
Guy Nordenson

Andy Altman

Gabriele Basilico
Richard Berenholtz
Purcell Carson
Majora Carter
Susan Fainstein
Hope Hall
Leah Meyerhoff
Alexander Weil

São Paulo
Prefeitura Municipal de São Paulo
Helena Maria Gasparian
Adriana Telles Ribeiro

Raul Juste Lores

Universidade de São Paulo
Regina Meyer

Carlos Calil
Rose Carmona
Giuliano Cedroni
Gustavo Cedroni
Otavio Cury
Roque Fernandes
Armin Linke
Regina Monteiro
Luiz Arthur Leirão Vieira
Milu Villela
Jacopo Crivelli Visconti

Shanghai
Qingyun Ma
Stephan Jentsch
Zheng Shiling

Olivo Barbieri
Peter Bialobrzeski
Bizart Center
Brancolini Grimaldi Arte Contemporanea
Andrea Cavazzuti
Yung Ho Chang
Yang Fudong
Tomasz Gubernat
Sze Tsung Leong
Ann Mu
Ryan Pyle
Davide Quadrio
Paolo Rosselli
StART
Caterina Tognon Pimpini
Paola Tognon
Alexander Weil
Lu Yue

Tokyo
Atelier Bow-Wow
Momoyo Kaijima
Yoshiharu Tsukamoto

Tokyo University of Science
Kaori Ito

Rumiko Ito

Hiroshi Ota

Mark Dytham
Tenrunobu Fujimori
Shigeru Itoh
Francesco Jodice
Miguel Kanai
Masahiro Katsuno
Marieke Kums
Naomichi Kurata
Takashi Machimura
Ryue Nishizawa
Takeo Obayashi
Miki Okabe
Akio Okamoto
John Parbury

Research Institute of Economy, Trade and Industry (RIETI)
Masato Hisatake
Masahiro Katsuno

Saskia Sassen
Norbert Schoerner
Kazuyo Sejima
Kimihiro Sonoda
Tomoaki Tanaka

Tokyo Metropolitan Government
Kenichiro Kawabe

Contents

AcoruñaAdelaideAlbaceteAlcobaçaAlmadaAlmeríaAmsterdamArcipelagoEgeoAscoliPicenoAscona
BadajozBallarat**Barcelona**BaselBe'erShevaBèglesBegurBeijingBelgradeBellinzona**Berlin**Bilbao**Bogotá**
BolognaBostonBragaBraunschweigBremenBrisbaneBrnoBrusselsBucurestiBudapestBuenosAires
CádizCaenCagliari**Cairo**CalaisCambridgeCapeTown**Caracas**ChiassoChiosChongqingChonlaDoCiudad
RealClaroCoimbraCologneCórdobaDarmstadtDetroitDresdenDubayyDubrovnikDunkirkDurbanDüsseldorf
EmeraldIsleFerraraFrankfurtFukuokaGandGattonGenovaGerraGambarognoGiurgiuGondolaGuadalajara
GuangzhouHakodateHaifaHalleHamburgHangzhouHellínHelsinkiHongKongIcheonIoannina**Istanbul**
IvanovoJerusalemJinHua**Johannesburg**KaiserslauternKanagawaKelerberrinKirunaKowloonKumamoto
KyotoL'HospitaletdeLlobregatLagosLasPalmasdeGranCanariaLefkosiaLeipzigLeiriaLinzLisboaLiverpool

LjubljanaLocarno**LondonLosAngeles**LouvainLaNeuveLuganoLugoLuxembourgMacauMadridManchester
MarseilleMelbourneMendrisio**MéxicoCityMilano**MinusioMontevideoMoscow**Mumbai**MunichNagano
NamurNanjingNant'ouNantesNapoliNeuchâtelNewOrleans**NewYork**NiigataNíjarNingboNovisadOita
OlotOuluPalenciaParisPatraPerthPescaraPoitiersPoitouCharentesPorthElizabethPortoPrahaP'yongyang
RabatRainbowRavnaGoraReykjavíkRigaRijekaRomaRoncasopraAsconaRosariodelTalaRotterdam
RoubaixSanSebastiánSantaDomingoSantanderSantiago**SãoPaulo**Sevilla**Shanghai**SheffieldShizuokaSibiu
SingaporeSiracusaSkopjeSeoulSplitStuttgartSydneyT'ainanT'aipeiT'bilisiTallinTarifaTartuTegnaTelAviv
ThessalonikiTirana**Tokyo**TongLi**Torino**TromsøTübingenValaeValenciaVancouverVeneziaVeniceVeronaVianado
CasteloVigoVilladoCondeVranceaWaggawaggaWarszawaWienXi'anYerevanYilanYinanZaragozaZürich

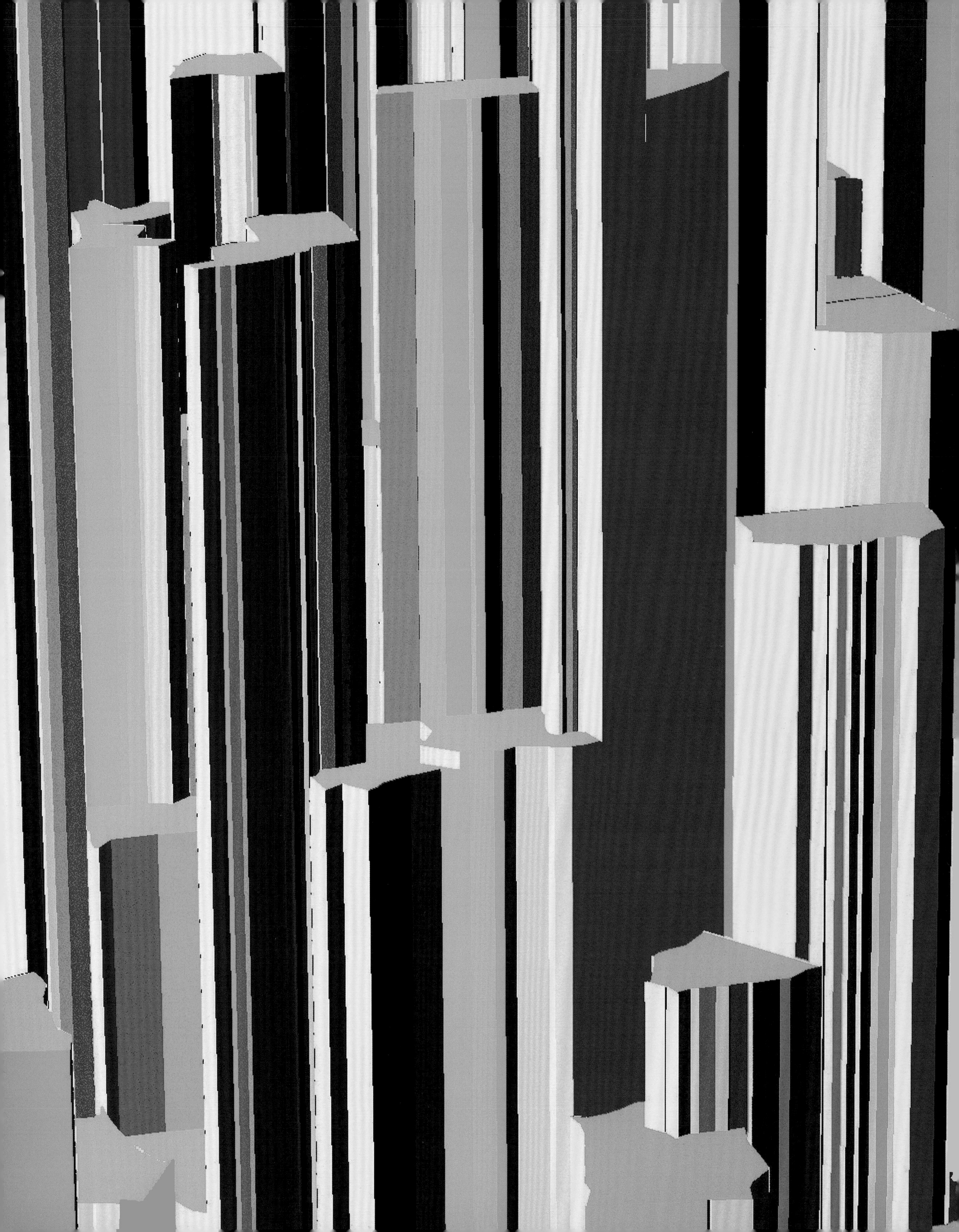

Cities of Stone

Section of the 10th International Architecture Exhibition
promoted by the project

sensi
CONTEMPORANEI

Venice, 10 September – 19 November 2006
Curator: Claudio D'Amato Guerrieri

la Biennale di Venezia

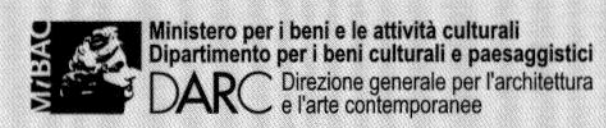

with

Main Partner

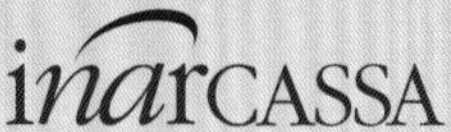

Sponsor

Cities of Stone

Curator: Claudio D'Amato Guerrieri

The *Cities of Stone* exhibition, promoted by the Venice Biennale, the Ministero dell'Economia e delle Finanze (Dipartimento per le Politiche di Sviluppo e Coesione, DPS) and the Ministero per i Beni e le Attività Culturali (Direzione Generale per l'Architettura e l'Arte Contemporanee, DARC), aims at improving architectural and urban contexts in the South of Italy.

The 'cities of stone' are by definition those cities that share the principle characteristic of having been conceived and constructed organically in stone, until the decline of structural concepts based on load bearing walls decreed the end of the (critical and construction) fortunes of this material.

This is confirmed by the apparent contrast between modern, light, artificial materials as opposed to pre-modern, massive, natural materials, whereby only the contemporary value of the former is now recognized.

The cities of stone are those Mediterranean cities that were directly generated by Greek and Roman civilizations, with their particular form of rationale and aesthetic values, which have over time become ideals shared by Western culture.

The architectural characteristics of the Mediterranean city are nowadays subject to unprecedented cultural aggression. New aesthetic and cultural models, based on hedonism and elevation of the relative to that of the absolute, impose on and undermine the concept of their very identity.

On one hand *Cities of Stone* aims to investigate what the dominant models are that govern the current urban and landscape transformation. On the other it attempts to investigate whether there are alternative hypotheses to those based on the myth of modernist, hi-tech, deconstructed architecture, stripped of memory, uprooted from its tradition, when not absolutely ideologically opposed.

The *Cities of Stone* exhibition, while taking all the necessary precautions within an as yet little researched thematic field, is aimed at posing the problem of critical recognition of the current potential of a stone wall culture, intended not only as continuity with traditional construction techniques but also their radical renewal.

It is an exhibition born from the conviction that Mediterranean architectural ideals still exist and are still vital, but risk being swept away. Furthermore, a high critical awareness is necessary to counteract the threat from the ongoing processes of planetary, cultural homologation.

The exhibition is divided into three sections:

1. Project South. International exhibition of architectural designs for the South of Italy
This exhibition proposes a series of projects expressly chosen for the Biennale aimed at the restoration of the coastal landscape of Southern Italian cities, which has as a prerequisite the demolition of incongruous buildings on the selected sites.

2. The other modernity. Characteristics of Mediterranean wall architectures in the twentieth century
This section will illustrate themes, problems and works from the grand season of Mediterranean wall architecture at the beginning of the twentieth century, which consisted of the modern planning response of countries with a Latin tradition to the 'white dream' of Nordic rationalism.

3. Stereotomic architectures. Building with stone today
This section will present prototypes of elements of stereotomic architecture, both full size and scale models made with cad/cam procedures. They are theses to illustrate the application potential of load bearing stone in contemporary architectural planning.

1
Portolago (Leros), three-dimensional reconstruction of city plant: the market square.
DIGITAL ELABORATION BY F. PAGANO, G. TAU, P. RIA, L.T. SIVO.

1
Project South. International exhibition of architectural designs for the South of Italy

2

Project South is directly inspired by *Progetto Venezia*, promoted by Aldo Rossi at the 3rd International Architecture Exhibition in 1985, and takes it as a model. In this sense *Project South* is also a tribute to Aldo Rossi, and is proposed with a continuity of cultural action.

The exhibition is intended to propose a series of projects specifically developed for the Venice Biennale, aimed at restoration of the coastal landscape of Southern Italian cities, whose prerequisite is the demolition of incongruous buildings on the selected sites:
- Bari: Punta Perotti;
- Crotone: the Waterfront;
- Siracusa: the Latomie dei Cappuccini;
- Pantelleria: the tourist port.

After the close of the exhibition these areas will be the subject of architecture competitions.

The exhibition is open to architects all over the world who are interested in these planning themes, regardless of their academic qualifications or professional standing.

The selection of projects for publication and exhibition will be carried out by an international jury chaired by the director of the Cities of Stone exhibition.

The projects selected for the exhibition will be awarded prizes, a tradition begun at the Third International Architecture Exhibition in 1985 with the award of the Leone di Pietra, instituted by Aldo Rossi.

Bari: Punta Perotti

After demolition of the buildings at Punta Perotti, the question is how to protect the site from building speculators and other unsuitable projects.

Punta Perotti is located between the place where the boat carrying the relics of Saint Nicholas landed from Myra in AD 1087 and the Basilica di San Nicola, which Abbot Elia began building immediately after to house the relics of the city's patron saint. But Saint Nicholas continues to be an important saint both in the Western Catholic and Eastern Orthodox Churches.

A religious meeting between believers from the East and West will be hosted in Bari, which has suggested as a theme for the project:
- a new Christian Orthodox Temple, which would magnificently close off the perspective of the Waterfront promenade facing onto a big piazza on the sea, along with buildings to accommodate the Orthodox clerics;
- completion of the Waterfront promenade as far as San Giorgio: a 'sacred way' that would lead to San Nicola, making it possible to revive the ancient procession along the sea shore.

3

2
Punta Perotti: the area Punta Perotti from the East seaside.
PHOTO BY MICHELE MONTEMURRO.

3
Punta Perotti: the demolitions of April 2, and April 23-24 2006.
PHOTO BY AGENZIA ARCERI

4
Crotone: view of the site from the Dock.
PHOTO BY CLAUDIO D'AMATO GUERRIERI.

5
View from above of the Latomie dei Cappucini.
PHOTO BY CLAUDIO D'AMATO GUERRIERI.

6
Spontaneous buildings along the margin of the Latomie dei Cappucini.
PHOTO BY CLAUDIO D'AMATO GUERRIERI.

4

Crotone: the Waterfront

The decommissioning of a large part of the industrial activity at the port of Crotone has led the city council to begin defining a demolition and reconstruction programme. The plan is to set up commercial and tourist activities in the area, a port terminus in the fish market, along with areas for parking and leisure activities that would redesign the strip between the old city and the sea.

The area involved is opposite the castle between the old port and the new Waterfront. It is at the centre of a gulf bordered on the south by the archaeological area of Capo Colonna and on the north by the mouth of the Neto river. The area is currently disused and was in the past occupied by fuel depots. Despite its central location in the landscape and urban fabric, the area has always been closed to the public.

The theme of the project is the conversion of the fuel depot area into a grand piazza between the inlets of the two ports and completion of the Museum of Contemporary Art included in the Urban Renewal Plan. This will consist of buildings and equipment for hosting artistic activities and exhibitions, along with community services.

Siracusa: the Latomie dei Cappuccini

The planned demolition of the buildings next to the Latomie dei Cappuccini is an opportunity to re-think the architectural and urban organization of the whole area and re-establish direct contact with the sea, now partly obstructed.

The area concerned belongs to the eastern-most part of a big system stretching from the ancient Latomie dei Cappuccini to the Neapolis archaeological park. It is a combination of archaeological and landscaped areas offering the most significant testimony of the ancient city's history.

The project themes are:

- redesign of the space occupied by the buildings to be demolished, possibly creating a new structure that will perform the dual functions of welcome centre and access to the Latomie through a 'Museum of the City of Siracusa'. The project may include redesigning the surrounding area with particular attention to the direct connection between the Latomie and the sea;
- redesign of the external margins of the Latomie and of the balza di Acradina with the creation of a pedestrian walkway, as well as areas for relaxation and socializing;

5

6

7

8

- redesign of the current access to the Latomie in Largo Latomie and on Via Politi Laudien. The main entrance may be part of a new building as defined in point a). The other entrance should include a mechanical lift for disabled access.

Pantelleria: the tourist port

The planned demolition of the service buildings (shipyards and building material warehouses) behind the tourist port and their subsequent transfer to the new light industrial zone, have been an opportunity to rethink the architectural and urban organization of the whole area, in order to promote all the activities related to the typical functions of a marina.

The project area is at the end of the fishing port: it is a site of great beauty, where it is possible to relate land and sea in an effective architectural synthesis.

The area intended for the marina may become an opportunity to rebuild a stretch of the urban fabric, as compensation for the ancient urban form destroyed during the second world war.

In terms of functional designation:
-the strip of land next to the sea will contain everything most directly related to the tourist port;
-the strip of land next to the hill will contain structures related to temporary residence (hotel, restaurants, shops etc.).

7
Pantelleria: the project site close to the turistic port.
PHOTO BY CLAUDIO D'AMATO GUERRIERI.
8
Pantelleria: view of the site from the Dock.
PHOTO BY CLAUDIO D'AMATO GUERRIERI.

9
Florestano Di Fausto,
Skanderberg Square,
Former Ministry of Foreign Affairs, Tirana, 1928-1932.
DIGITAL ELABORATION BY MARCO STIGLIANO.
10
Saverio Dioguardi,
Project for the Palazzo del Littorio in Bari,
1934.
DIGITAL ELABORATION BY ANNALISA MAIORANO.

2.
The other modernity. Characteristics of Mediterranean wall architecture in the twentieth century

In this section, the characteristics of some significant Mediterranean cities that represent the other side of modern architecture between the end of the 1920s and the beginning of the '40s are investigated through the analysis of exemplary case studies.

Only cities on the South-East Mediterranean have been taken into consideration:
- the North African coast (Tangiers, Algiers, Tunis, Tripoli, Benghazi, Alexandria);
- the coast of the Middle East (Tel Aviv, Beirut);
- Greece (Athens, Thessaloniki, the Dodecanese Islands: Rhodes, Kos, Leros);
- Albania (Tirana);
- Central and Southern Italy (Rome-E42, Latina, Bari, Taranto, Reggio, Messina, Catania, Palermo, Naples)

The exhibition is divided into five thematic sub-sections:

9

Style

This sub-section – dedicated mainly to the architectural organism – illustrates the style of modern Mediterranean architecture in relation to the languages and architectural types adopted.

10

11

11
Portolago (Leros), three-dimensional reconstruction of the urban system: the seafront.
DIGITAL ELABORATION BY F. PAGANO, G. TAU, P. RIA, L.T. SIVO.

Newly-foundation cities
This sub-section illustrates the idea of the modern Mediterranean city through some examples of newly-foundation cities, the organic nature of which will be explored by relating the unbreakable bonds that link their architecture to the town plan (urban architecture).

The city and the sea
In this sub-section significant Waterfront projects of the urban type intrinsic to the idea of the Mediterranean city are illustrated.

12
Kos, Government Palace on the city seafront.
DIGITAL ELABORATION BY ANNALISA GIGLIO.
13
Bari, Nazario Sauro promenade.
PHOTO BY MICHELE MONTEMURRO.
14
Taranto, Vittorio Emanuele III promenade from the sea.
PHOTO BY UBALDO OCCHINEGRO.

12

13

14

15

Modes of construction

Some typical modes of construction of modern Mediterranean architecture are illustrated in this subsection through the analysis of some example projects.

Origins: the Hellenistic city; architecture and archaeology

This section deals with the origins of the Mediterranean city, through the exploration of one of its most interesting models, that of the Hellenistic city. It will be investigated on different dimensional scales, from the truly urban to that of its grand monumental complexes. The cities of Alexandria and Kos will be analysed in particular.

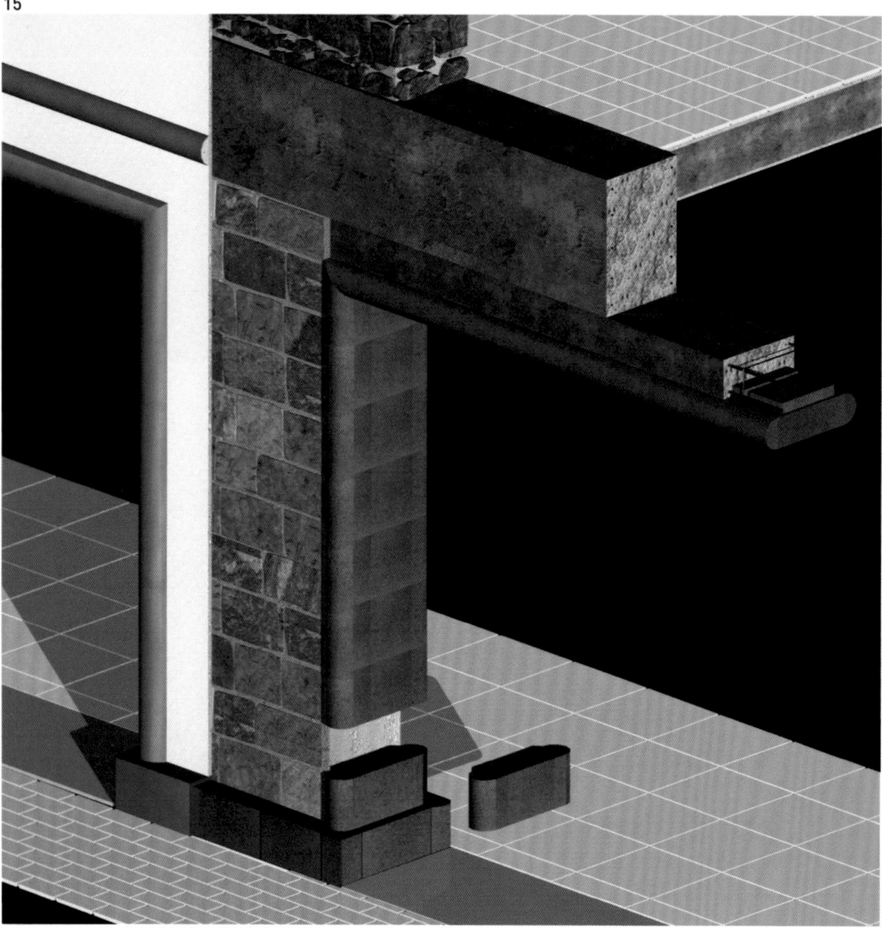

16

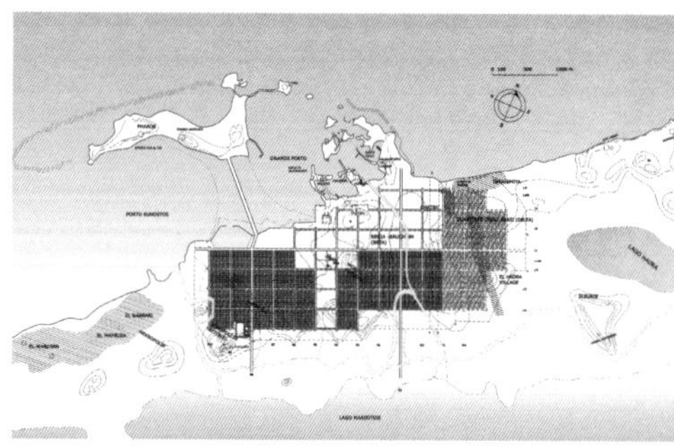

17

3
Stereotomic architectures. Building with stone today

The aim of this section is to demonstrate some possible uses and the potential of structural stone in contemporary architecture using full size and scale models, uniting traditions and technological innovation.
The full size structures and the scale models will be made entirely using cad/cam procedures.
The full size models are designed as an integral part of the exhibition layout:
-an obelisk made of six large reinforced stone pieces;
-an entrance arch that will become the intrados of a small bridge in Venice after the exhibition.

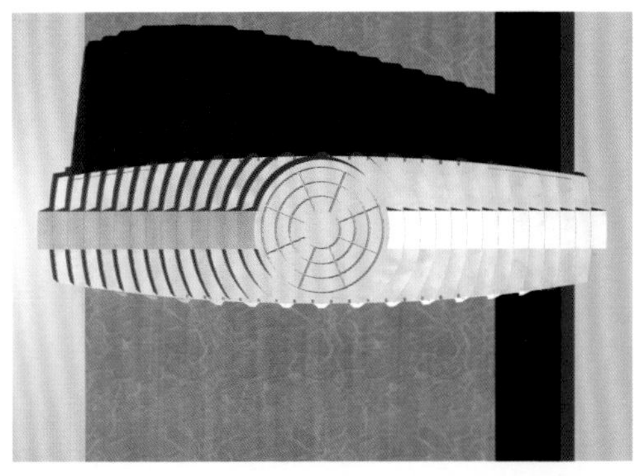

18

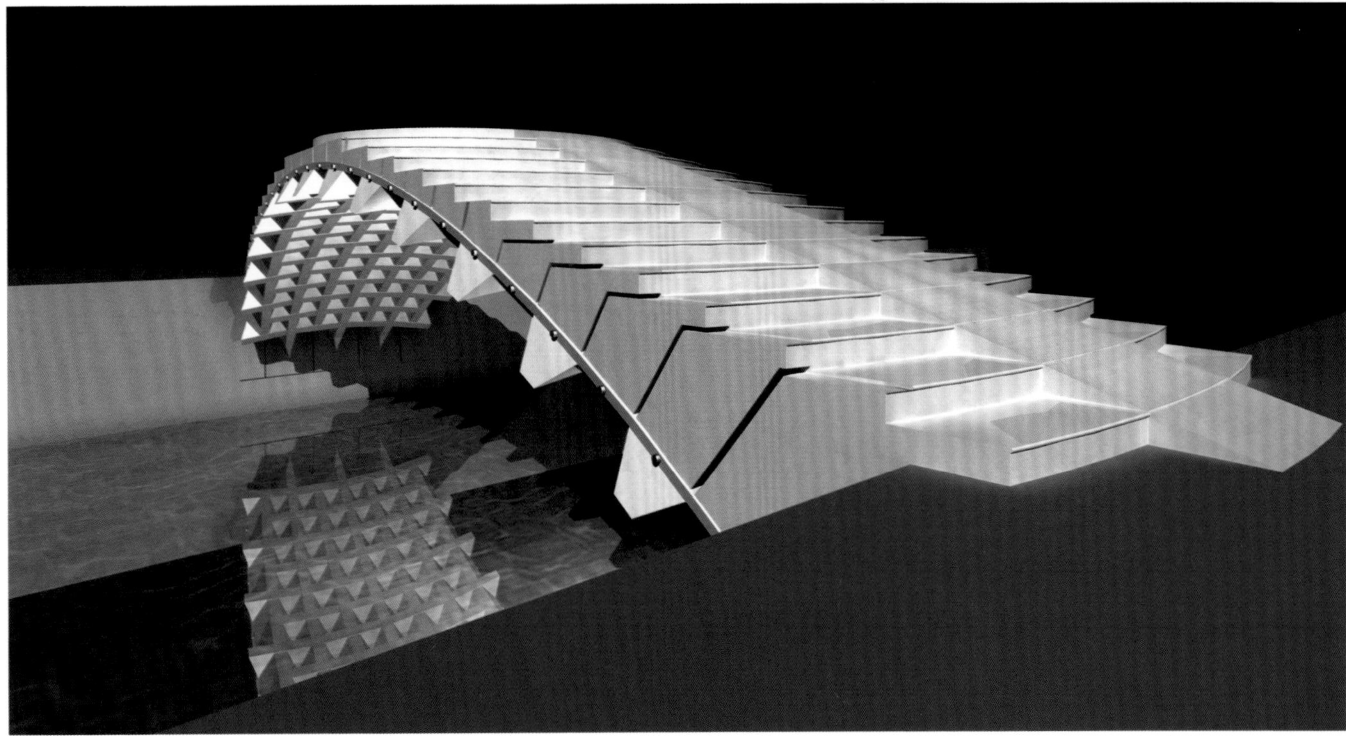

19

15
Portolago (Leros), I.N.C.I.S. building for petty officers, 1936-1938, detail of the corner solution with cantilever roof and junction with the exterior stair.
DIGITAL ELABORATION BY F. PAGANO, G. TAU, P. RIA, L.T. SIVO.

16
Portolago (Leros), Casa del Fascio, 1935-1938, structural detail of the arcade.
DIGITAL ELABORATION BY F. PAGANO, G. TAU, P. RIA, L.T. SIVO.

17
Deinocrates of Rhodes, 331 b.C. Alexandria of Egypt: map of the Hellenistic-Roman city.
PLAN REALIZED BY MARIANGELA TURCHIARULO (GRADUATE STUDENT OF ARCHITECTURAL DESIGN FOR MEDITERRANEAN COUNTRIES, POLITECNICO DI BARI, 2006). ON THE BASIS OF THE TOWN PLANS OF MAHMOUD BEY EL FALAKI, P.M. FRASER, A. ADRIANI, G. GRIMM, W. HOEPFNER, UPDATED BY THE RELIEVES OF THE DIFFERENT ARCHAEOLOGICAL MISSIONS INCLUDED THE FRENCH ONE OF 1996 WHICH HAS RESTORED THE EASTERN PORT OUTLINE.

18
Ponte Canocia: aerial view.
DIGITAL ELABORATION BY GIUSEPPE FALLACARA.

19
Ponte Canocia: perspective view.
DIGITAL ELABORATION BY GIUSEPPE FALLACARA

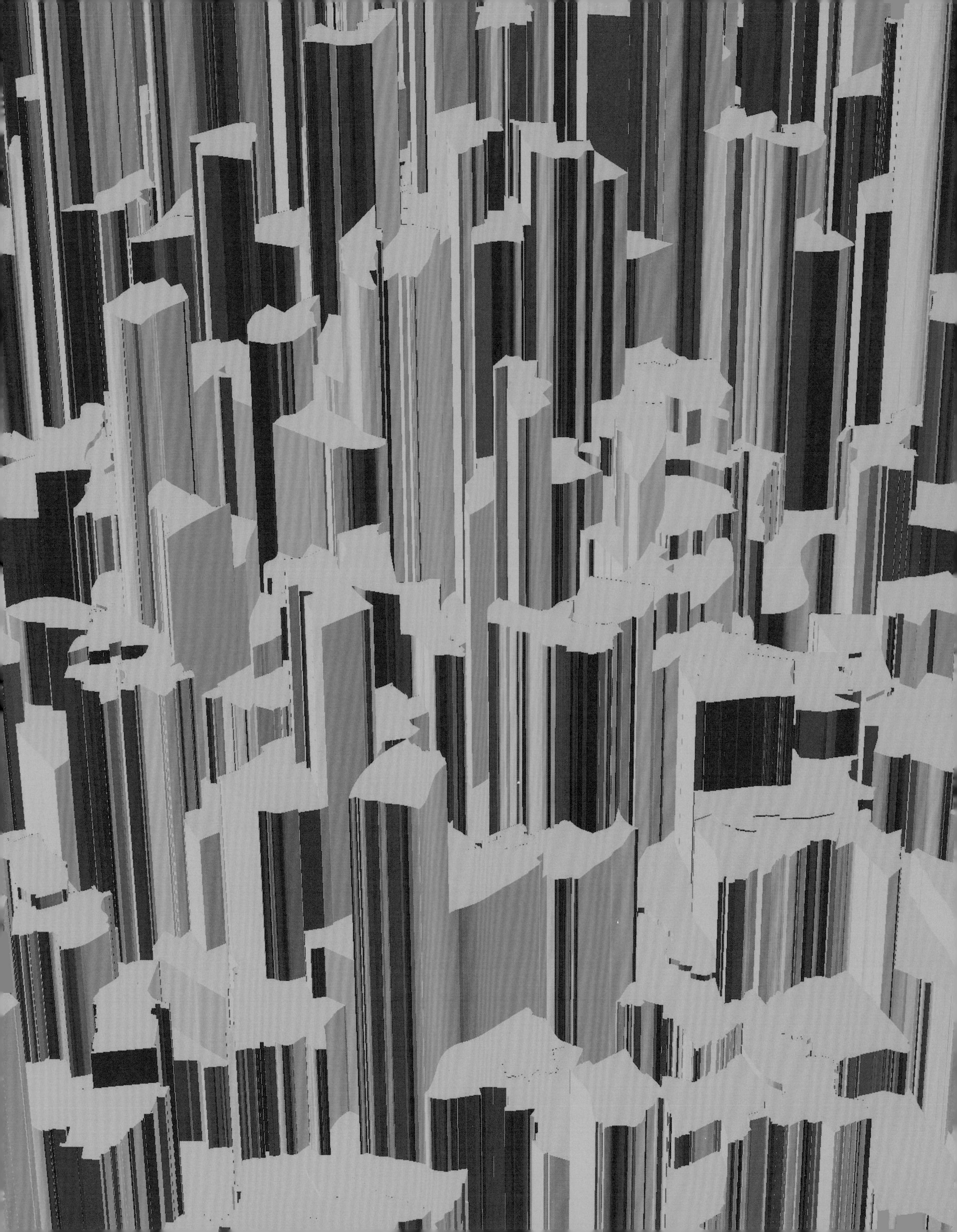

City-Port

Section of 10th International Architecture Exhibition
promoted by the project

sensi
CONTEMPORANEI

Palermo, 15 October 2006 – 14 January 2007
Curator: Rinio Bruttomesso

la Biennale di Venezia

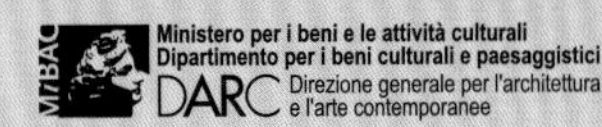

with

Regione Siciliana
Assessorato dei Beni Culturali,
Ambientali e della Pubblica Istruzione

and with

Main Partner

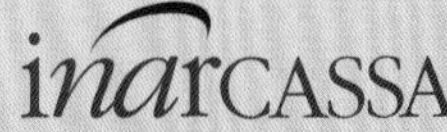

Partner

TARGETTI

Sponsor

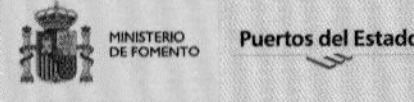

1

1
Sydney, aerial view.
Sydney is Australia's iconic face to the world and international gateway.

City-Port

Curator: Rinio Bruttomesso

Introduction

City-Port is the programme of events planned by the Venice Biennale's 10th International Architecture Exhibition and the *Sensi contemporanei* project for the Italian South, taking place in 2006-2007.

Sensi contemporanei was launched in 2003 to promote the spread of contemporary art and the improvement of architectural and town planning contexts in South Italy. It is supported by the Ministero dell'Economia e delle Finanze (Dipartimento per le Politiche di Sviluppo e Coesione, DPS), the Ministero per i Beni e le Attività Culturali (Direzione Generale per l'Architettura e l'Arte Contemporanee, DARC) and the Fondazione La Biennale di Venezia, with the participation of eight regions in South Italy (Abruzzo, Basilicata, Calabria, Campania, Molise, Apulia, Sicily and Sardinia).

The main aim of *City-Port* is to develop a greater awareness of the urban situation in South Italy and encourage assessment of the various views on the cities' future so that actions can be taken to improve their town-planning order and quality of life.

City-Port continues the theme of the *Città d'Acqua* exhibition at the 9th International Architecture Exhibition in 2004 and that of this year's event – *Cities. Architecture and Society* – while also offering a reflection on urban contexts in the South and the upgrading work taking place there.

Particular attention is focused on the important but complex relationship between cities and their ports. This is strategic to the development of all urban centres that are closely linked to the water and that draw considerable benefits for their socio-economic growth from the functional presence of a port.

The 'port-city' is certainly not a modern urban phenomenon. This combination was of considerable importance in past centuries, too, when port cities competed with others both in Italy and around the world.

But the close relationship between port and city has often taken on a new and significant meaning in recent decades. This marks a new stage in its history, with very interesting consequences and outcomes worthy of further study and illustration to a wider public, such as at the Architecture Biennale.

Water cities and port-cities

Like coastal cities all over the world, many of these in the South of Italy have port facilities for goods and passenger traffic, fishing, tourism and recreation.

In recent years the port functions in these places have undergone radical changes, profoundly altering their place within the urban area and, consequently, their relationship with the physical fabric and overall activities of the city.

The level, type and consequences of such changes are now extremely significant.

Works to transform Waterfront urban-port areas are among the most interesting examples of town-planning changes in water cities. They have been taking place since the middle of last century and are still going on, with the participation of public bodies and private business.

The port-city

The problems pertaining to the port-city are the focus of various projects being promoted during 2006-2007 as part of *Sensi contemporanei* and the 10th International Architecture Exhibition.

This is because the changes made in coastal/port cities have given rise to a new kind of city, a new 'port-city'. Although this still has many similarities to those of the twentieth century, it certainly has some specific and distinctive aspects, such as: the repositioning of some important port functions, a different relationship between port and city, the urban use of important port areas, their more incisive role in the city's economy and a greater influence of port activities on the outlying area beyond the city.

These new port-cities have in recent years become synonymous in many parts of the world with major new development and modernization of the urban structure, which was previously unbalanced and subject to the many evils of the twentieth-century city. The image of the cities themselves has in this way been transformed, resulting in international visibility and renown.

The new version of the port-city has developed from a simple working port, often of limited scope, into a genuine 'door' to the whole world and, consequently, to the global market.

2

3

4

5

The port-cities in the Italian South

In this context, *City-Port* directs attention to the urban contexts of coastal cities in South Italy, which have recently been subject to important interventions on both the renewed town-planning of their physical-morphological order and their socio-economic relaunch, significantly transforming their image.

The main force behind such transformations has been local bodies (city councils, provincial and regional administrations), which have planned, promoted, financed, carried out and managed such projects, at times also in close cooperation with private sector partners.

City-Port aims to maintain and encourage the view of the South as a 'great system of relationships'; as a mosaic of ideas and conditions for building a shared future. The aim is to find the basis for relaunching the local economy and a new image of regions with extraordinary opportunities for growth and investment, in places already known for the quality of their natural and artistic heritage.

The *City-Port* action is seen as an opportunity for the cities of the South to make themselves better known, both in Italy and abroad, for their urban transformations.

Many European cities are part of a big 'urban market' dimension, where investments, economic resources and all kinds of opportunity are linked to mechanisms regulated by quite precise factors. These include the image of the city, its capacity for attraction and its ability to present its unique, 'niche' aspects – or at least those that distinguish it from others.

The port cities in the southern regions of Italy are here taken as a laboratory for making a closer study of the conditions, methods, character, outcomes and consequences of such development already accomplished or planned in these cities.

An effort will also be made to focus on similarities to and differences from international examples, selected for having obtained levels of excellence in implementing policies for the renewal of port-urban areas.

The aims of *City-Port*

The main aims of the *City-Port* action, which have inspired the programme's various projects, may be summarized as follows:

a. organization of a range of activities, referring particularly to architecture and town planning, to stimulate development processes in specific urban centres in South Italy based on measures to improve urban quality;
b. creation of opportunities for comparison and debate, also at an international level, on urban and environmental renewal, with particular reference to the coastal towns of the Italian South;
c. organization of training and updating events, open particularly to the staff of public bodies involved in urban-port Waterfront renewal works;
d. definition of actions to be taken in association with university departments and research institutes in the South, in order to ensure that the southern academic world has a central role in the proposal of ideas for the new ordering of the cities under consideration;
e. promotion of actions aimed at gaining real participation in the decision-making processes of urban renewal and of projects to upgrade important public environments in the cities of the South.

It is evident that this project is not intended as something ephemeral, limited to just a few months, but as the start of a permanent operation that will gradually develop and consolidate, promoting the capacities and autonomy of the local towns involved.

The *City-Port* projects

The *City-Port* projects open in Palermo in October 2006 before moving to other cities of the South during 2007. They consist of the following activities:

a. four exhibitions on the relationship between city and port. After Palermo, these will be presented in other port cities in the South of Italy;
b. Portus Architecture Prize, open to designers under 40, for proposals to upgrade urban Waterfront areas in small and medium towns in the Italian South;
c. an international conference on the main themes of the exhibitions, to be held in Palermo in late autumn 2006;
d. updating and training courses on the port-city relationship, open mainly to local body and port authority experts;
e. www.citta-porto.tv web television providing information on the activities of the *City-Port* section.

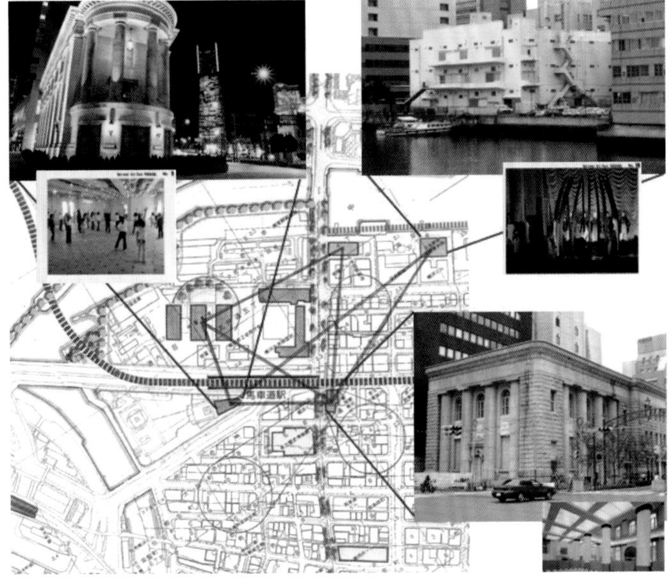

6

7

8

2
Pierhead with Table Mountain backdrop, V&A Waterfront Cape Town.
© VICTORIA&ALFRED WATERFRONT.

3
Genova, aerial view of the Old Port area.
© ARCHIVIO CITTÀ D'ACQUA.

4
Valparaiso Waterfront Development today.
© PUERTO DE VALPARAISO-EMPRESA PORTUARIA VALPARAISO.

5
Rotterdam, Port-city area.
© STADHAVENSROTTERDAM.

6
Yokohama, the 'Creative City Yokohama' project.
© CITY OF YOKOHAMA.

7
Edinburgh, rendering of Leith Docks Development Framework.
© WATERFRONT COMMUNITIES PROJECT, EDIMBURGH.

8
Venice, aerial view of the city and its harbour.
© ARCHIVIO CITTÀ D'ACQUA.

The four exhibitions

The international exhibition: *City-Port. Maps for New Urban Routes*

This exhibition presents significant examples of upgrading works to urban-port areas that have managed to combine two aspects. The first is that of the demanding but compelling challenge of 'globalized' urban marketing, which international cities cannot ignore, as such competition between them is the authentic scenario on which their destiny is played out.

The second aspect is the importance of the local element, in the process leading to insertion in an international context. This entails a reappraisal of the elements of identity and their appreciation as a distinctive asset.

The exhibition presents significant international examples of the construction of a new port-city and is divided into three sections:

- introductory;
- a presentation of 15 port cities in different continents:
  Europe: Oslo (Norway), Helsinki (Finland), Liverpool and Edinburgh (UK), Rotterdam (Holland), Istanbul (Turkey), Genoa and Venice (Italy);
  South America: Rosario (Argentina), Valparaiso (Chile), Rio de Janeiro (Brazil);
  Africa: Cape Town (South Africa);
  Asia: Incheon (Korea), Yokohama (Japan);
  Australia: Sydney;
- a space dedicated to Spain.

The Spanish port system is being represented at the 10th International Architecture Exhibition, thanks to the important contribution of the Ministerio de Fomento entity, Puertos del Estado, because of its important international role in the specific city-port relationship. Spanish port-cities have gained vital experience in this field over the past ten years, both in the modernization of working ports and the upgrading of urban-port Waterfronts.

The exhibition is being staged by the architect Italo Rota and presented in the Palazzo Forcella-de Seta, made available by the ANCE of Palermo.

9

10

11

9
View of Istanbul and the Golden Horn.
© MARA VITTORI.

10
Oslo, Aker Brigge.
© ARCHIVIO CITTÀ D'ACQUA.

11
Rosario (Argentina), Sunchales Park, Museum of Contemporary Art, Collectivity Park, 2004-2006.
©MUNICIPALIDAD DE ROSARIO.

12

13

12
Helsinki, rendering of the Kalasata project.
© CITY OF HELSINKI.
13
Liverpool, proposed Mann Island Development project.
© LIVERPOOL CITY COUNCIL.
14
Barcelona, aerial view of Port Vell.
© PUERTOS DEL ESTADO.
15
Bilbao, the river and the Guggenheim Museum by Frank O. Gehry.
© PUERTOS DEL ESTADO.
16
Malaga, project for Docks 1 and 2.
© PUERTOS DEL ESTADO.

14

15

16

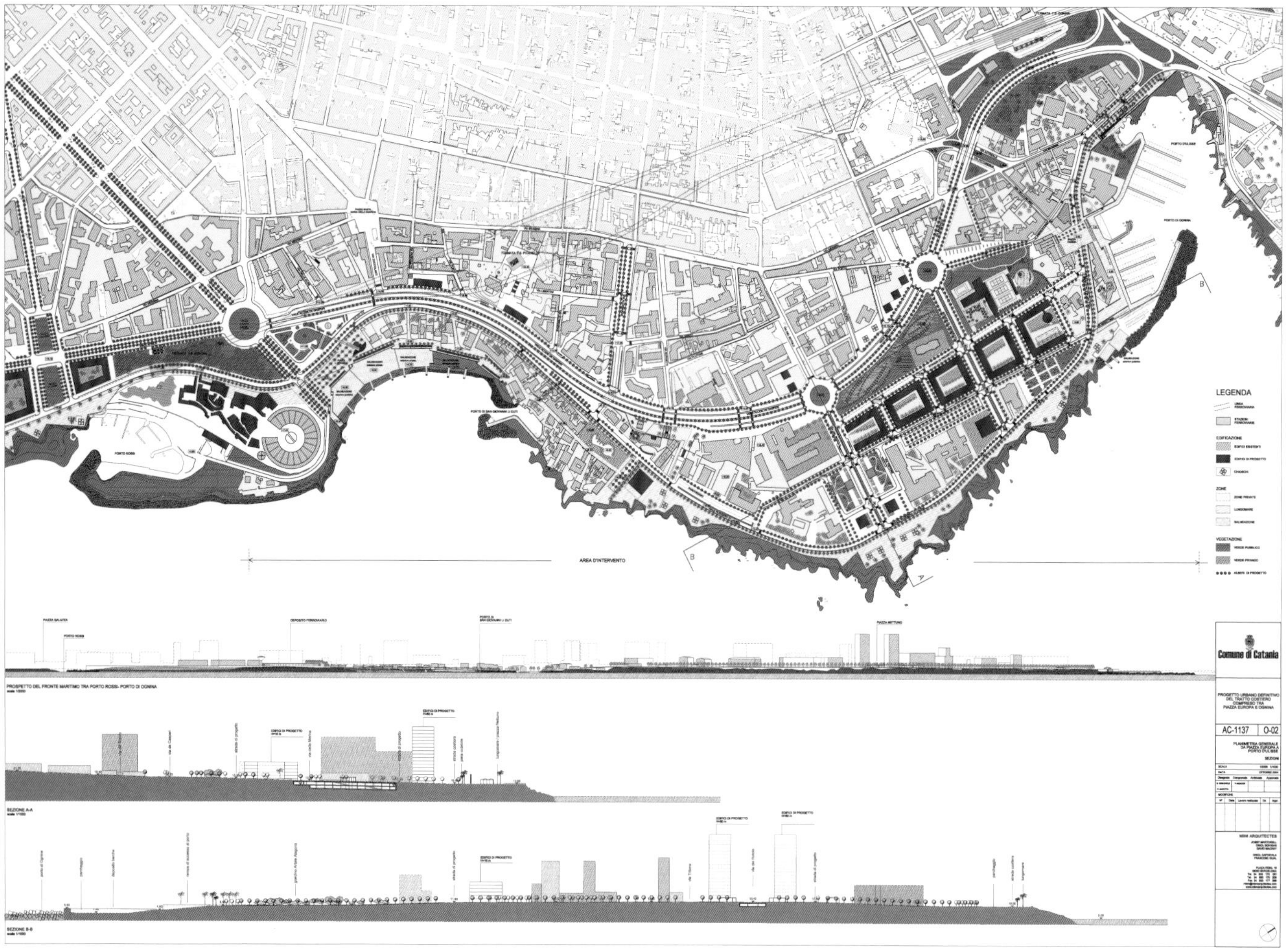

17

17
Catania, Plan for the advancement of the coastal strip between Piazza Europa and Ognina (MBM ARQUITECTES).

18
Aerial view of the city of Brindisi showing the natural shape of the port with the ramification of its two bays: east and west.

The exhibition on South Italian port-cities: *City-Port. Great South*

The exhibition is on South Italian port cities with some of the largest port facilities:
Abruzzo: Pescara;
Campania: Naples and Salerno;
Apulia: Bari and Brindisi;
Calabria: Reggio Calabria;
Sicily: Catania, Messina, Siracusa and Trapani.

The exhibition presents an overall image of the actions taken or planned to upgrade the urban-port Waterfront of coastal towns in South Italy.

Great South is being staged in the old Sant'Erasmo train sheds, with installation designed by the architects Alessandra Raso and Cliostraat.

18

19

19
Bari, the port and the city.

20

21

20
Pescara, Proposal for the new arrangement and the new Port Master Plan.

21
Napoli, rendering of the winning project for the new monumental Waterfront of Naples (architect Michel Euvé).

22

22
Aerial view of the Waterfront of Palermo.
ELABORATION BY OFFICINA DI ARCHITETTURA DEL PORTO.

23
3D model of the port area theme of the pilot-project for the rearrangement and strenghtening of port functions: the new "three harbours".
ELABORATION BY OFFICINA DI ARCHITETTURA DEL PORTO.

The exhibition on the experience of the port-city of Palermo: *City-Port. Palermo, Mediterraneo*

The *Palermo, Mediterraneo* exhibition is completely devoted to the ongoing work in Palermo to redefine its port area and Waterfront. The *Officina di Architettura del Porto* recently set up by the Port Authority, in collaboration with Palermo City Council and supported by other important city institutions, has offered new opportunities to find new solutions for the relationship between the city and its port.

Palermo, Mediterraneo is also being staged in the old Sant'Erasmo train sheds, again with layout designed by Alessandra Raso and Cliostraat.

Palermo has launched an innovative plan to upgrade its Waterfront as part of an overall renewal of the port-city interactions. The guiding idea of the pilot projects is the vision of a new 'city of trade and innovation' as one of the main driving forces of urban creativity. The 'design engine' for renewal of the new port-city is the *Officina di Architettura del Porto* as a laboratory for planning and for stimulating communication.

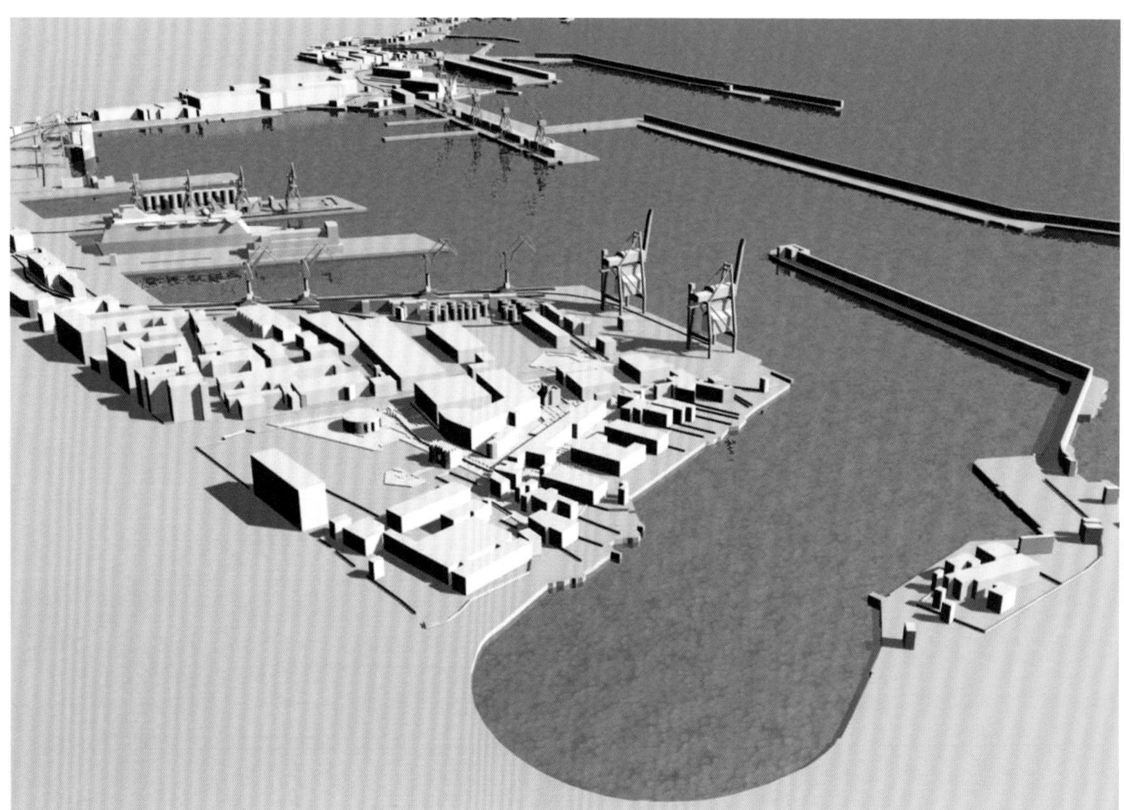

23

24

24
The trapezoidal Dock and the old port of the Cove: the areas of the main urban transformations of the activities for the yachting and for the historical center of Palermo.
© SANDRO SCALIA.

Portus Prize: The exhibition of the winning designs for the Portus Architecture Prize

An important role can be played in various spheres by young people in the urban renewal now taking place in many South Italian cities: from architectural design to business enterprise, creative and artistic work and social engagement.

This is why *City-Port* is dedicating a special area to the proposals of the young Italian professionals who took part in the Portus architecture prize with upgrading projects for Waterfront areas in small and medium urban contexts in eight regions of South Italy. Architects, engineers and landscape architects under 40 presented designs intended to resolve precise problems and offer quality solutions for potential development extended to an urban and district scale.

The exhibition on the outcomes of the Portus architecture Prize presents the winning and highly commended designs and is being staged in the EXPA architecture gallery in the old city of Palermo. The exhibition design is by Tiziano Di Cara and Giuseppe Romano.

Premio di Architettura
Portus

Home page | Documenti | FAQ | Iscrizione | Risultati

sensi CONTEMPORANEI

Premio di Architettura Portus

Nel quadro delle iniziative di 'Città – Porto', sezione curata da Rinio Bruttomesso per la 10. Mostra Internazionale di Architettura della Biennale di Venezia e nel contesto del progetto Senzi Contemporanei, viene promosso il Premio di architettura Portus, rivolto ad architetti, paesaggisti e ingegneri under 40.

I professionisti sono invitati a presentare proposte di riqualificazione per aree di waterfront in contesti urbani di piccole e medie dimensioni del Mezzogiorno italiano (con popolazione inferiore a 100.000 abitanti) scelte a propria discrezione. Si richiede di definire soluzioni di riassetto delle zone individuate nelle regioni del Sud Italia, e più precisamente nelle Regioni Abruzzo, Molise, Campania, Basilicata, Puglia, Calabria e Sicilia, con proposte che superino criticità esistenti, avanzando progetti e programmi di sviluppo eventualmente replicabili in altri contesti urbani.

Il Premio di architettura è indetto da Sensi Contemporanei e gode del patrocinio del Consiglio Nazionale Architetti, Pianificatori, Paesaggisti e Conservatori (C.N.A.P.P.C), che assicura altresì un sostegno scientifico all'iniziativa.

Il Premio è patrocinato inoltre da Inarcassa, dalla testata settimanale Edilizia e Territorio - Il Sole 24 Ore e da In/Arch - Istituto Nazionale di Architettura.

È previsto un montepremi complessivo di 49.000 euro. I migliori progetti saranno esposti in una mostra che sarà allestita a Palermo nell'ambito delle iniziative della sezione 'Città – Porto' e tutte le proposte candidate, e in linea con quanto richiesto dal bando, saranno presentate in un catalogo dedicato.

Le proposte saranno valutate da una giuria internazionale, presieduta da Richard Burdett, direttore della 10. Mostra Internazionale di Architettura della Biennale di Venezia.

Tutte le procedure del concorso saranno svolte interamente dal C.N.A.P.P.C per via telematica. Il periodo stabilito per la registrazione e la trasmissione degli elaborati va dal 26 giugno al 6 luglio 2006.

Data e ora ufficiale:
2/5/2006 - 08:49:24 AM

Calendario

12 Maggio 2006
Termine entro il quale i concorrenti potranno inoltrare i quesiti.

05 Giugno 2006
Termine entro il quale sarà fornita risposta ai quesiti ricevuti mediante pubblicazione sul sito internet di una raccolta di domande e risposte di carattere generale predisposte dalla Segreteria tecnica.

26 Giugno 2006
Apertura del sistema telematico per l'iscrizione e la trasmissione telematica degli elaborati.

06 Luglio 2006
Chiusura del sistema telematico per l'iscrizione e la trasmissione telematica degli elaborati.

15 Luglio 2006
Inizio dei lavori di selezioni da parte delle Giurie.

31 Luglio 2006
Conclusione dei lavori delle Giurie e comunicazione dei progetti selezionati.

14 Ottobre 2006
Inaugurazione della Mostra e cerimonia di premiazione.

14 Ottobre 2006
Proclamazione dei vincitori e dei segnalati da parte della Giuria.

Ministero per i beni e le attività culturali
Dipartimento per i beni culturali e paesaggistici
DARC Direzione generale per l'architettura e l'arte contemporanee

inarcassa

25

25
Home-page of Portus Architecture Prize.

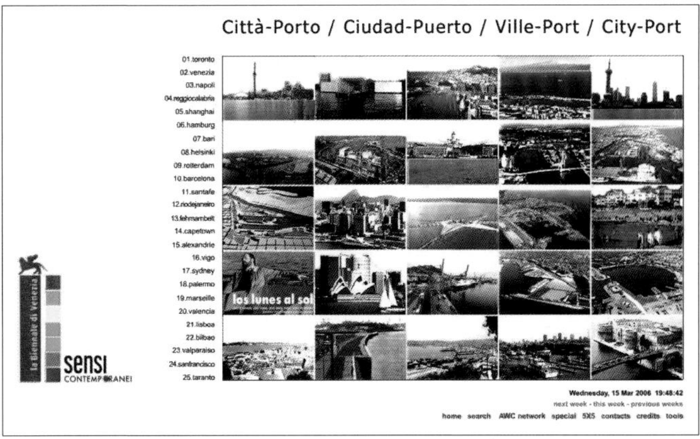

26

26
Screen of the home-page of citta-porto.tv.

www.citta-porto.tv

The creation of WebTV that precedes and follows the exhibitions and events in Palermo is intended to project the visitor into the world of flows and emotions produced and aroused by old and new port cities. One hundred videos from those the network holds have been selected to describe these 'feelings', to stimulate discussion, to make known distant realities and to entertain the eyes and mind. This complex presentation will be made monthly: 25 videos in original language, accompanied by fast files and bibliographic references on the net will accompany the exhibition and Biennale visitors. The format used will be that adopted by Archiworld Channel on archiworld.tv: 5x5 videomagazine.

Seminars and courses

During the exhibition period, Palermo will host conferences on port-city themes and seminars addressing specific questions on Palermo, with the essential participation of university departments and local associations.

Palermo and other port cities involved in *City-Port* events will hold updating and training courses on the city-port relationship and on questions concerning the renewal of urban-port Waterfronts.

The *City-Port* action launched in Palermo will move to the other South Italian port cities taking part in the initiative throughout 2007.

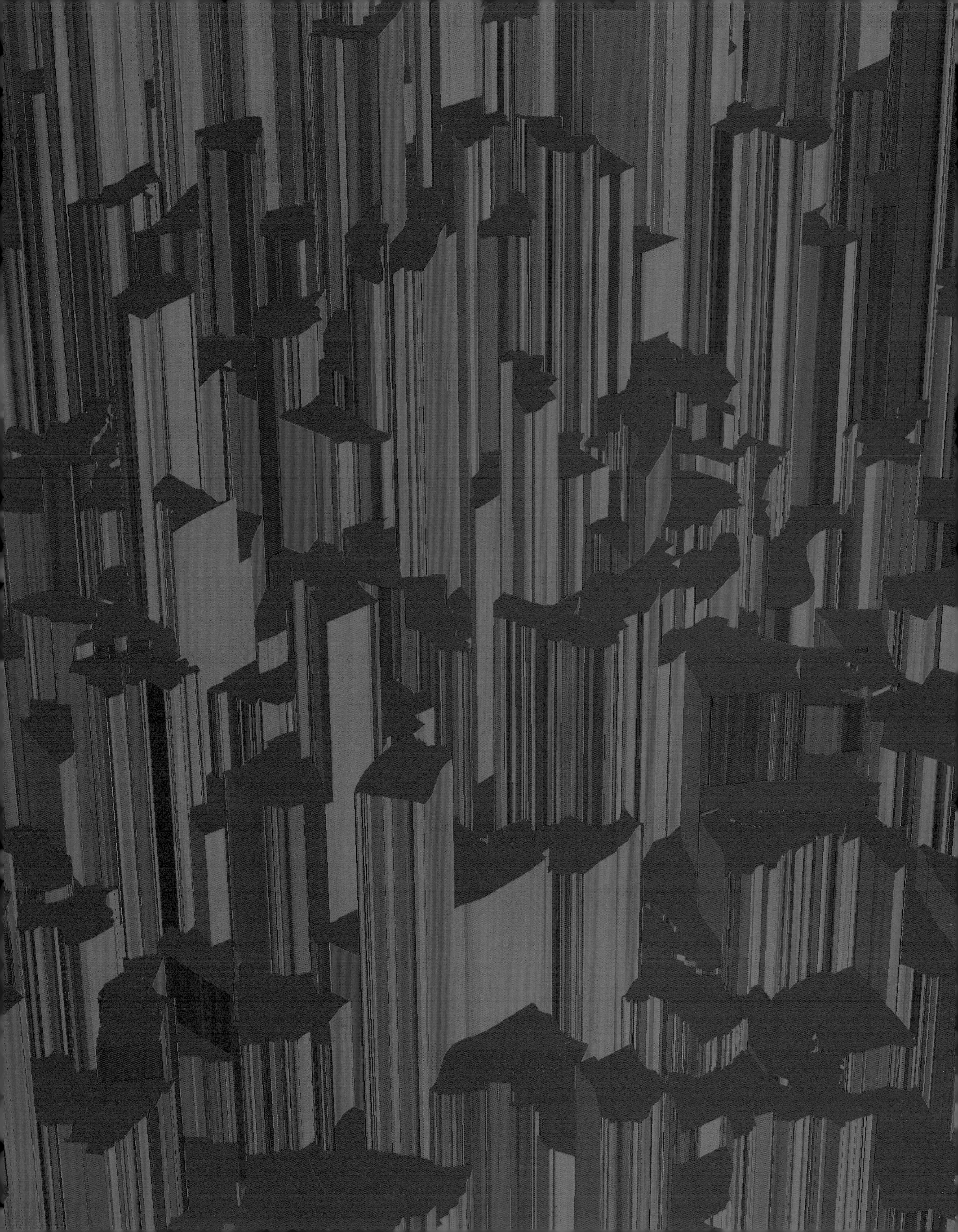

Italian Pavilion

Venice, First Tesa delle Vergini at the Arsenale
10 September - 19 November 2006

Commissioner: Pio Baldi
Curator: Franco Purini

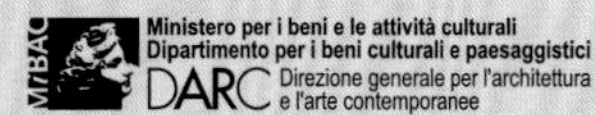

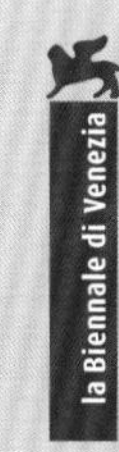

Main Partner

Partner

TARGETTI

Sponsor

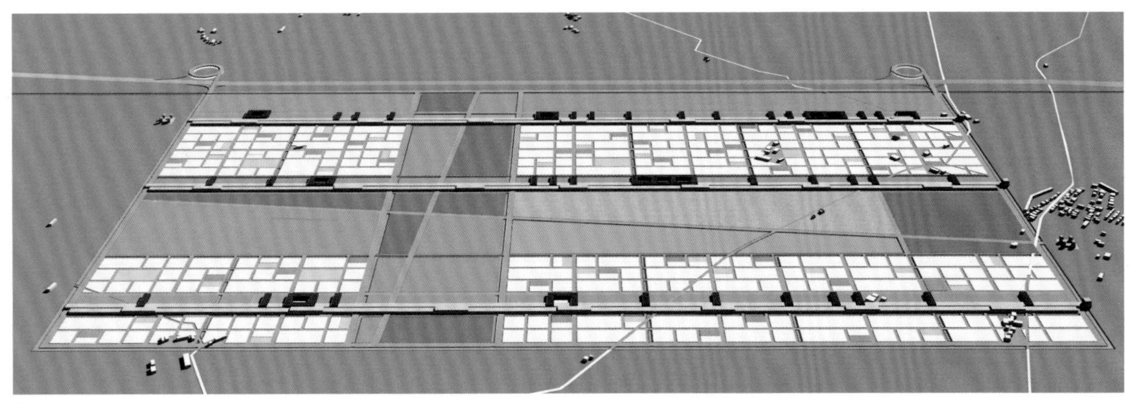

1

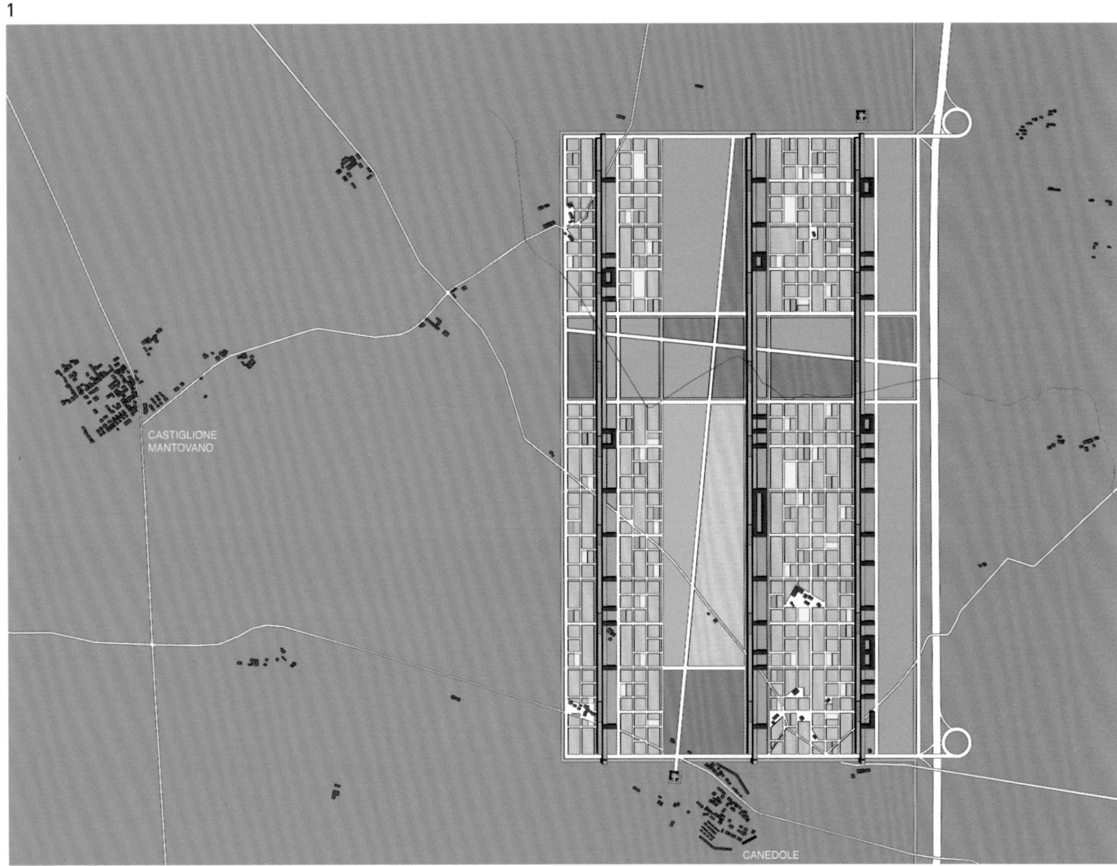

2

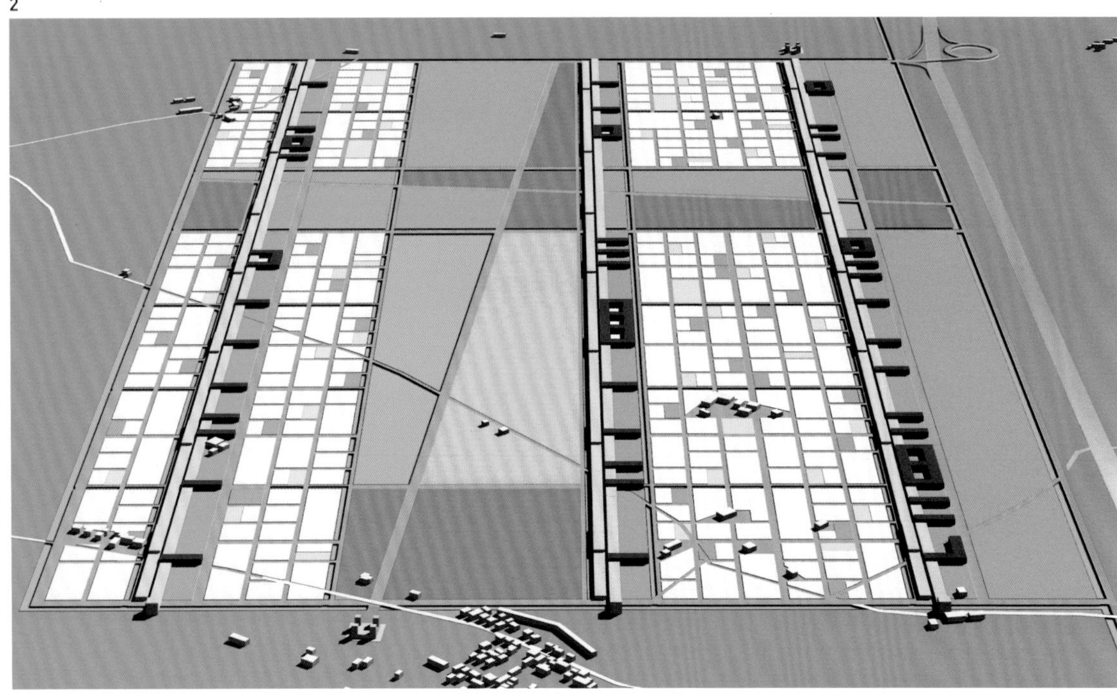

3

1
Vema 2026,
aerial view of the city.
2
Vema 2026,
plan of the city within its territory.
3
Vema 2026,
aerial view of the city.

Italia-y-2026. Invitation to Vema

Curator: Franco Purini

Vema, a new Italian city for the Venice Biennale

The most difficult task now facing Italian architecture is to encourage greater experimentation in the spheres of language and technology, and the regulatory, administrative and production procedures through which architecture is accomplished. The task is aggravated by the current global situation, with fierce competition between the design schools it gives rise to. Italy's consistent, often precious and exceedingly bountiful design offer needs to be put to the test of European and international competition in a more advanced, integrated and open context. But it is heavily penalized by the Merloni law – without whose abolition Italian architecture can have no future on a par with its past. The big exhibitions like the Venice Biennale and the Milan Triennial are important stimuli for this, because of the themes they suggest and the media interest they arouse. They are the most important institutional theatres of Italian architectural debate and among the most recognized places of disciplinary exchange at an international level.

Recent Venice Biennale architecture exhibitions, starting from that of 1996 curated by Hans Hollein and following those curated by Vittorio Gregotti, Paolo Portoghesi, Aldo Rossi and Francesco Dal Co, have increasingly focused on designs by the most famous architects in the world. They have been presented as often impressive summaries of important town planning and architectural works. Such works, generally already known, have been recontextualized within special problematic frames. This formulation is certainly of considerable documentary interest and undoubted dramatic effect, but one of its effects has been the failure to look into new planning problems and offer emerging architects an opportunity to present their ideas in a prestigious and media savvy context like that of Venice. Taking up the tradition of previous Biennali, though locally, as compared to the global picture proposed by the 10th International Architecture Exhibition curated by Richard Burdett, the Italian pavilion, curated by myself, wishes to reverse this trend.

The intention is to stage an experimental exhibition featuring future oriented projects by young architects of great inventive energy that are easily decipherable by the general public.

The Italian Pavilion, promoted by Venice Biennale and DARC (Direzione Generale per l'Architettura e le Arti Contemporanee), is starting out this year on what will hopefully be a long and successful life, full of innovative content. The curator is being assisted by Nicola Marzot, Margherita Petranzan and Livio Sacchi on a project that promises to be difficult, but rich in stimuli for reflection.

The title of the exhibition is *Italia-y-2026. Invitation to Vema*. The 'y' is intended to subliminally suggest the reading 'Italy', as an amplification beyond the nation, as creative transcendence of its borders. The theme is the design of a new city. A city of foundation, but also an ideal, utopian city – that of Ernesto Nathan Rogers – situated near the intersection of the Lisbon-Kiev and Berlin-Palermo European rail corridors.

The city will be between Verona and Mantua and be called Vema. It is being designed by 20 architects or groups of architects between 30 and 40 years of age, who will look at the same number of problems, including the house, work places, the body, art, infrastructure, the media, green areas and leisure time. The invited architects were provided with an installation outline by the curator and Francesco Menegatti, city manager of the operation. This is a very simple, flexible directional model, based on the alternation of parallel green bands or crossed by another green belt corresponding to the border between the two regions.

Served by a network of roads flanked by canals that connect it to the Mincio and Po rivers, Vema takes up and reproposes the urban world of the Po plain in a structurally more articulate and complex manner. The area is marked by strong environmental and architectural uniformity, unfailingly contradicted by subtle differences and enlivened by important monuments. The outline for the city is a rectangle of 2.26 by 3.7 kilometres for 30,000 inhabitants. It incorporates several existing roads and buildings, with the intention of ensuring deep roots in the area by paying attention to these and reinterpreting their structures and textures.

The decision to propose a weak design is based on the desire to leave the planners the greatest freedom to introduce variants, alternatives, combinations and hybridizations, and not overwhelm the architecture with an overly assertive urban picture.

On the more strictly architectural level, the 20 groups have been asked to formulate exemplary solutions from a typological and linguistic point of view, and advanced solutions based on a distinct thematic acceleration, on a calculated heterotopical detour and on an extended recognition of contributions from other disciplines. Vema is also intended to offer an alterative to the sprawling city, replacing the uncontrolled, confused proliferation of houses, factories and shopping malls with finite, recognisable urban entities able to institute new territorial relations and make explicit what is now already in existence as imprinted potential.

The venue for the exhibition is the grand evocative space of the Tese delle Vergini, where a panorama will be created with images of the new city. There will also be a kind of big folk-story, a layered visual performance recounting the stories, faces and buildings of twentieth-century Italian architecture. There will then be models of individual buildings and a big model of the city itself, crossed by the border between Lombardy and Veneto. The exhibition is intended to suggest a possible hypothesis of Italy in 20 years' time, the centenary of Gruppo 7, the progenitor of modern Italian architecture, which is the ideal reference for the entire exhibition programme.

The architects invited to design Vema are: Avatar Architettura+PTL, Lorenzo Capobianco, Dogma|Office, ELASTICO SPA+3, Giuseppe Fallacara, Santo Giunta, Iotti+Pavarani Architetti, Raffaella Laezza, Michele Moreno, Giovanni Santamaria, liverani / molteni architetti, ma0 / emmeazero studio d'architettura, Antonella Mari, Masstudio, Stefano Milani, Moduloquattro Architetti Associati, Tomaso Monestiroli and Massimo Ferrari, OBR Open Building Research, Gianfranco Sanna, Andrea Stipa, studio.eu, Alberto Ulisse, unoaunostudio, laq_architettura. They are young people who have already produced significant works, but have not yet had a chance to take on the challenge of a complex project on an important stage like that of the Venice Biennale. The Vema planners belong to the Erasmus generation, are at home in the international dimension and have grown up within the digital revolution. They have the task of reproposing in new terms that organic but critical relation between city and architecture: the element on which Italian design culture built its theoretical and linguistic identity in the twentieth century.

Exhibitors

Avatar Architettura (Nicola Santini, Pier Paolo Taddei)
Collaborators: Diana Lombardi, Juan Seara Oro, Anna E. Poullou
PTL - Peter Thomas Lang
Mauricio Cardenas (bamboo construction's advisor)

Lorenzo Capobianco
Collaborators: Fabio Baratto, Matteo Belfiore, Raffaele Capasso, Marco Fabio De Lillo, Sabrina De Martino, Giovanni Fasanaro

Dogma|Office
Dogma (Pier Vittorio Aureli, Martino Tattara, Sabina Tattara)
Office (Kersten Geers, David Van Severen)

ELASTICO SPA (Stefano Pujatti Architetti)
Collaborators: Corrado Curti, Valeria Brero, Daniele Almondo, Elena Ferrari
ELASTICO 3 (Alberto Del Maschio)
Collaborator: Marco Burigana

Giuseppe Fallacara
Collaborators: Nicola Parisi, Marco Stigliano, Marco Orsini, Marco Lomascolo

Santo Giunta
Collaborators: Domenico Falcetta, Viola Avvento, Mariano Capitummino, Giuseppe Cardillo, Francesca Crocco, Andrea Liguori, Massimiliano Masellis, Sebastiano Raimondo, Giampiero Riggio, Riccardo Scalisi, Domenico Scirica, Fabio Vella, Calogero Vetro

Iotti+Pavarani Architetti (Paolo Iotti, Marco Pavarani)
Collaborators: Valentina Adami, Anita Cova, Matteo Francesconi, Fabrizio Gruppini, Cristina Haumann, Carlotta Meneguzzo, Federica Pennacchini, Perla Rebecchi, Giulia Sacchetta, Simone Tortini

Raffaella Laezza, Michele Moreno, Giovanni Santamaria
Collaborators: Alberto Casarotto, Alberto Cosatti, Valentino D'Osualdo, Andrea Trolese

liverani / molteni architetti (Andrea Liverani, Enrico Molteni)
Collaborators: Giovanni Podestà, Martino Sacchi, Gianfranco Orsenigo, Elena Ruotolo, Sebastiano Conti Gallenti

ma0 / emmeazero studio d'architettura (Massimo Ciuffini, Ketty Di Tardo, Alberto Iacovoni, Luca La Torre)
With: Enrica D'Aula, Diane Jaeger, Lisa Pavanello, Giacomo Pietrapiana, Carlo Tancredi, Piero Ventura

Antonella Mari
With: Matteo Lorusso
Collaborator: Marcello Reina

Masstudio (Simone Colombo, Chiara Martini, Lorenzo Rossetti, Gabriele Sposato)

Stefano Milani
Collaborators: Filip Geerts, Arek Seredyn, Radek Brunecký

Moduloquattro Architetti Associati
(Fabrizio Ciappina, Giuseppe Fugazzotto, Antonello Russo, Gaetano Scarcella)
Collaborators: Monica Bellantone, Rosaria Antonella Testaì, Umile Molinaro, Santi Maggio Savasta

Tomaso Monestiroli, Massimo Ferrari
Collaborators: Chiara Besozzi, Claudia Tinazzi

OBR Open Building Research (Paolo Brescia, Tommaso Principi)
Veronica Baraldi, Matteo Casavecchia, Dahlia De Macina, Andrea Malgeri Margherita Menardo, Gabriele Pitacco, Chiara Pongiglione, Paolo Salami, Izabela Sobjerai, Luca Vigliero, Francesco Vinci, Barbara Zuccarello

Gianfranco Sanna
With: Giovanni Curreli, Vladimiro Frau, Gemma Paone, Fabrizio Pusceddu, Mauro Quidacciolu, Silvia Serreli, Michele Valentino

Andrea Stipa
Collaborators: Tommaso Battista, Alessandro Casciotti, Sara D'Innocenzo, Martina Fiorentino, Matteo Grimaldi, Francesca Luciano, Stefano Noccaro, Gianluca Pelizzi, Gabriele Settimelli, Valentina Ticino

studio.eu (Paola Cannavò, Maria Ippolita Nicotera, Francesca Venier)
Collaborators: Maria Moreno Garcia, Simona Stortone

Alberto Ulisse, unoaunostudio, laq_architettura
With: Marino la Torre, Marco Morante, Maura Scarcella, Giuseppe Marcotullio, Andrea Mezzaroma, Annalisa Taballione

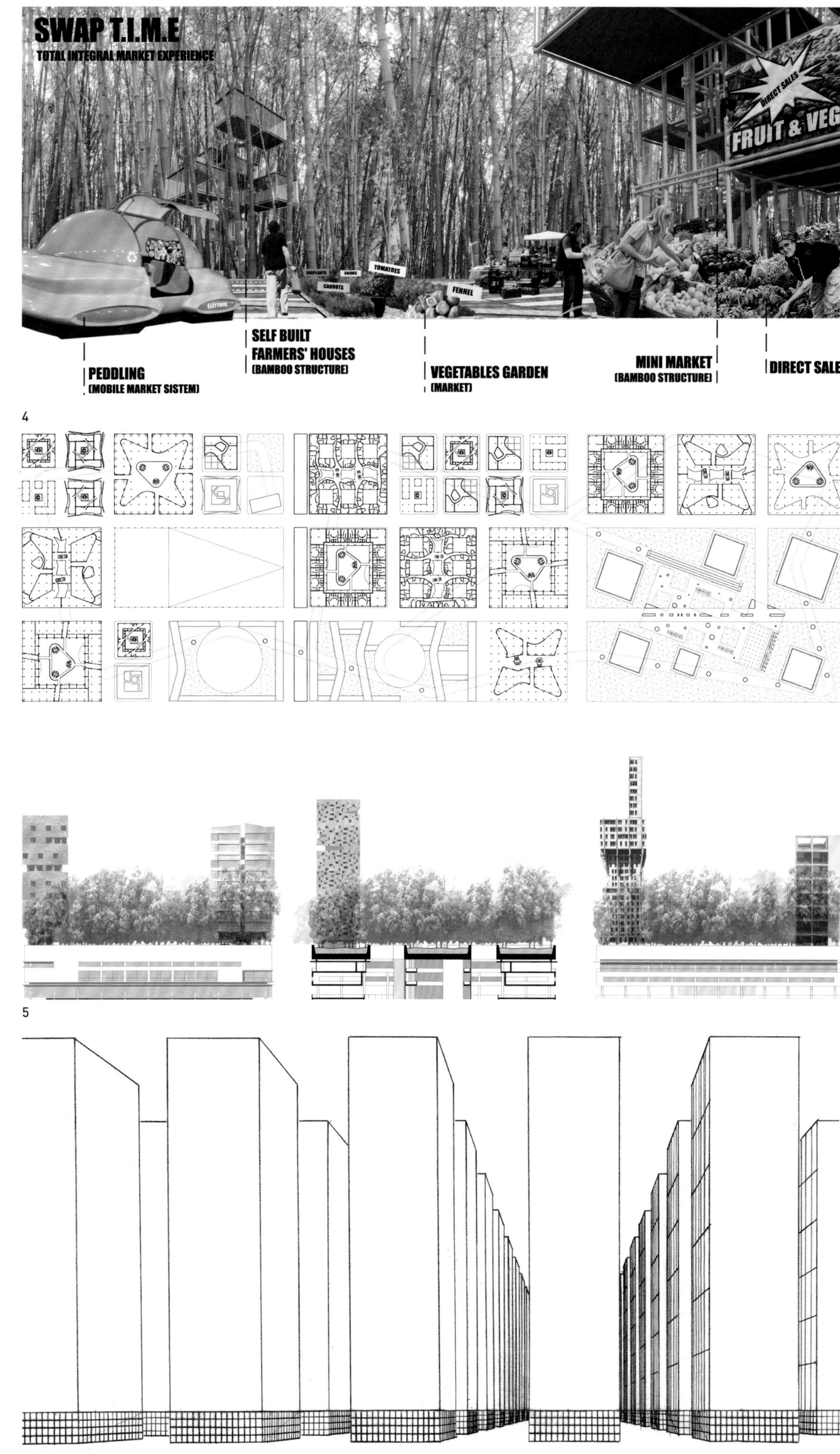

4

5

6

4
Avatar Architettura + PTL,
T.I.M.E. Swap ©,
(the market),
Vema 2026.

5
Lorenzo Capobianco,
Sottobosco [Underbrush],
(the radio/tv studio),
Vema 2026.
Morphological map and section plan (work in progress).

6
Dogma|Office,
Liberté, Fraternité, Egalité,
(the cemetery),
Vema 2026.

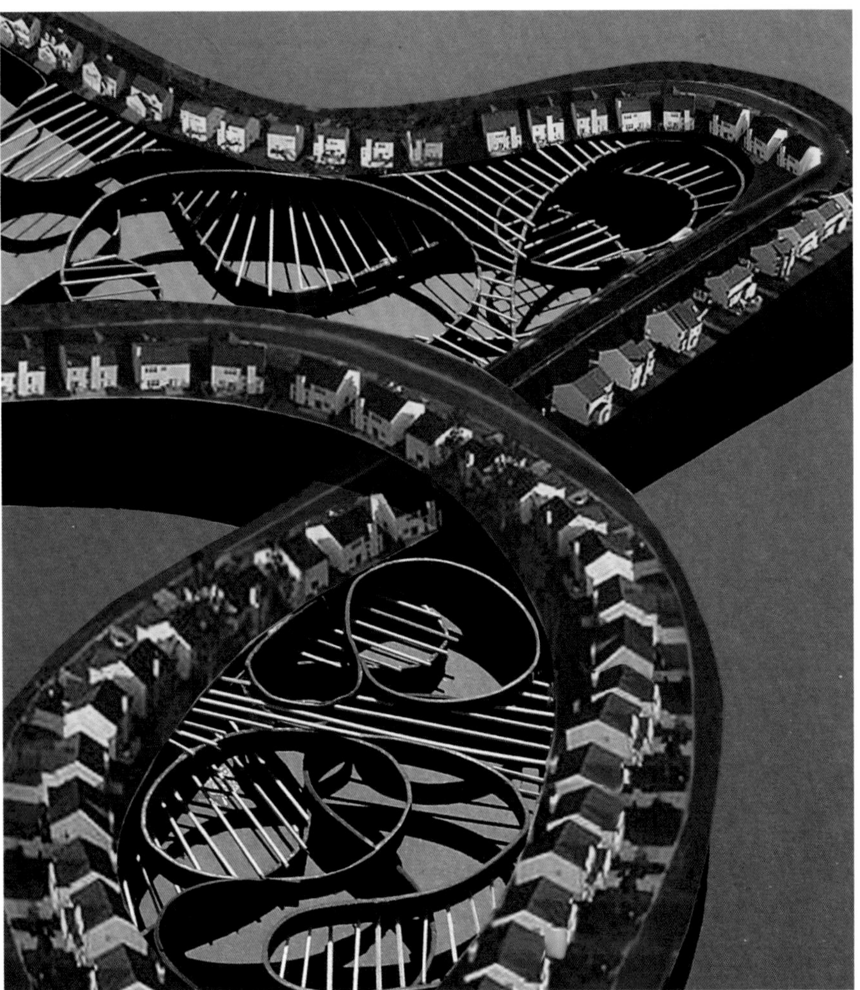

7

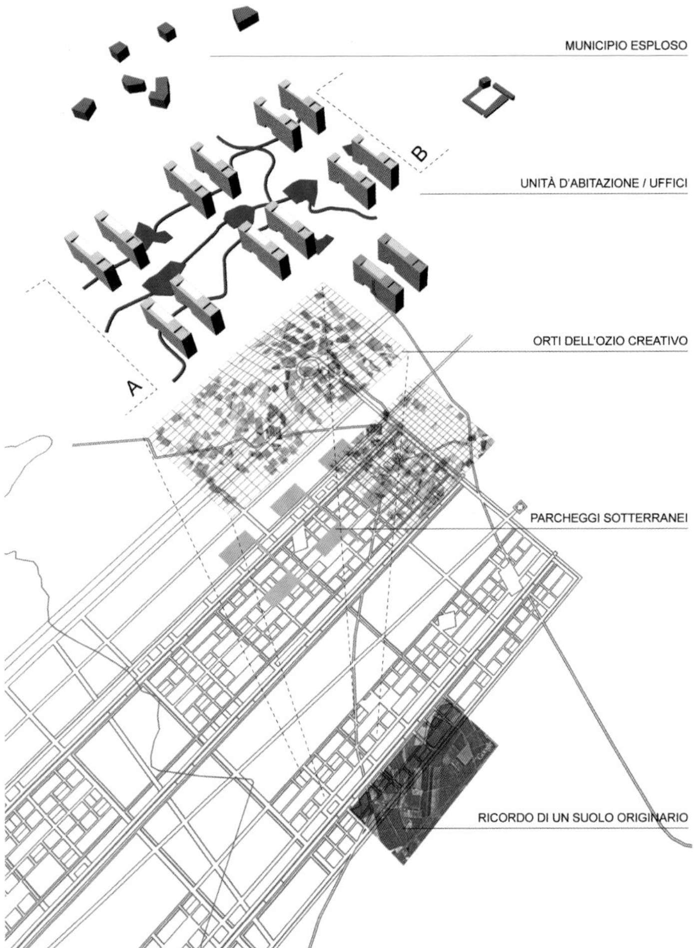

9

8

7
ELASTICO SPA
+ELASTICO 3,
The roads to speculation are endless,
(the school pole)
Vema 2026.

8
Giuseppe Fallacara,
Rgone Lake,
perspective view of the "inhabited wall" and of the "vault-shelter" from Energy Park, Vema 2026.

9
Santo Giunta,
Creative idleness gardens,
(offices and town hall),
Vema 2026
(work in progress).

10

11

10
Iotti+Pavarani Architetti.
Slow Town,
(shopping mall),
Vema 2026
(work in progress).

11
Raffaella Laezza,
Michele Moreno,
Giovanni Santamaria,
Sacred You.
Multireligious Urban Space,
Vema 2026.

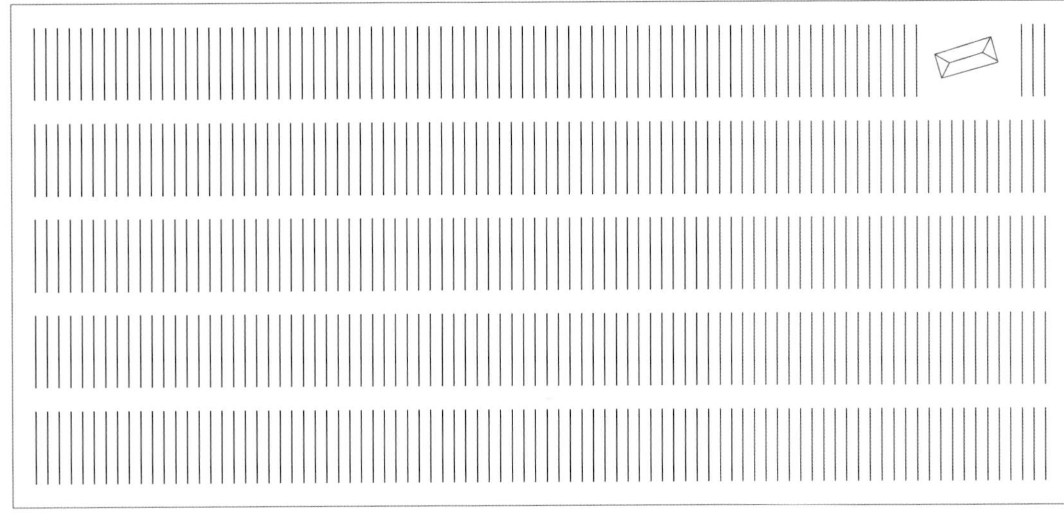

12

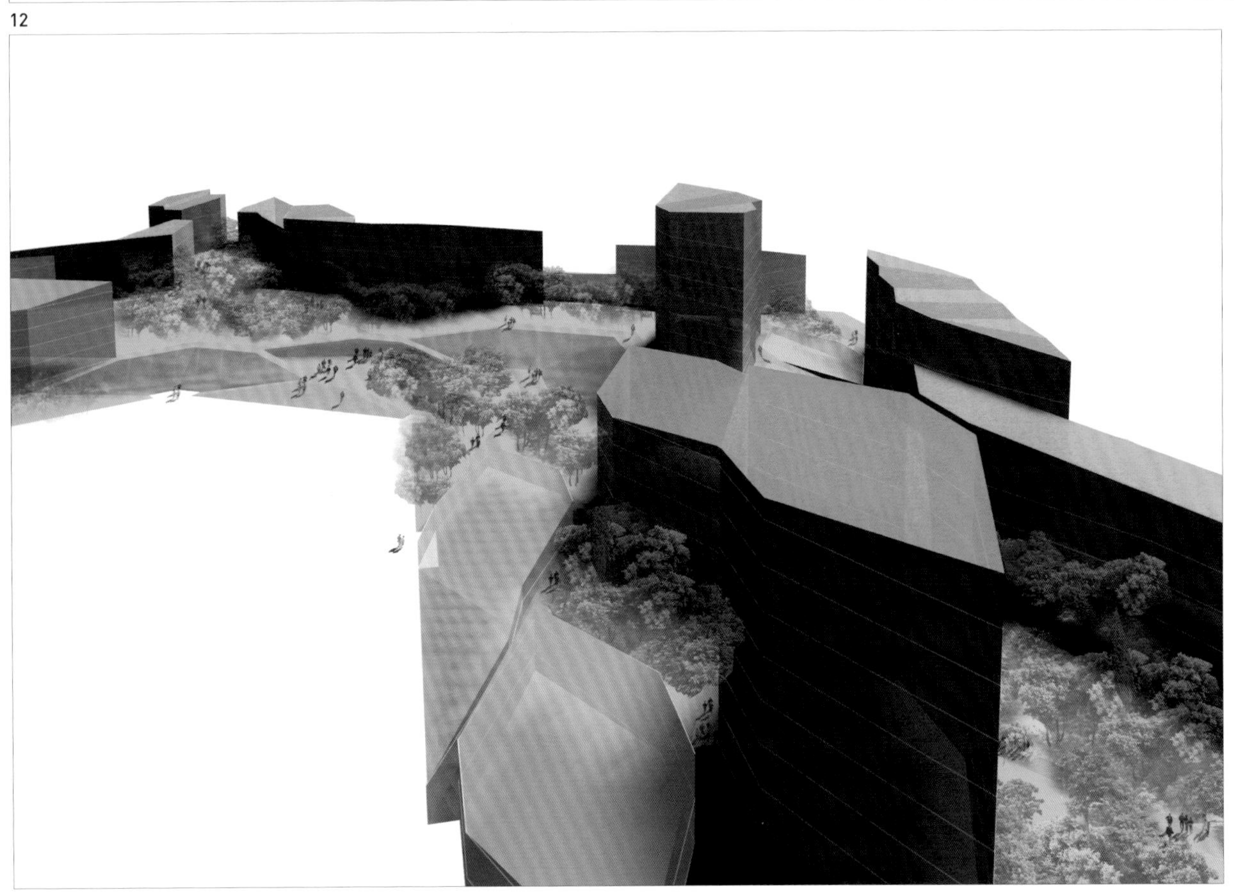

13

12
liverani / molteni
architetti,
The City / Factory,
Vema 2026
(concept work
in progress).

13
ma0 / emmeazero studio
d'architettura,
Continuicity,
(the museum),
Vema 2026
(work in progress).

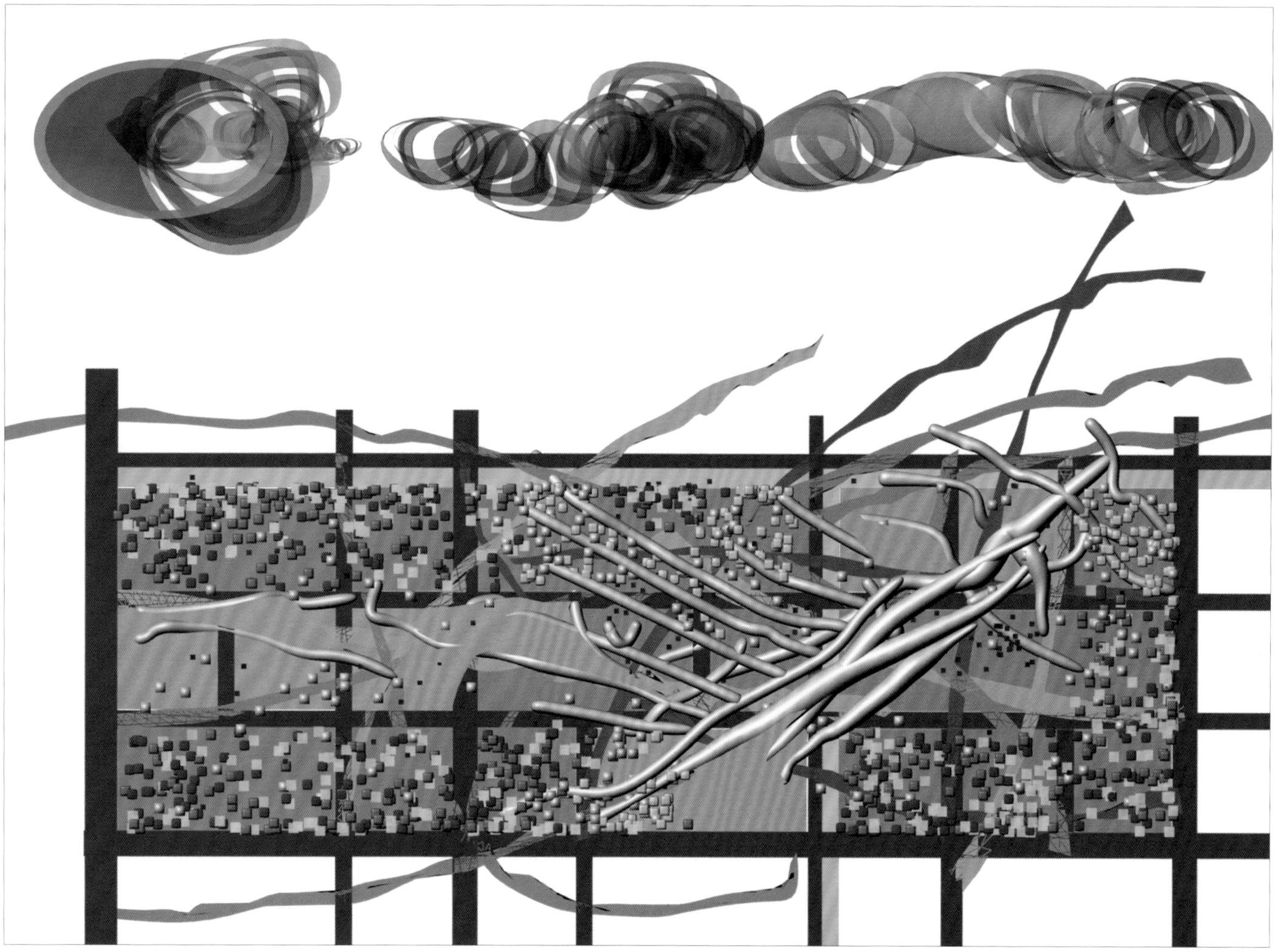

14

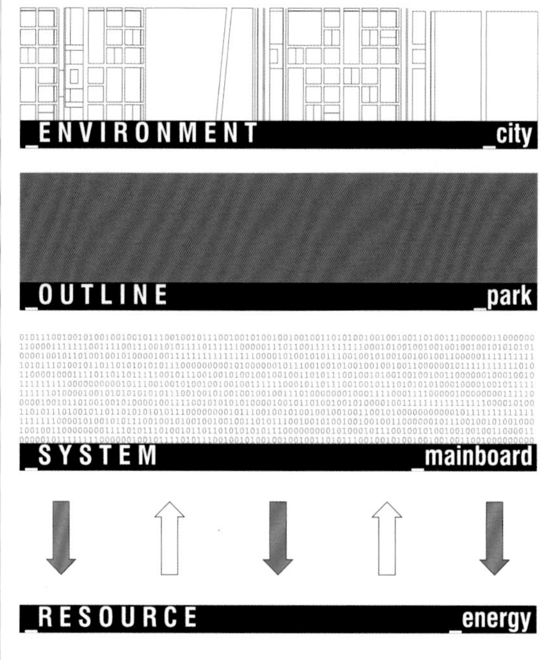

15

14
Antonella Mari,
Psychological turbulence fields - Hospital,
Vema 2026
(work in progress).

15
Masstudio,
The park and the resources system,
Vema 2026
(concept).

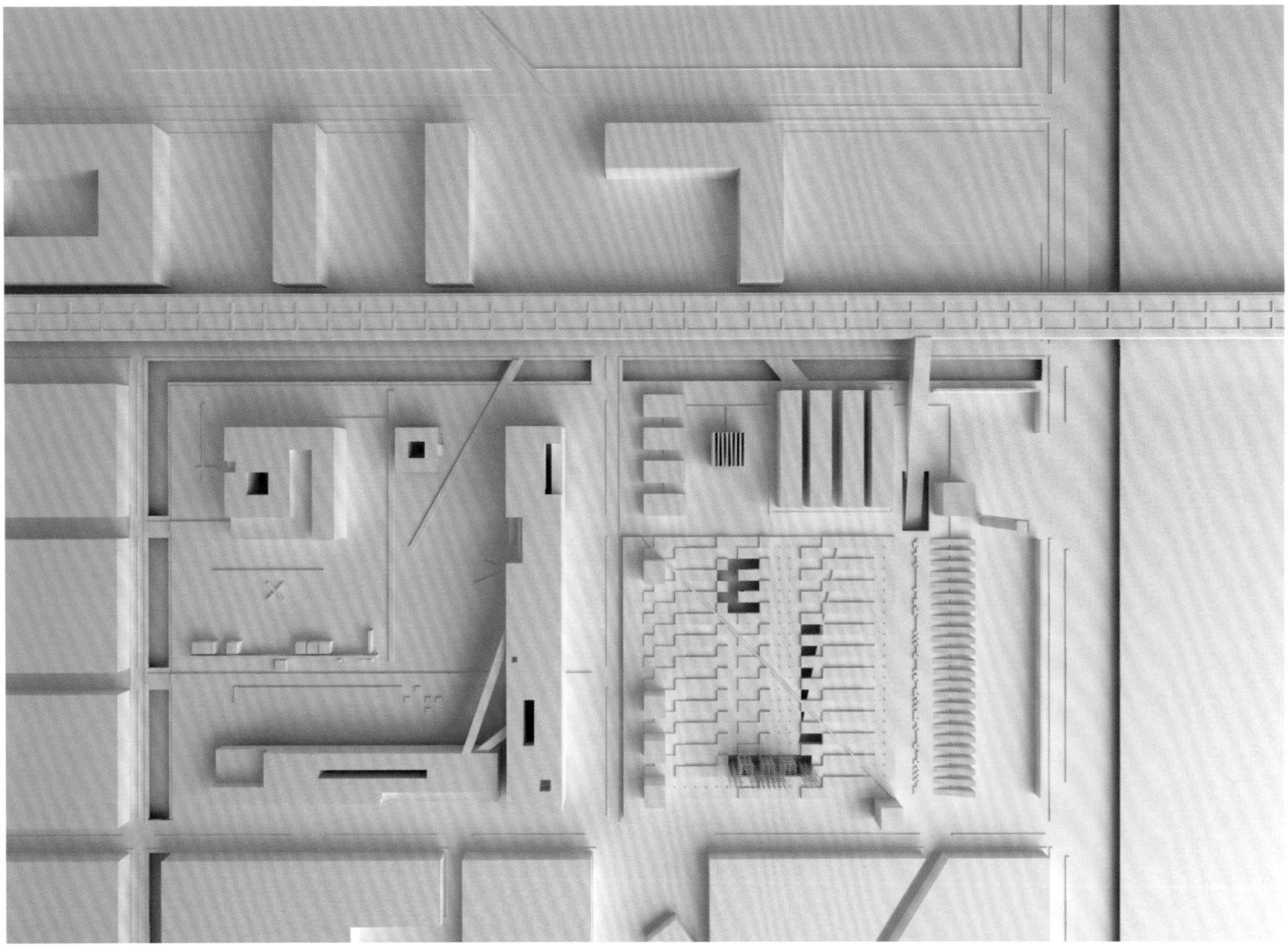

16

17

18

19

16
Stefano Milani,
Insieme vuoto,
(the warehouses),
aerial view of the area of the warehouses and of one of the residential areas,
Vema 2026
(work in progress).
Sponsored by TU Delft Holland.

17
Moduloquattro Architetti Associati,
Layers,
(Video and tape library, the media forum with works by Roberto Pietrosanti), artistic coordination Galleria A.A.M. Architettura Arte Moderna - Rome,
Vema 2026
(work in progress).

18
Tomaso Monestiroli, Massimo Ferrari,
A theatre for Vema,
Vema 2026
(work in progress).
Collage with the little theatres by Fausto Melotti.

19
OBR Open Building Research,
2026.09.06 18.00.00,
(Park of the Sport),
Vema 2026
(work in progress).

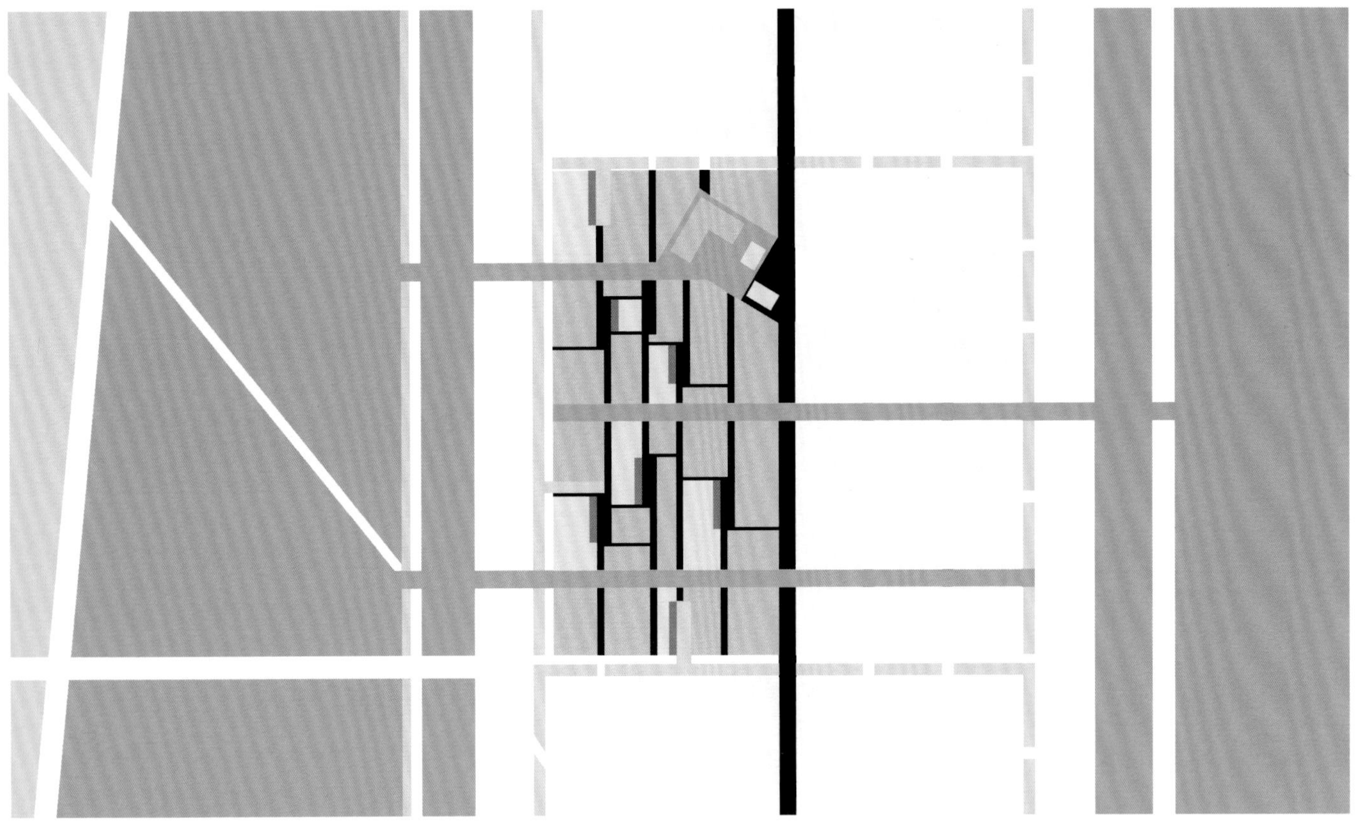

20

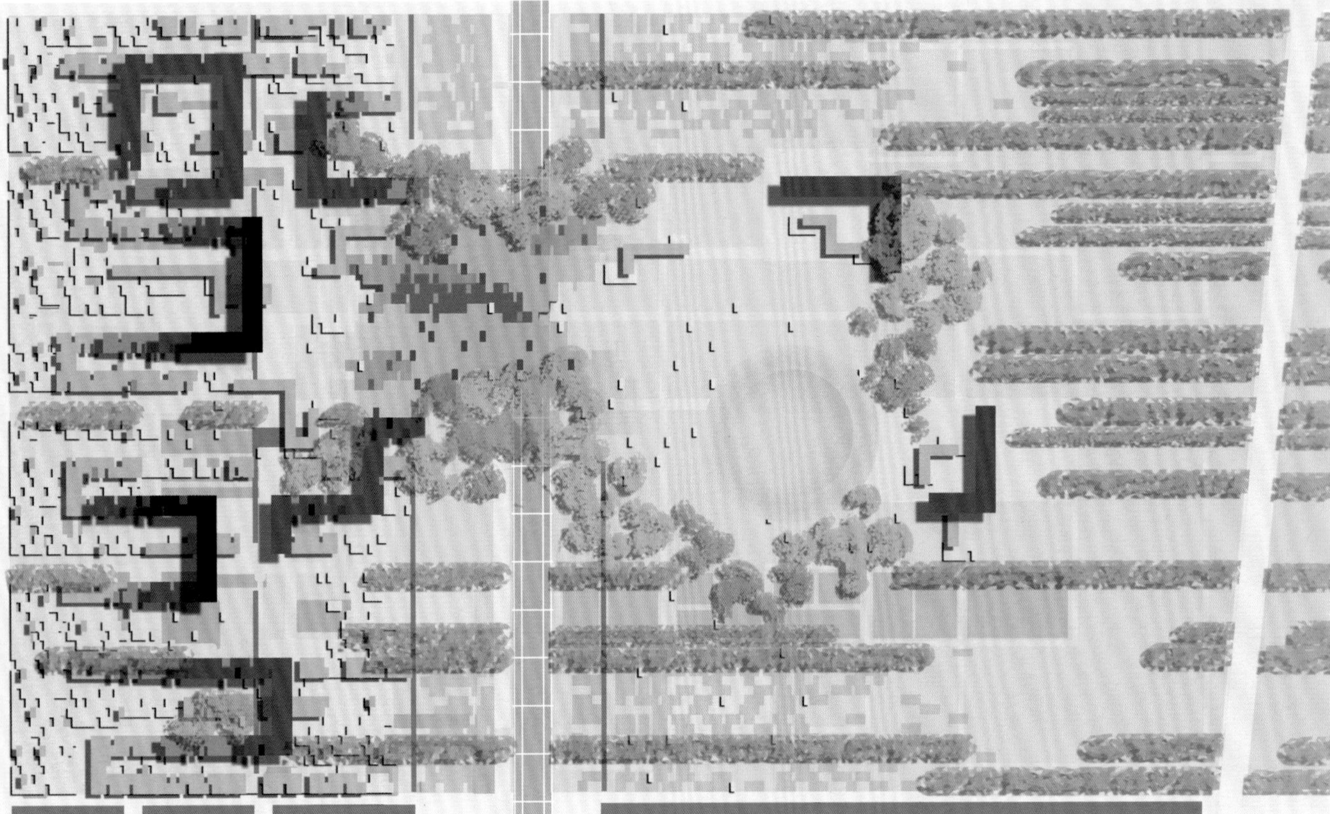

21

20
Gianfranco Sanna,
Vema 2026,
Environmental dimension and future living forms,
(Residential system for tourists and hotel), general plan of the settlment and of the connections with other parts of the city, Vema 2026.

21
Andrea Stipa,
Sound landscape,
(the entertainment pole), Vema 2026
(work in progress).

22

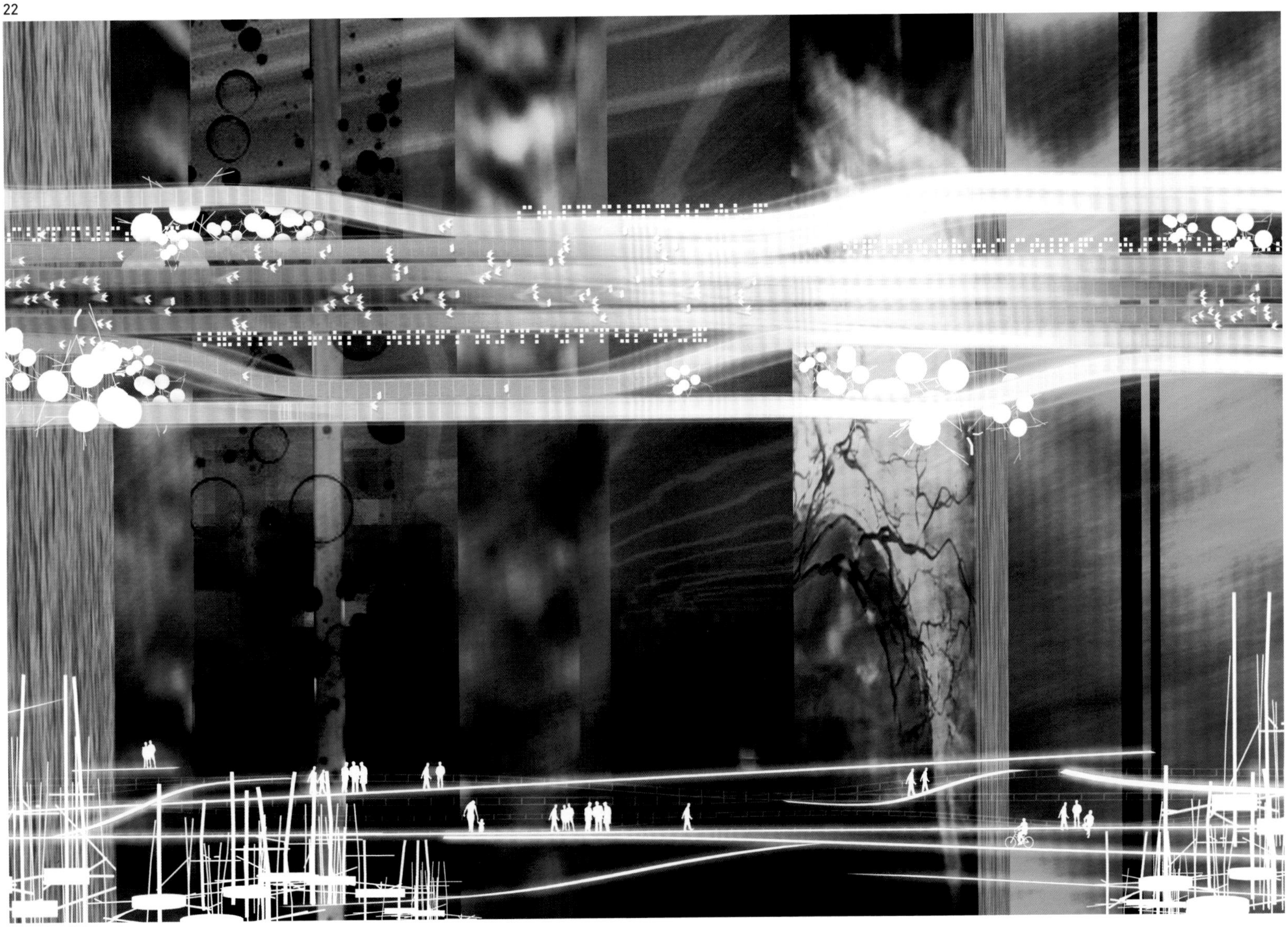

23

22
studio.eu,
Flower, power,
(Energy Park),
Vema 2026.

23
Alberto Ulisse,
unoaunostudio,
laq_architettura.
Velo.city.
(mobility machine),
allowing to live at
different speeds, in
a nomadic way, the
apartment building of a
urban natural/artificial
forest in progress, Vema
2026 (work in progress).

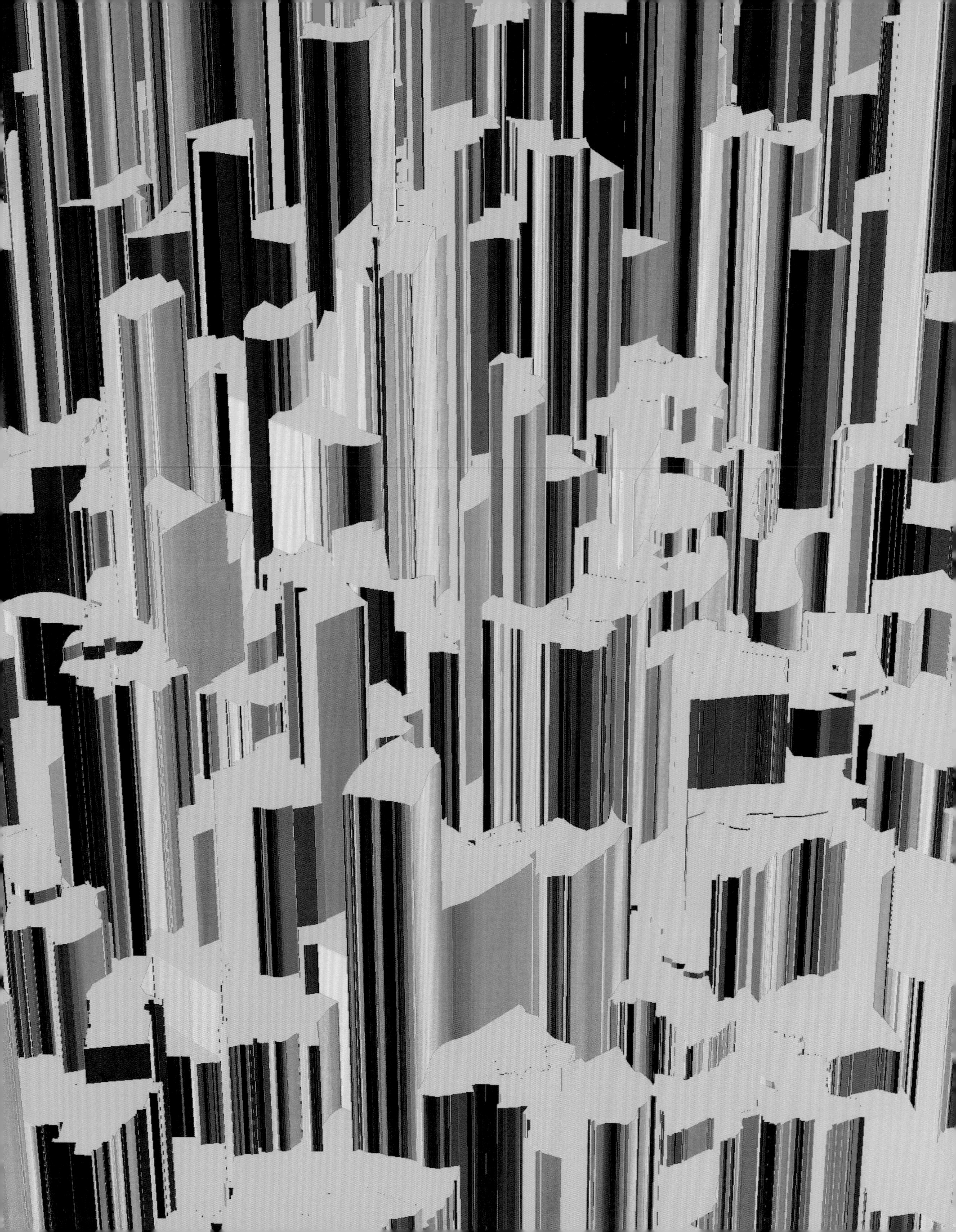

Participating Countries

Latitud 33° 41′ S, longitud 59°41′ O

1.
The 'Cuenca del Plata' (Plate River Basin) is one of the six biggest reserves of food and water in the world and is noted for its biological, cultural and economic diversity. It covers an area of almost 4,000,000 square kilometres in highly populated parts of Brazil, Argentina, Uruguay and Paraguay, and has a growing population of 60,000,000 inhabitants.

The Plate-Paraná river system is 8,990 km long, consisting of the Paraguay (Bermejo and Desaguadero), Paraná (Paranaiba and Tiete), Uruguay and Plate rivers running through those four countries.

The Paraná river is the second longest in South America after the Amazon. It extends for 4,000 kilometres and has a basin of 2,800,000 square kilometres, taking in most of south-east Brazil, Paraguay, eastern Bolivia and northern Argentina. Together with its tributaries, it forms the biggest of the two fluvial systems flowing into the Plate (the other one is the Uruguay river).

The basin is a strategic resource in itself for Argentina as it not only contains the country's largest fluvial and pluvial wealth, but also about 70% of its population, in 37% of the national territory (918,900 km^2).

2.
The Buenos Aires and Rosario metropolitan areas are the biggest urban developments in the Plate River Basin. This explains the planetary scale of the Plate Region in terms of the availability of non-renewable resources and its potential as a supplier of food, energy, manufactured and other goods, originating in the cultural diversity of the people settled on its banks.

3
There has been great expansion (extensive urbanization of rural areas) and consolidation (of the urban network) in Buenos Aires and Rosario, leading to an increase in replacement of the urban areas and infrastructure and the upgrading of large structures. This was firstly due to the renewal of obsolete infrastructure (harbours, railway, etc.), but is now stimulated by economic pressure and the overvaluation of real estate, resulting in private projects to replace large buildings. It seems the right time to question ourselves about the image and territorial balance we may aspire to.

4
The Argentine exhibition shows the current state of affairs and the plans both cities have developed during recent years. It also proposes a development scheme projected toward 2050 that is in line with the macro-economic projections for the area and closely linked to the growth of MERCOSUR. In this idea-presentation, speculation is made about a near future of solid growth and economic concentration in the Plate Basin and the physical encroachment of the urban sprawl from both cities along the Paraná river and National Highway 9 - with high impact on the riverside cities and villages settled between those routes and the metropolitan areas themselves.
Daniel Silberfaden

Argentina

COMMISSIONER/CURATOR
Daniel Silberfaden

SCIENTIFIC COMMITTEE
Alberto Varas
Jorge Sarquis
Pablo Sztulwark
Claudio Robles

DEPUTY COMMISSIONERS
Hernán Bisman
Roberto Busnelli
Julia Cabral

IMAGE SOURCE: VISIBLEEARTH.NASA.GOV

Nature Featuring City, City Featuring People

It is not by chance that we chose the Armenian Pavilion's motto, Nature Featuring City, City Featuring People. The link between humans and nature that has so naturally existed during the millennia of human development is something to be sought and rehabilitated. Today this link is marred. Humans continuously move away from nature, they distort the landscape, contaminate the environment and alienate themselves from nature. In this process of alienation, the artificial environment created by people in the course of their activities, including those related to town-planning issues, has a significant role.

Yerevan's current urban development is the result of such a process.

The natural landscape with its 'amphitheatre' layout seems to turn one towards the Biblical Mt Ararat, on the top of which people are still striving to find Noah's Ark. In between the amphitheatre and Mt Ararat is the Ararat plain, through which the Arax flows: one of the four rivers of Paradise. Mt Aragats, which holds Grigor the Illuminator's lantern, is in the northern part of this unique area. It would be only natural to expect that ancient and contemporary city planners, inspired by or feeling responsible for this area, should make an effort to preserve this tiny though precious piece of nature. Especially because it has been attracting people's attention since the Stone Age. However, Yerevan's current architectural appearance has diverged so far from the primeval state of this heavenly corner of the world that it is becoming more and more like a desert. This puzzle grows even more difficult to solve, given the high level of seismic risk, the dense population, different cultural layers, monuments of historical and archaeological value, the high level of underground water, the inflow of modern technologies, the unmanageable and unpredictable 'progress' of market relations, the limitless social needs of humans and their clashes on the crossroads of the traditional, individual and international, as well as the frequently conflicting political and economic interactions and interests of national, community and religious entities and neighbouring states.

What should be done to find the right development schemes for the urban infrastructures and communication networks? What should be done to improve the urban structures? Yerevan is a capital city, also serving as a refuge of hope for all Armenians all over the world. In fact, it does not envisage becoming a 'world or planet city', because of both its size and the town-planning challenges, but the tendencies of its development, together with the existence of solved but mostly unsolved problems (like erecting multi-storey buildings in a seismic zone, air pollution, hyper-density construction, traffic jams, clashes of public and personal interests in the implementation of town-planning principles) come within the same area and require solutions here and now.

With the help of the samples presented in the pavilion, an attempt is made to forecast ways for solving the problems by showing the current state of things; and to expose the importance of the efforts made in this area by Armenian architects and planners of various generations.

Our hope is that mankind will eventually move nearer to its natural state, so the features of nature, urban life and people will once again become common, thus leading to the linkage of People-City-Nature, flowing within the natural circle of all.

Ashot Haykazun Grigoryan

Armenia

COMMISSIONERS
Ashot Haykazun Grigoryan
Arà Zaryan

EXHIBITORS
Gagik Hovhannisyan and Levon Mrikyan
Gurgen Musheghyan and Petros Soghomonyan
Levon Vardanyan, Lilit Vardanyan and Ara Avetissyan
Hovhannes Mutafyan
David Baier Hotson

1

2

3

4

5

1
Gurgen Musheghyan and Petros Soghomonyan,
General layout of Yerevan city
future development concert.

2
Gagik Hovhannisyan and Levon Mrikyan,
Public and Residential Complex on the Main Avenue
Yerevan, 2005-2006. Construction in progress.

3
Levon Vardanyan, Lilit Vardanyan, Arà Avetissyan,
"Buzand de Luxe" Public and Residential Complex on the Main Avenue
Yerevan.

4
Hovhannes Mutafyan,
Residential complex in Zorap Street
Yerevan.

5
David Hotson, Gerard L. Cafesjian
Museum of Art
Yerevan.

Micro-macro city

The inhabitation of Australia is often portrayed through romantic images of isolated dwellings located in its vast interior or at its spectacular beaches. In reality only 7% of Australia's enormous land area is arable and more than 85% of its population lives on the thin coastal fringes of the continent, resulting in one of the most highly urbanized societies in the world.

Conversely, Australian cities demonstrate some of the lowest urban densities in the world and these conditions have led to very particular forms of urban settlement that elude many of the conventional categorizations of urban form. In this urban condition, a range of urban relationships and corresponding architectural responses have evolved.

Our response for the Australian Pavilion, within the broader Biennale theme of *Cities. Architecture and Society*, has been to look closely at the conditions of the Australian urban environment and focus on its specificity and differences. Our exhibition asks what unique attributes and possibilities are to be found in Australia's peculiar combinations of density, extreme spaciousness, cheap land, relative affluence and widespread access to technology. Our exhibition establishes a framework for seeing and understanding the contemporary Australian urban condition through case studies of precise moments within it.

Micro-macro city presents the Australian urban condition as a matrix of inter-relationships between urban cores, suburban sprawl, regional centres and rural hinterland. The concept of this field as a continuum of inhabitation across a range of densities and settlement types bypasses traditional distinctions between city and country, town and suburb, centre and periphery, metropolitan and non-metropolitan. Rather than separations, this idea of a dispersed urban continuum highlights connections and inter-relationships.

The workings of complex economic, demographic, social, governmental, environmental and cultural forces are revealed at certain precise moments within this framework. It is through the close study of such distilled environments that useful applied knowledge about our cities can emerge.

We present a series of eight case studies, called micro-systems, of particular urban environments from a wide range of contexts, which together form a cumulative and comparative macro-representation of our cities. Each case study reveals and provokes latent potential within our broader urban situation. In parallel with this process, eight

Australia

COMMISSIONER
Lucy Turnbull

SPONSORS
This is an initiative of the Royal Australian Institute of Architects. The RAIA would like to thank the Australian Architecture community for their significant support for this event. The Royal Australian Institute of Architects gratefully acknowledges the support of the Australia Council for the Arts for the use of the Pavilion for this exhibition

WEBSITE
www.architecture.com.au

EXHIBITORS
Nigel Bertram
Shane Murray

1

2

3

4

significant works of architecture representing a range of scales, programmes and locations, and which understand and engage their urban field, are coupled with these micro-systems in a dynamic relationship.

Our curation of the pavilion comprises two strategies: one atmospheric and one specific.

The 'atmospheric' is conceived as an environment that immerses the visitor in a range of experiences, providing a general understanding of the urban environments under consideration. These elements are not intended to be the subject of intense study; as an ensemble they visually and aurally evoke the qualities and differences of these specific environments.

The 'specific' consists of eight irregularly shaped tables distributed through the exhibition space. It is here that the details of each micro-system and its urban-architectural engagement are presented. Each table is dedicated to an urban micro-system and comprises representation of a particular aspect of that situation; drawings of the selected architectural work that demonstrate how its relationship to urban context is analogous to the chosen micro-system; and commissioned photographs and models depicting the building to foreground this particular relationship.

Shane Murray & Nigel Bertram

1
Ring-Road
FOTO BY MARIKA NEUSTUPNY

2
Station Entrance.
PHOTO BY DIEGO RAMIREZ.

3
Level Crossing.
PHOTO BY DEAN MACKENZIE.

4
High Street.
PHOTO BY JUNITA ABDUL RAHMAN.

City = Shape Space Net

The terms *shape*, *space* and *net* express the three ideas that have formed our view of the city's organization since early modernism. By thematizing these terms, reference is made to works by Austrian architects who have been capable of achieving a concise visualization of their era's contemporary architectural discussion. Additionally, this selection of exhibits also evokes Austria's spectrum of possibilities, offering a description of its culture based on three examples, which can be considered paradigmatic attempts to understand the mechanics of the city and comprehend its specific effects with the help of a concise picture.

Friedrich Kiesler's *City in Space* from 1925 is representative of the experiential space of the modern metropolis, as influenced by the dramaturgy of the stage. Built in the Grand Palais, it was part of Austria's presentation at the Exposition Internationale des Arts Décoratifs in Paris. Kiesler drew the urban viewer's gaze, accelerated through mechanization, onto the stage. According to him, *City in Space* was the first demonstration of his vision of time-space architecture. For Alfred Barr, it presented the technically and conceptually most daring spatial realization of De Stijl's ideas.

Hans Hollein's *Flugzeugträger* (aircraft carrier) of 1964 comprehends the city as a functional shape. Hollein recalls Le Corbusier's use of a ship as a model for the city's spatial complexity and economy. In the aesthetics of the ocean liner, Le Corbusier celebrated in 1923 the liberation of outdated images in architecture. In the early 1960s, Hollein used mechanical engineering details to transform Kiesler's fragile structures into massive, down-to-earth city nodes. This realism progresses further in the re-contextualization of an aircraft carrier, which, transplanted onto a green field, comments in a Pop Art, ironic gesture on the relationship of city and nature. Hollein finds expression for the city's energy by condensing it into a mobile object.

Gregor Eichinger's Net
1. In a group of bridges across the Danube Canal in the centre of Vienna, the 2005 project *Trialto* connects a number of directions and brings together the urban network that has long been missing.
2. The Viennese 'XXX Parties' activated left-over urban space and expanded the city into new patterns of usage for the event culture. In 1982, the *For Sale* workshop, co-organized by Christian Knechtl, Bepi Maggiori and Marco Zanuso Jr., gathered almost an entire generation of European designers around a copying machine in a remote gas station in nowhere land, 50 kilometres east of Vienna.
3. In Venice, a network will be created, which will generate a moving festival during the pavilion's opening. The intensity of making contact as an indicator of a society that is being set up will be visible as a structure in the pavilion. A newly opened bar in Venice serves as a meeting point for this community for the entire duration of the Biennale.

Vienna. Intensities: The ordinary city, when examined with unusual parameters, reveals a wealth of unexpected relations and possibilities. The exhibition undertakes the attempt to comprehend Vienna's latent intensities, giving them shape and comprehensible presence in a three-dimensional depiction.

Rock over Barock: this exhibition in the Magazzini del Sale supplements the programme shown in the Austrian pavilion.
Wolf D. Prix

Austria

COMMISSIONER
Wolf D. Prix

CURATOR
Reiner Zettl

COLLABORATORS
Markus Pillhofer (Project Architect)
Andrea Börner
Bärbel Müller (Research)
Katharina Müller
Eva Diem (Project Coordination)
Cynthia Kallmeyer
Paulus M. Dreibholz
Thomas Kramer
Roswitha Janowski-Fritsch

EXHIBITORS
Hans Hollein/Shape
Friedrich Kiesler/Space
Gregor Eichinger/Net

1

2

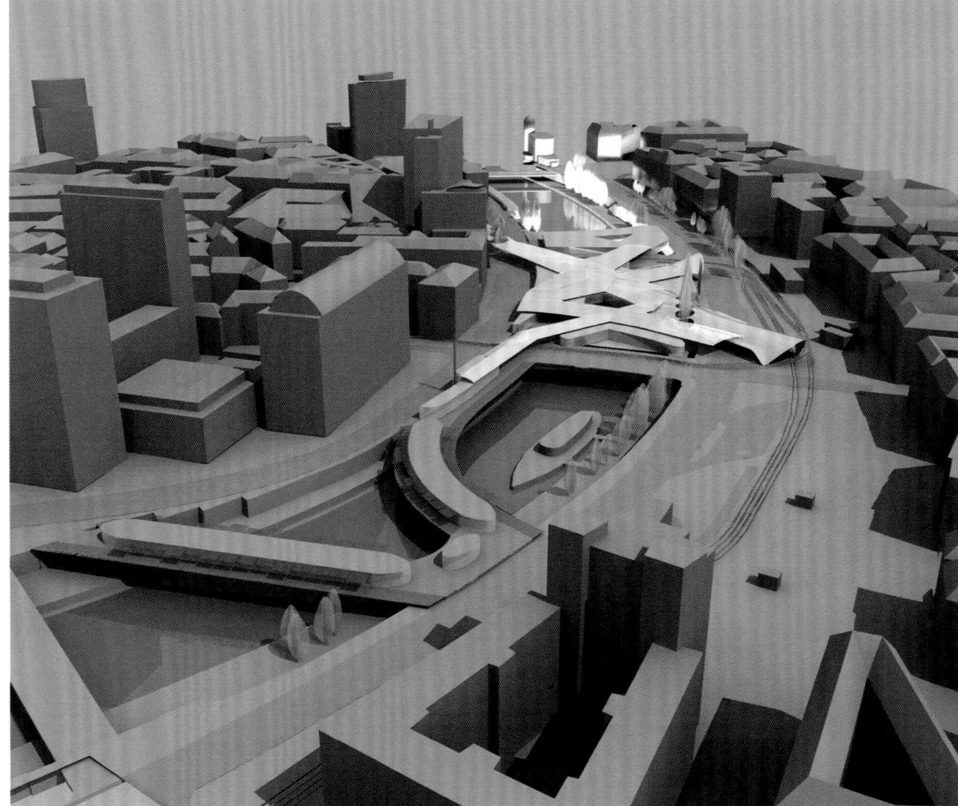

3

1
Hans Hollein,
Aircraft-Carrier-City in landscape,
1964. Collage, 56 x 66 cm. Collection Museum of Modern Art, New York.
COURTESY HANS HOLLEIN.

2
Friedrich Kiesler,
Raumstadt,
1925. Silbergelatine/ Barythpapier.
COURTESY KIESLER FOUNDATION
PHOTO BY J. ROSEMAN, PARIS.

3
Gregor Eichinger,
Trialto,
Rendering.
COURTESY GREGOR EICHINGER

Rock over Barock

The desire to celebrate space: based on 7+2 examples, the exhibition *Rock over Barock* at the Magazzini del Sale will convey what could comprise a specific, shared, distinctive Austrian architecture. These young architects show that for all their diversity, it is nonetheless possible to discover a distinct quality in Austrian architecture: the architecture of the spatial sequence.

Although architecture, too, must be thought of in global terms, it is becoming increasingly important to develop the unmistakable uniqueness of an authentic architectural language, one that can be defined only in the context of a cultural background. We can embark upon the attempt to define the world's architects who determine the architectural discussion at the moment through their cultural roots. We can call the Dutch and the Swiss, in contrast with the Austrian space inventors, strict 'diagram Calvinists'; a Rietveld in Vienna is just as unthinkable as a Kiesler in Rotterdam. We can call Frank Gehry, Eric Moss, and Daniel Libeskind Cabbalists and mystically describe their architecture as powerfully literate and eloquent. And Zaha Hadid's designs are clearly the spatial signs of Arabic calligraphies.

Yet in the search for the uniqueness of Austria's architecture, we constantly stumble upon the missing theoretical foundation that would allow an interpretation and stylization of the architects' clearly evident qualities in such a way that a sharply contoured image appears of what might make Austrian architects distinguishable on the global scene: namely, the desire to redefine built space.

Although the lack of a supporting theory might open up individual possibilities, the often acclaimed diversity—perhaps otherwise a sign of strength—is ultimately just the sum of lone warriors, which opens the gates to international recognition for only very few Austrian architects.

Whereas in other places young architects learn to ride the slipstream of their country's greatest names, in Austria we practice patricide. However, this patricide is not an act of liberation: it is simply an unruly defiance of tradition, a reflection of Austria's anti-intellectual stance. This prevents a discursive confrontation with innovative architectural qualities that risk being novel.

EXHIBITORS
ARTEC Architekten
Urs Bette
DELUGAN MEISSL ASSOCIATED ARCHITECTS
the next ENTERprise architects
Klaus Stattmann
stiefel kramer, Wien/Zurich
Wolfgang Tschapeller
Sophie Grell
Tercer Piso Arquitectos

1

What madness to build immensely heavy domes and have them vanish under heavenly visions! By taking the desire for spatial design evident in baroque structures as a starting point, a particular skill of Austrian architects becomes clear: designing complex space rather than the simplified box. From Fischer von Erlach to Rudolph M. Schindler and Friedrich Kiesler through to Hans Hollein, Walter Pichler, Raimund Abraham, Günther Domenig, and Coop Himmelb(l)au, the buildings of these architects are structural evidence of the existence of a formal language that unmistakably places Austrian architecture on the global scene.

Consciously or unconsciously, in ways appropriate to their era, young architects follow the baroque traces of the spatial sequences—and change them. *Rock over Barock*, with its 7+2 examples, shows that there is an Austrian tradition, as it were, which goes beyond the scattered battles of lone warriors: it is the shared desire to celebrate space.
Wolf D. Prix

2

1
Stiefel Kramer,
Kunsthaus Graz
"Promenade médiale - A Continuos House",
2000. Scale 1:500.
Plaster, plexiglass.
18 x 19 x 10 cm.
PHOTO BY MARKUS PILLHOFER.

2
Sophie Grell,
Raum oder Vorfeld (Symbol and announcement) system on the site before the MuseumsQuartier,
Vienna, 2004-2005.
Scale 1:200. Foamboard, plastic. 30 x 15 x 10 cm.
PHOTO BY SOPHIE GRELL.

La beauté de l'ordinaire
Perspectives on Belgium's territory and its small particularities...

The exhibition *La beauté de l'ordinaire* gives us the opportunity, during the 2006 Venice Architecture Biennale, to pause and consider the beauties of Belgian territorial banality.

Having been engaged in profound changes for many years, in a similar way as those territories described by Richard Burdett, Belgium is seeing noticeable change in its territory, at a pace that is certainly slow but potentially relevant.

The installation presented in the Belgian Pavilion is designed to offer visitors to the 2006 Biennale several, unashamedly modest perspectives that allow us to uncover a culture and society. We are also given a glimpse into that society's membership of an urbanity to which the neologism of the Brussels artist Juan d'Oultremont, 'abruxellation', could be applied and extended to the whole of Belgium, as the distinctive love/hate relationship that Belgians enjoy with their territories in everyday life.

Envisaged as the spatial, political and cultural expression of the Belgian collectivism, the territory in question is characterized by a whole series of particularities that can be drawn on to reveal the special nature of a framework for life and constitute its charm and its assets. These can come under the heading of, in turn, spatial banalities, ordinary appropriations and improbable confrontations... This condition, and more particularly the observer's view of it, allows us to examine the extraordinary that is contained in numerous ordinary situations, and vice versa. *La beauté de l'ordinaire* seeks to question this context: in a generic society engaged in the globalised phenomenon of the aestheticization of everyday life, how can one bring out the particularities arising out of the involuntary, the improbable, the anecdotal, the indefinite or the absurd and, without engaging in an exhaustive or incantatory discourse, move towards a possible identification, however relative?

It is, moreover, pleasant and interesting to live on this unstable, flawed territory that is defined in terms of its 'vacancies' through wastelands that are as much material as geographical and gaps in the organization of its social and cultural life. This situation offers numerous opportunities for action. It also allows us to envisage the anecdotal, beyond its generic character, as an element of both identification and recognition. If the Belgian territory is not a priori distinctive, it has the capacity to transform itself into spaces that combine lived experience, culture and political expression. Contrary to numerous standardized European territories, which are producers of established ideologies, this territory continues to destabilize the status quo and to inspire the imaginary. It also allows the most varied, individual, collective, cinematographic, novelistic, artistic – and potentially architectural and urban – projects.

Despite the fact that several among us may experience a certain discomfort or annoyance at the impossibility of establishing order in what seems an inevitable territorial disorder, we have to accept both that we are at the beginning of that process and, for reasons that often escape us, that we like it here. More fundamentally, we can accept the daily reality of this territory, observe the existing situation and play around with its possibilities, enjoy its richness, take inspiration from it and display its most (extra)ordinary and most beautiful aspects.
Label Architecture

Belgium

COMMISSIONER
Label Architecture (Jean-Didier Bergilez, Michel Lefèvre, Thibaut Rome, guest Véronique Patteeuw)

IN COLLABORATION WITH
Stefan Liberski

WITH THE SUPPORT OF
Ministère de la Culture de la Communauté française Wallonie-Bruxelles

EXHIBITOR
Label Architecture (Jean-Didier Bergilez, Michel Lefèvre, Thibaut Rome, guest Véronique Patteeuw)

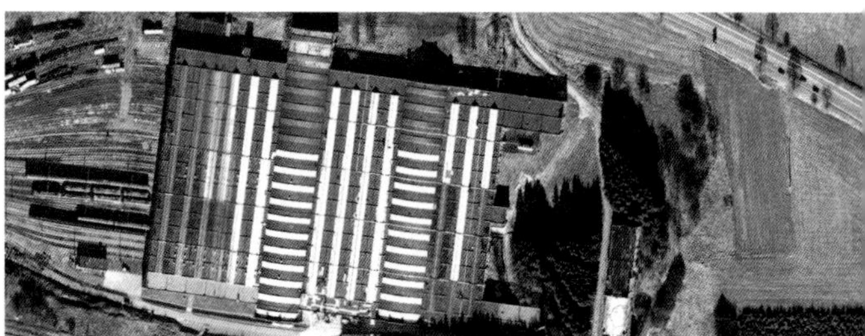

2

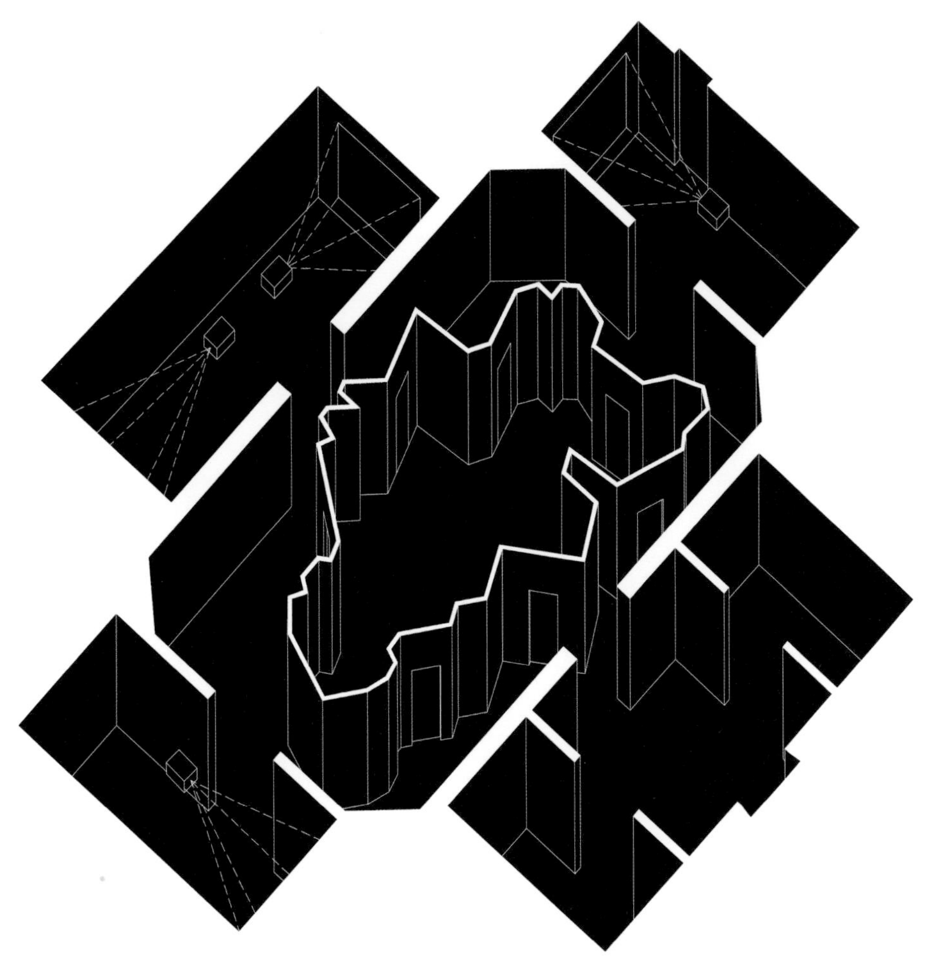

1

1
Label Architecture.
Belgian pavilion,
Axonometry, 2006.
© LABEL ARCHITECTURE.

2
Belgium. Orthophotos.
© IGN, 1997-2005.

Brazil's representation at the 10th International Architecture Exhibition seeks to evoke the transformative power of São Paulo's constructed space. In this metropolis, the structuring of the urban space can be understood in terms of the writing traced on a specific territory by the main infrastructure systems. São Paulo was built as a series of concrete responses to the demands of a late but extremely fast process of industrialization. As a result, construction of the material basis to enable production was one of the main factors guiding the development of this industrial metropolis.

We know that the systems include attributes with the power to organize the physical, spatial, functional and symbolic interrelations of a significant part of the elements belonging to the metropolis. Therefore, one idea to be investigated is how intervention on the ways these systems are used can be a feasible strategy for dealing with the issues raised by transformation from an 'industrial metropolis' to a 'contemporary metropolis'. The idea is to approach the day-to-day dimension of life in the city by bringing new values to the constructed space.

These and other collective reflections studied by a group of professionals invited by the Fundação Bienal de São Paulo resulted in an exhibition consisting of two blocks. Its theme is the borderline position of designing actions that coincide in the complexity of the metropolis.

The first room presents the transformation of the original site of the São Paulo basin by its technical construction. It points to its capacity to articulate on a territorial scale and questions its reflections in the fraying of local urban relations. The forms of occupation of this territory are clearly shown by a set of maps and aerial photographs.

The second room reveals the construction of the places. That is, it seeks to recognise the moments when the qualified city was constructed by long-range planning, not limited exclusively to technical sectoral responses; moments when the formulation of multiple, diverse programmes, simultaneous in space and altered by time, offer usages that transform spaces into places with an empowered urban condition.

Brazil

COMMISSIONER
Manoel Francisco Pires da Costa

CURATOR
Jacopo Crivelli Visconti

PRODUCTION AND ORGANIZATION
Fundação Bienal de São Paulo

EXHIBITORS
Vinicius Andrade
Fernanda Barbara
Marta Bogéa
Martín Corullon
Luciana Carvalho Pinto
Fernando de Mello Franco
Marcelo Morettin
Juan Pablo Rosenberg
Fabio Valentim
Fernando Viegas
Guilherme Wisnik

1

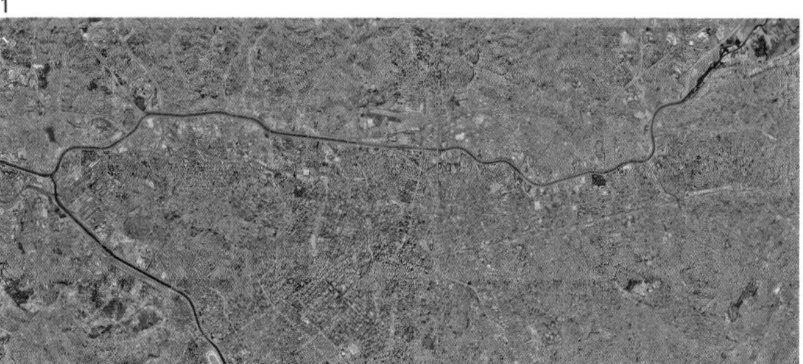

2

3

4

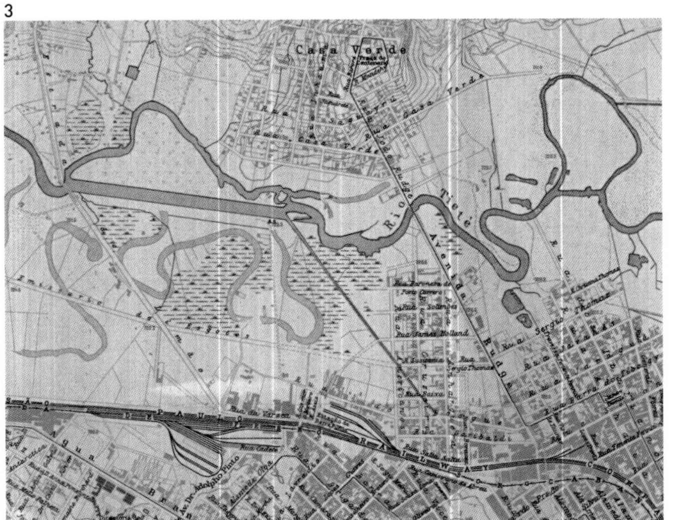

5

6

7

8

1
Theatre performance BR-3.
Teatro da Vertigem.
PHOTO BY EDOUARD FRAIPONT.

2
Aerial view of the city of São Paulo with the rivers Tietê, Tamanduateí and Pinheiros.
SOURCE: BASE.

3
PHOTO BY BEBETE VIÉGAS.

4
Banks of the Tietê river, in the neighborhood of the Manoel Feio underground Station, São Paulo, 2006
PHOTO BY CRISTIANE MUNIZ.

5
Canalization of the river Tietê, near Casa Verde and Água Branca.
Fragment of the *Mapa Topographico do Municipio de São Paulo*, Sara Brasil, 1930.
SOURCE: ACERVO BIBLIOTECA DA FAU USP.

6
Part of the railway line Sorocabana over the river Pinheiros, where it meets the river Tietê, a/d, 1937.
SOURCE: ACERVO ELETROPAULO.

7
Deforestation of the canalization line of the river Pinheiros, a/d, 1930.
SOURCE: ARQUIVO ELETROPAULO.

8
Marginal Pinheiros near the University of São Paulo - USP,
Detail.
PHOTO BY BEBETE VIEGAS, 2000.

Sweater Lodge

The installation at the Canadian Pavilion for the 2006 Venice Architecture Biennale has been fashioned by the Vancouver based practice Pechet and Robb Studio.

The primary and most arresting manifestation of the project is the insertion of a hugely overscaled polar fleece sweater inside the pavilion. The literal legibility of the sweater is supplanted by the creation of a sensually engaging backdrop. The work inside references the emerging design culture of the city of Vancouver - a city in which an extravagant geographic setting establishes an unflinching measure of the activities associated with settlement and building. Vancouver's urbanity is vitally contaminated by ever-present leisure activities, a pervading concern for environmental propriety and the essential optimism of a hugely diverse population preoccupied with fabrication of the home.

While exhilarating in its expression of capital flow and conventions of domestic taste, design speculations often locate themselves along a cultural perimeter. The essentially blunt nature of current city building is probed through more agile explorations associated with landscape, furniture, set design and public art installation - always maintaining a critical and at times quizzical regard for the brittle experiences of this place.

Pechet and Robb's accomplishments include a number of installations within the public landscape that anticipate and provoke the invention of new social practices. Within an urban realm that is largely unprecedented, such installations could be considered provisional invitations - awaiting the forcefulness of their built presence to be fully accommodated in daily lives.

This regard between the routine and the improvisational not only characterizes the nature of Pechet and Robb's practice, but also draws a direct resonance between the actions of the designer and those of the citizen. Each is obliged to undertake a revision of the environment *as found* in order to cultivate personal and nuanced meanings. The reading of the city is forged by individual and particular vested interests, which, in turn, intersect and collide to create a collective identity of layered communities.

In its allusion to the aboriginal constructions known as *sweatlodges* – structures built for the purposes of ritual purification and communal association – the *SweaterLodge* installation evokes another powerful strain of native American culture, that of the *trickster*. In their use of puns, arcane allusions and double entendre, Pechet and Robb make manifest one valuable strategy for minority interests to maintain a degree of invisibility within the realm of the dominant. Allied with shifts in scale and a general inclination to decontextualise the familiar and everyday, the work operates as both visceral and intellectual stimulus – its final meaning constructed again and again by visitors to the Biennale.

The exquisitely ephemeral material of recycled plastic drink containers rendered in the monumental scale of a titan's sweater transformed again into a comforting interior that evokes Barbarella while reminding us of architecture's ultimate affiliation with the essential shelter of clothing and invites a moment of repose and reflection... a cipher for that order of complexity and substance that lies at the heart of this project we call architecture.
Christopher Macdonald

Canada

COMMISSIONER
Greg Bellerby

CURATORS
Christopher Macdonald
Greg Bellerby

SPONSORS
Canada Council for the Arts, Foreign Affairs Canada
Emily Carr Institute of Arts and Design
UBC School of Architecture and Landscape Architecture
Aeroplan
Global Mechanic
Mountain Equipment Co-op
Spot Brand Bikes
BlueImprint Books
Tugboat Media
Sydney's Sweatworks

WEBSITE
www.sweaterlodge.ca

EXHIBITOR
Pechet and Robb Studio (Bill Pechet and Stephanie Robb)

1

2

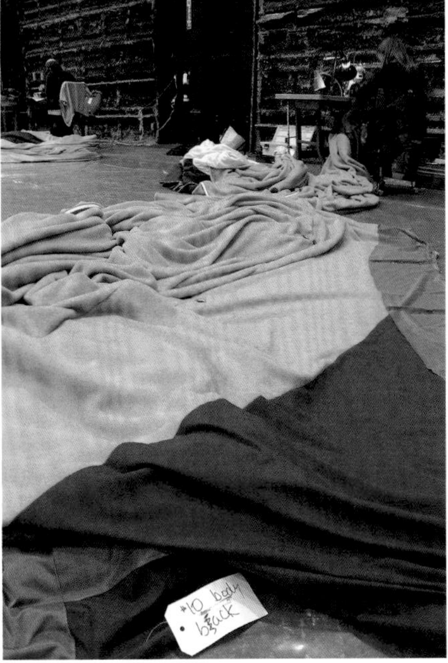

3

4

5

1
Sweater for SweaterLodge.
PHOTO BY SCOTT MASSEY.

2-3
Sweater Construction.
PHOTO BY SCOTT MASSEY.

4
SweaterLodge Label.
PHOTO BY SCOTT MASSEY.

5
Pavilion Model.
PHOTO BY BILL PECHET.

Plaza de la Ciudadanía y Centro Cultural Palacio La Moneda

The historic events of political life in Chile in the second half of the twentieth century have profoundly affected Chilean society. For many years the restoration of democracy to civic institutions lacked a similar vital sign in the condition of urban and public space in this country. Tragic images reminiscent of war, the bombing of the government palace, made a much more lasting impression on the collective eye than did the subsequent restoration.

In contrast with the imposing expanse and geographic silence of the regions, Santiago, the sole metropolis in Chile, exhibits a dearth of public spaces within a classic Hispanic layout. Such dense construction, however, frames the most extensive empty urban space in the heart of the city: the *barrio cívico* comprises an area of public buildings conceived by city planner Karl Brunner in the 1930s. A vast space to the south of the magnificent eighteenth-century government palace, the Palacio de La Moneda, built by Joaquín Toesca, extends beyond Avenida Libertador Bernardo O'Higgins, which forms the structural axis of the city. Here the sum of the greatest urban linear infrastructure and the most valuable piece of civil architecture in the country come together in full force. As in so many areas elsewhere in the city, time has erased intentions and the automobile has destroyed its vitality.

Plaza de la Ciudadanía and Centro Cultural Palacio de La Moneda are the most important public works built recently in the central area of Santiago, in the framework of the works that the Chilean government is promoting for the coming celebration of Chile's bicentenary.

We see the new square as the vital urban sign designed to establish in the collective consciousness the restoration of democracy and civic traditions in the country. The process began with an open architecture competition, won by Cristián Undurraga – Undurraga Devés Arquitectos. The preliminary design, supported by specialists, included the study of social considerations and was followed by a call for bids coordinating public and private interests to ensure execution of the works through a regular concession process.

The architectural project restored pedestrian use of the extensive public space by means of three distinct operations. The first was to build a *piano nobile* next to the Palacio de La Moneda, a terrace shading and extending the inner courtyards to the outside, a necessary step given that President Lagos had reinstated public circulation across the palace ground floor. Next came the creation of a tissue of hard lines and stretches of green with a twofold guideline: a regular order extending the present main lines of pedestrian circulation beyond the square; and a random, less emphatic, order diagonally joining specific urban features. The third operation was demolition of the monument known as *Altar de la Patria*, or altar of the motherland, built by the military regime, which completes the continuity of the Bulnes promenade ending in the square.

Where the city plan is designed for continuity on the surface, a number of parts of the program are clearly identifiable underground. The new *Centro Cultural Palacio de La Moneda* at the foot of the government palace and the associated public parking space, the new infrastructure for traffic and metro station under the square, in addition to the new tomb of Libertador Bernardo O'Higgins on the south side are all parts of the overall architectural project.

The clear-cut subterranean figures, like tapestry motifs, reveal on the underside of the square the continuous urban threads that support them. Urban and historic continuity that – since the experience of man in outer space – extends beyond the limits of the project, beyond its architectural scope.

Chile

COMMISSIONERS
Patricia Rivadeneira
Alejandro Manriquez

CURATOR
Pablo M. Lopez

WITH THE SUPPORT OF
Government of Chile
Department of Cultural Affairs

EXHIBITOR
Cristián Undurraga

Bogotá: From Chaos to Meta-City

This exhibition shows the radical transformation of Bogotá by an urban strategy combining physical interventions, civic culture, good governance and social inclusion. These meta-practices go beyond traditional planning discourses, while at the same time are inspired by the city's own urban experience in order to redefine it as a physical, social and mental construction.

Bogotá's modern urban history has included some remarkable planning initiatives (Brunner, Le Corbusier, Sert) and periods of good government (mayors Gaitan Cortés and Virgilio Barco during the 1950s and 1960s), both in the context of an active civic culture. These meta languages and practices were lost during the 1970s and 80s in a context of explosive rural-urban migration and increased insecurity, sharpening contrasts between formal and informal, legal and illegal, secure and insecure. The 1980s were characterized by a critical degradation of Bogotá as public space, collective experience and administrative entity, with accompanying high murder and other crime rates, deterioration of public space, traffic chaos, absence of organized mass transport and loss of urban identity.

Since the mid-1990's, Bogotá has succeeded in radically transforming this city in crisis by implementing fiscal-administrative decentralization and other national reforms. The comprehensive urban strategy was highly original and extremely effective in restoring the city as a physical and mental whole. It was inspired by earlier local experiences, and made non-dogmatic use of urban renewal processes elsewhere. The resulting combination of urban projects, educational programmes and institutional reforms managed to increase public security and revitalize social dynamics and citizenship.

Under new forms of city administration, demographic and physical urban growth were made manageable again by intervening at the same time on a macro level (parallel to this process, the first overall spatial planning policy document, POT, was formulated) and on the micro level of neighbourhood and community, and by promoting social equity and social inclusion policies. On all these levels: high quality architecture, urban landscape design, including works by Colombia's best architects, and new ways of conceiving the public's relations with the city administration were part of a cultural offensive to promote equality, identity and self consciousness. Sparkling new public libraries in peripheral neighbourhoods, two million square metres of new public space, a mass transport system (Transmilenio),

Colombia

COMMISSIONER
Embassy of Colombia in Italy

CURATOR
Luis Carlos Colón Llamas

CURATORIAL TEAM
Juliana Forero
Gerard Martin
Marijke Martin
Diego Amaral
Alberto Escovar

WITH THE SUPPORT OF
Instituto Distrital de Cultura y Turismo-IDCT
Museo de Bogotá
Corporación La Candelaria-CLC
Ministerio de Relaciones Exteriores de Colombia
Embajada de Colombia en Italia
Georgetown University
University of Groningen
Istituto Italo-Latino Americano - IILA

COLLABORATORS
Pablo Burgos (videos)
Pablo Castillo (multimedia animations)

hundreds of kilometres of sidewalks and cycle paths and the implementation of new ways of participation in public decisions are the physical and social pendent of the city's revival. As a result, crime rates have decreased, quality of life and public trust in the city administration have increased, and the 'Bogotá model' is being seen by other (Colombian) cities as an example to follow.

The comprehensive strategy to rescue the city has guaranteed sustainability of the process; different mayors have changed priority, but not the model.

This exhibition underlines the idea that the loss of meta languages and practices on behalf of the city were the central cause of the crisis, and that their reintroduction guaranteed its renaissance. While in the mid 1990s Bogotá was among the most dangerous and unliveable metropoli in Latin America, it is now a reinvented city, loved and cared for by its citizens.

Parallel to this contribution to the Biennale, a larger travelling exhibition Bogotá: *The Renaissance of a Proud City* will open in Bogotá (October 23-25, 2006) and in the US and the Netherlands.

Luis C. Colón Llamas, Juliana Forero Bordamalo, Alberto Escovar Wilson-White, Diego Amaral, Marijke Martin, Gerard Martin

In-Between the Systems

Even a brief survey of Croatian history will reveal a condition of permanent instability that has had a significant impact on the extent and form of the territory. Croatian cities in turn have been shaped in accordance with shifts in their geopolitical positions and consequent economic resources and systems. The intensity and continuity of this tradition of instability led to the specific layering of both the built and the programmatic structures of the cities. Recent events related to the independence of Croatia combined with the introduction of a new political system and the free market compounded these changes, even if they have not necessarily led to expansion, urban sprawl or visible development. Inevitably, transitional processes have resulted in the restructuring of systems and procedures in the fields of the economy, demographics and a variety of social practices. These processes have not necessarily changed the actual shapes of the cities, but have changed the ways in which urban areas are used or even comprehended. Especially vivid examples of these processes can be found in three major costal cities: Dubrovnik, Split and Rijeka. The exhibition will focus on their harbours, emphasizing the different characters and dynamics of these cities, each of which derives its identity from its historical genesis, iconic urban image and localized economic assets, also inevitably depending on structural shifts from the inherited conditions of instability to the present hybrid forms of tradition and new impossibilities. Analyses will try to detect and interpret the sets of parameters affecting the current functional and morphological fluxes of traits in Dubrovnik, Split and Rijeka, all of which are trying to adjust to a new reality. The changing destinies of these three harbours, which are currently experiencing differing degrees of prosperity or decay and stagnation, will show mutual affiliations between ports and their surrounding contexts and illustrate authentic local situations in contemporary Croatian cities.
Maroje Mrduljaš

Croatia

COMMISSIONER
Andrija Rusan

CURATOR
Vedran Mimica

COLLABORATORS
Randič-Turato arhitektonski biro, Rijeka (Research)

PRODUCTION
K.LJ.B.
Damir Martinovič
Saša Randič
Ivan Šarar
Idis Turato

COORDINATION
Ana Šilovič

EXHIBITORS
Saša Randič
Idis Turato

1

2

3

1
Dubrovnik.
PHOTO BY DAMIR FABIJANIĆ.

2
Rijeka.
PHOTO BY DAMIR FABIJANIĆ.

3
Split.
PHOTO BY DAMIR FABIJANIĆ.

CO-EVOLUTION
Danish / Chinese collaboration on Sustainable Urban Development in China

The world is evolving at an explosive pace and our towns and cities are growing in size and number, as is the desire to create growth and prosperity.

Within the next 20 years, some 400 million Chinese are expected to join the urbanization race, and China's government has set itself the goal of creating appreciably better living conditions for its entire population of 1.3 billion people.

But what happens if a country the size of China initiates a development process aimed at giving 1.3 billion people access to modern living conditions like housing with its own bathroom and toilet, heating in winter and air-conditioning in summer, electric lighting, transport facilities and so on?

If traditional urban development models and production methods continue being used in China, the result could be global environmental and resource problems of unpredictable dimensions. We therefore raise the question: how can China proceed with its ambitious project of improving the living conditions of its population without exhausting the very resources needed to sustain a better life?

With *CO-EVOLUTION* we are highlighting the fact that achieving the greatest welfare boost of the twenty-first century without causing major environmental and social consequences is a joint global challenge. It is therefore a task that calls for strong interdisciplinary and international alliances, drawing on the cream of the experience we already have today. More particularly, it makes demands in terms of innovative thinking and the development of new models for large-scale, sustainable urban development.

The *CO-EVOLUTION* project is the result of Danish-Chinese collaboration between some of the most talented young Danish architects and Chinese students and professors from four of China's largest universities. Together – and sparring with experienced consultant engineers, researching and exchanging ideas and know-how – they have created four visionary concepts for sustainable development on four very different sites in the four largest cities in China.

CO-EVOLUTION is more than these four concrete projects, however. It's all about what it takes to create new models for sustainable urban development in the twenty-first century. Therefore, the Equator Principles – a set of international guidelines 'established by and for financial institutions to minimize the negative environmental and social impact of development project activities' – have also been integrated to form part and parcel of the project.

CO-EVOLUTION is the first step towards the formation of a unique, long-term network of top Chinese universities and young Danish architects. Moreover, it is an obvious way of linking young people's holistic and sustainable problem-solving approach in to the explosive growth in Chinese construction. Such an encounter may mark the birth of entirely new know-how within sustainable urban development at a world level.

Henrik Valeur and Kent Martinussen

Denmark

COMMISSIONER
DAC/Danish Architecture Centre
Kent Martinussen

CURATORS
UiD (Henrik Valeur, Uwe Wütherich, Lea Bolvig, Annelie Håkansson, Karin Lindgren, Ma Liang, Liu Hanxin, Haydar Al-Khatib, Christoffer Pilgaard)

ENGINEERING CONSULTANTS
Carl Bro Group

COORDINATION IN VENICE
M+B Studio (Daniela Murgia, Troels Bruun, Luca Delise, Ines Tolic)

SPONSORS
The Danish Ministry of Culture
Realdania
The Danish Arts Foundation
The Committee for Architecture

EXHIBITORS
CEBRA / Tsinghua University, Bejing
CEBRA (Mikkel Frost, Kolja Nielsen, Carsten Primdahl, Anders Lonka, Jacob Ulvsrod Sørensen, Kim Bangsgaard Olesen, Nikolaj Harving, Peter Jørgensen, Peter Neckelmann, Rasmus Andersen)
Tsinghua University team (Liang Wei, Liu Wan, Yang Jun, Meng Yu, Feng Jie, Gao Wei, Sun Shimeng, Li Ting)
TRANSFORM / Xi'an University of Architecture and Technology (XIAUT)
TRANSFORM (Lars Bendrup, Søren Leth, Maria Thye-Petersen, Marie Ørsted Larsen, Rikke Jeppesen)
XIAUT (Liu Linan, Hao Li, Junhuan Li, Jingheng Chen, Zonggang Liu, Qian Wang, Jing Chen, Liyan Qi, Ke Ma, Hui Cheng)
COBE / Chongqing University
COBE (Dan Stubbergaard, Vanessa Miriam Carlow, Caroline Nagel, Kristian Elleby Sundquist, Mads Rudi Lassen, Jakob Nørbjerg Madsen, Mikkel Olsen, Kristine Annabell Torp, Rong Bin, Manon Fantini)
Chongqing University (Zhao Wanmin, Wang Jiwu, Zhou Xuehong, Huang Ling, Liu Jianmin, Dai Yan, Li Jin, Huang Yong, Yangqinchuan, Wangjian, Menjiaorong, Fangyu, Zuoxiaojian, Pengweiyin)
EFFEKT / Tongji University, Shanghai
EFFEKT (Kristoffer Lindhart Weiss, Sinus Lynge, Tue Foged, Kevin Hviid Nielsen, Maria Ahn Walther, Anders Bergmann, Ditte Bendix Lanng)
Tongji University (Pan Haixiao, Liu Bing, Yu Yifang, Zhang Qi, Sun Jie, Ye Keyang, Liu Zhao, Hou Mingming, Na Taesoo, Chui Yongjoon, Noritaka Maeshiro, Fu Qing, Qi Jun, Yang An, Lian Xing)

1

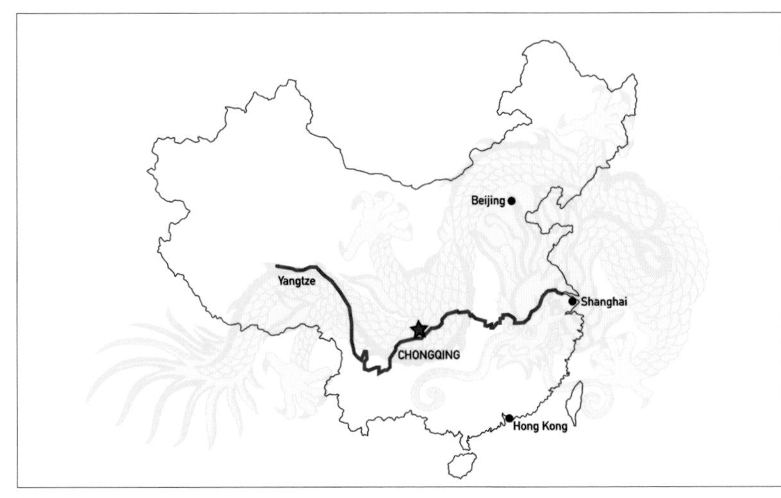

2

3

4

5

6

1
CEBRA/
Tsinghua University,
Made by China, 2006.
Project concept.

2
COBE/
Chongqing University,
High-speed Urbanism,
2006. Project concept.

3
uid©2006,
housing conditions.
PHOTO UID.

4
EFFEKT/
Tongji University
Shanghai,
SubCity,
2006. Project site.

5
CO-EVOLUTION.
Workshop in
Copenhagen, April 2006.

6
TRANSFORM / XIAUT,
Mass and Monument,
2006. Project site.

Cairo's cities in the shadow, redefining its new urban morphology

The capital of Egypt for over a thousand years and with a population of approximately 17 million inhabitants, Cairo is now the largest urban metropolis in Egypt, Africa and the Middle East. Historically, the Islamic traditional city expanded since the mid-nineteenth century along European models defining the urban morphology and character of its centre and its suburban districts.

In the last five decades, as in most developing cities, Cairo has experienced high population growth rates (about 3% per annum) and intensive rural migration of people seeking employment opportunities, better services and urban lifestyles. The government is unable to capitalize on investment opportunities for the provision of housing and cope with the demand, (government housing is estimated not to exceed 30 % of the total provision of housing) so a real housing crisis has emerged. And in the absence of effective town planning and management controls, the urban poor rely on self-help initiatives, petty contracting and informal access to government or agricultural land, usually available on the periphery of the formal city.

The 'ruralization of cities' is a phenomenon that is widely regarded as typical of the informal, uncontrolled growth patterns of most Egyptian cities, including the capital city, whose informal sector today houses over 62% of its population and takes up more than 52.8% of its total surface area. While the production of such informal housing is cost effective, affordable and compatible with the economic needs of the urban poor, there is much criticism about its inhabitants' poor quality of life. Most such settlements suffer from serious environmental hazards, infrastructural deficiencies and inadequate transport facilities, along with acute unemployment, high illiteracy rates, poverty and a lack of social and community services.

The urban morphology of such settlements is characteristically dense, lacking basic health needs (sun, ventilation...etc). Their narrow linear streets and grid pattern usually follow the initial borders of agricultural land, were housing blocks replace plots and streets replace irrigation networks. The housing blocks are five storeys high on average and take up the entire plot, leaving no room for open space or green areas. The blocks are built with an exposed concrete skeleton and redbrick infill, usually with no external finishing, giving them the permanent appearance of unfinished building sites.

Informal and squatter settlements also exist today in some of Cairo's inner districts, in the form of roof-toppers, cemetery dwellers (in the City of the Dead), in other areas associated with professions such as garbage collectors (El Zabaleen), in and around industrial areas and along major transportation routes. Such settlements live in the shadow of Cairo's formal, visible city.

Connected in many ways to the urban culture, while still retaining traditional and rural values, dwellers of the informal settlements have shaped their specific cultural identity to accommodate their semi urban/rural lifestyles, recreating their traditional environments in the new urban context. The formal and informal sectors experience interdependency and cohabitation, their cultural interaction seems to work both ways extending influences to the two sectors.

Government policies to deal with the problems of informal settlements balance between slum clearing, self-help building, community participation, the provision of core housing, improvement and upgrading, site and services programmes, management of human settlements and enabling approaches, but the informal settlements continue to expand.

So what is the future of Cairo?

Egypt

COMMISSIONER
Mohamed Awad

DEPUTY COMMISSIONER
Yasser Aref

EXHIBITORS
Hatem El Said
Mohamed Abul Seoud

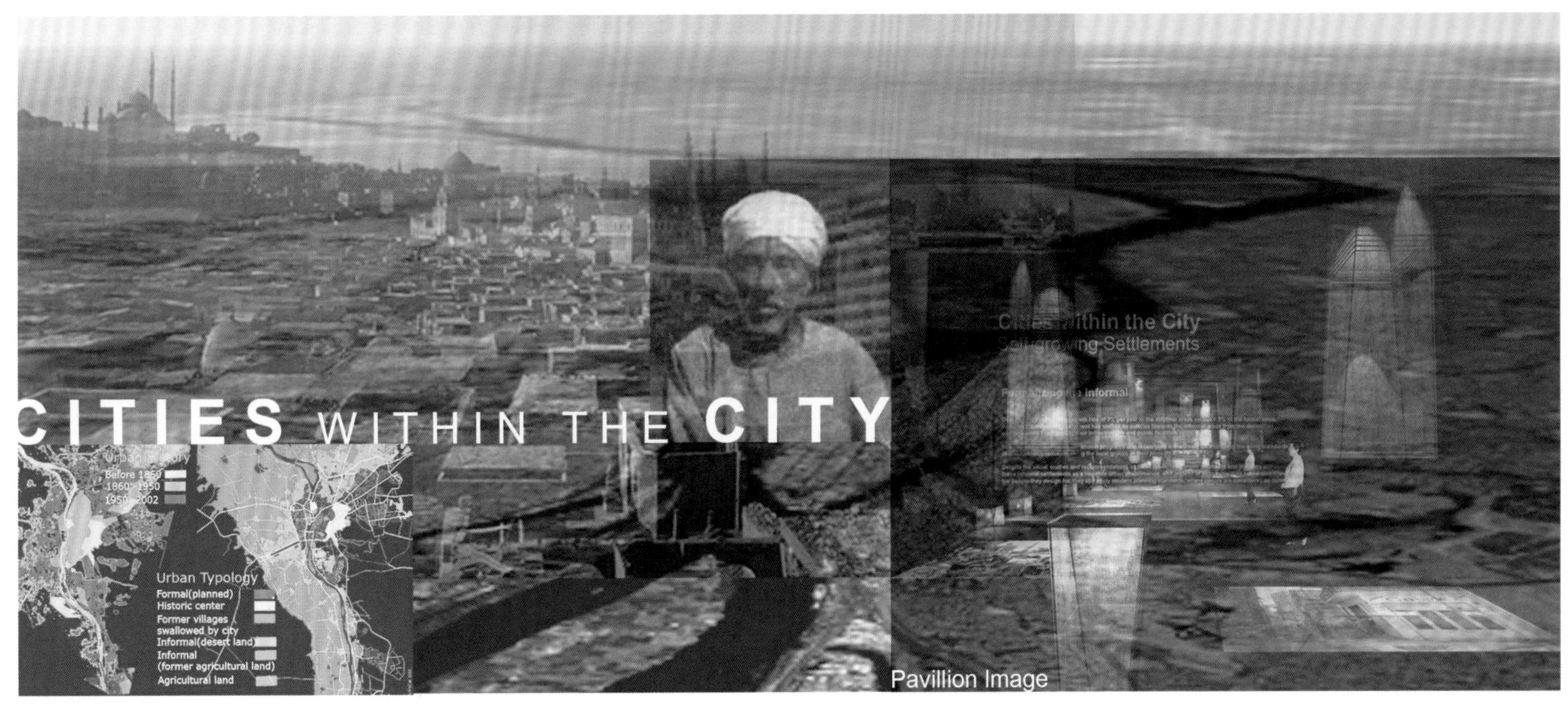

Pavillion Image

JOINT SPACE

The Estonian exhibition *Joint space* searches for ways of creating suprapersonal space combining mobile positioning with an online medium. Architects, town planners and geographers have worked with geo-IT specialists to cut through the lifelessness of traditional planning.

Estonia is at the forefront of new technology applications. Parking, bus-tickets and banking by mobile phone are everyday matters in this small north European country. Mobile phone and internet usage is among the highest in the world: even the government is elected and works online. At the Architecture Biennale the latest ICT technology meets city-planning.

85% of all phone calls start with 'Hi! Where are you?'. But why ask? Your mobile phone can locate your position. 750 people have given us 450,000 positionings over the last few years.

This input has created a real-time medium – www.POSITIUM.ee.

An interface creating quality through feedback while also mapping quantity.

What are the possibilities for personality in the cityscape today? A space reflecting and recognized by the individual, her cultural background, social identity etc. How can such a multi-faceted space be created?

Personality can today be realized by expanding the consciousness of space usage; by clever intensity of time and space; an instantaneous transformation of space. By joining real-time positions and social identity in www.POSITIUM.ee as a medium, we have tried to create a possibility for the realization of such personal space. Personal space creates additional value, diversity. It embodies our personal history.

Surveillance fear interests us: is location really so important, so private? Why do people choose to show, why not? What are the possibilities for positive creation when choosing to show, without ignoring possible drawbacks?

THE EXPO

The main element of the exhibition www.POSITIUM.ee is an on-line website displaying and exploring real-time movement. The sub-projects shown are based on data gathered by mobile positioning and show different applications of such information.

- SOCIAL NETWORKS – possible new locations of the Estonian Academy of Art
- ECOLOGY – evaluate your ecological footprint
- PARTICIPATION DEMOCRACY – voting on bicycle routes
- LEISURE TIME SPACE – tourism analysis
- THE DISPERSAL OF CITIES' SPATIAL CONCENTRATION - suburb analysis

Decision-making in local government is an inadequate category or means of organizing space. The aim of pleasing the majority of people is the drawback of policies. We believe there is a personal space for every individual.

Consumption is a confluence all can understand: the acquisition of functions, spaces, infrastructures and prefabricated models of being this/doing that. People can be seen unconsciously adapting to situations forced upon them. In other situations they use the minimal remaining possibilities to outmanoeuvre. Tactical behaviour, searching for instantaneous actuating codes, can act against constructed frames.

It is a question of how groups of individuals can make their voices heard. Not with once-only actions when the critical limit is reached and people rush to the barricades, but through systematic everyday participation.

Pille Epner

Estonia

COMMISSIONERS
Estonian Ministry of Culture
Pille Epner

CURATOR
Ülar Mark

WEBSITE
www.positium.ee

EXHIBITORS
Urban Mark Architectural Office (Ülar Mark, Indrek Tiigi, Kaja Pae, Yoko Alender, Raul Kalvo)
University of Tartu Institute of Geography (Rein Ahas, Anto Aasa, Siiri Silm)
Positium ICT Research (Margus Tiru, Erki Saluveer)

1

1
IMAGE BY KAJA PAE.

The City of *Possible* Worlds

Skopje: The thing we see in the cityscape of Skopje is a fragmentary reality of the city, a product of a century of modernization: traces of various political, social and cultural ideas of the twentieth-century city.

The changes in cities do not refer only to their demographic, social and physical contents, but to the changed perception of the city and the way it is presented. The changeable dynamics of its representation has a key role in its new state. The twentieth century is a century of extreme scenarios for the redefinition of cities. The twenty-first century is a century of correlations, once exclusively spatial systems converge in real experience. That which Skopje shows on its surface are the fragmented contents of a city construct of long ago.

How can we convert that contradictory complexity of a multitude of conflicting systems into a multitude of coexisting systems? Out of a city from a vision into a city of a multitude of possible worlds.

Skopje 2km^2: Scenery of various ideas of the city. In the last 100 years, the modernization process marked the metastable state of the city, the ideal desired city and meant negation of the existing one through a model of tabula rasa.

A series of extraordinary models strengthened the ambivalence of the city, swinging between what it was and what it desired to be.

Exploded base of the city: a city of various pieces, a multitude of conflicting systems as shadows of former visions of the city. City of fragments = city of shadows.

How can one act in such a city, composed of a multitude of various pieces?

Tactics: de-centred procedures of the city's new reality. The transition period related to the political and economic aspects, and acquired dramatic consequences in space. The new method of the city refers to a series of correlations: building-in, building-out, building-up, building under, which produces atypological configurations further on.

Can this practice be the new model of the city, a new way of reacting to the articulation of its parts? Can the lack of an a priori concept generate a new narrative of the city?

This project proposes a series of tactics of the city in a transition period, acts through its hybrid reality and through atypological correlations.

City of possible worlds: Five young architects: Saša Tasič & Dimitar Papasterevski; Mihajlo Zinovski; Jovan Ivanovski; Vladimir Petrovski
Territory: SK2km^2
Tactics: building-in, building-out, building-up, building-under
New city index: updating, space=information, shopping guide, reinventing mobility, the revenge of the ignored traffic participants, linking-urbanudism
Hypothesis: city of fragments→ city of possible worlds
Minas Bakalčev & Mitko Hadži Pulja

Former Yugoslav Republic of Macedonia

COMMISSIONER
Frosina Zafirovska

CONSULTANT
Vlatko P. Korobar

CURATORS
Minas Bakalčev
Mitko Hadži Pulja

EXHIBITORS
Jovan Ivanovski
Vladimir Petrovski
Saša Tasič & Dimitar Papasterevski
Mihajlo Zinoski

1

2

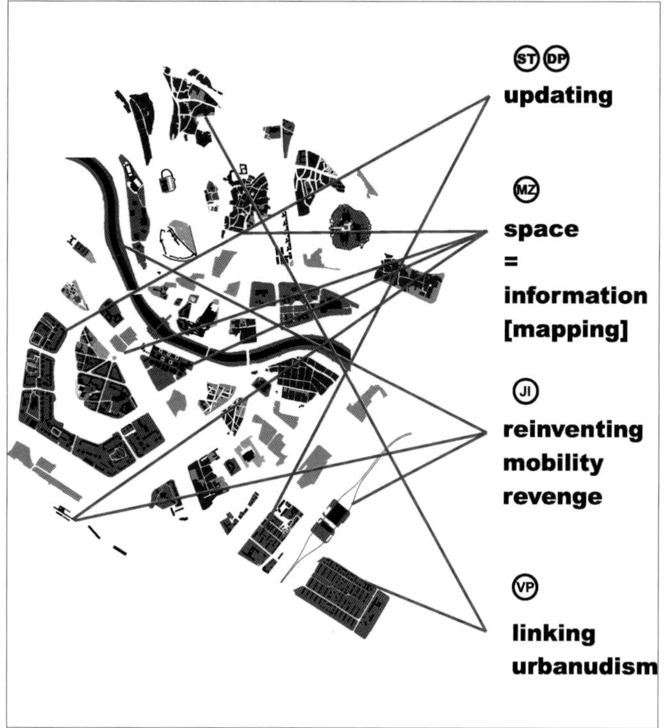

3

4

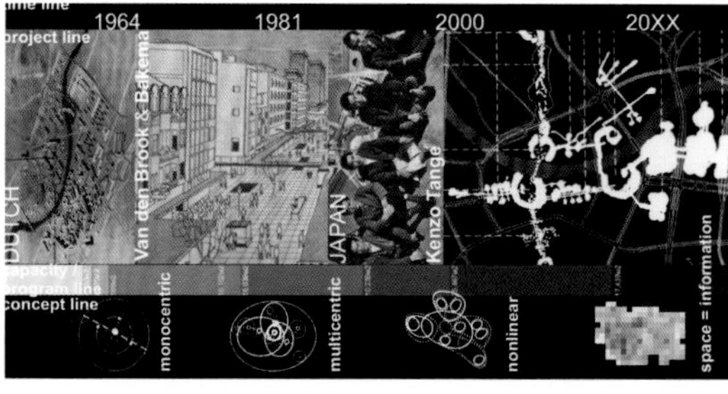

5

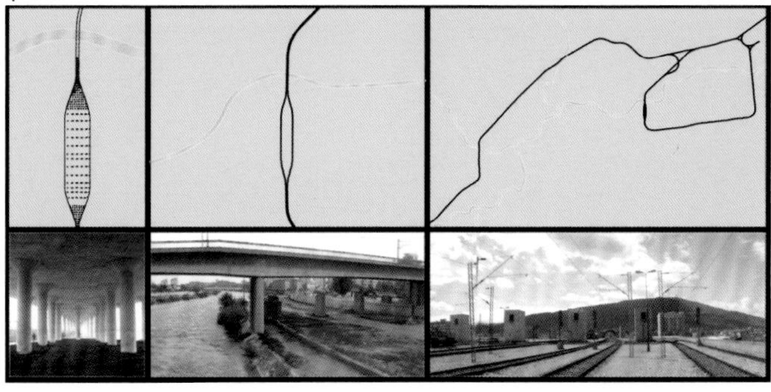

6

7

1
Skopje satellite image, reference area of urban transformations.

2
Urban map of Skopje 2 x 2 km.

3
SK exploded urban fragments.

4
Semi-detached house project, Skopje 2005, upgrading of existing house.

5
Collage of plans and conceptual diagrams for city centre.

6
Potential of river corridors and railway networks.

7
Undressing the city.

City Home

As an environment, the city is both rewarding and demanding. Its main property is density. Density creates efficiency. Distances are short, services are abundant and the costs of municipal engineering can be shared.

On the other hand, the simultaneity of different activities calls for tolerance. Traffic and proximity lead to disturbances, to wear on the immediate surroundings and its pollution.

Habitation is private in nature, and therefore easily disturbed. In the city, public and private seek to overlap. Mutual flexibility makes urban living adaptable and interesting.

In the Finnish tradition the boundary between public and private has been particularly distinct. However, as 80% of Finland's population now lives in built-up areas, urban habitation is becoming more public and tolerant in nature.

Urban identity presents itself not only as the density of built form but also as the density of services. Providing a wide range of services calls for a solid population basis. As habitation becomes more spacious through increasing affluence, the density of population will decrease. Decreasing population cannot support the former standard of services. To end this vicious circle new residents must be attracted.

A dynamic city is in continuous flux. Ports, railway yards and warehouses are moving outside the clogged fabric of city centres. Industries are vacating their old facilities. Large sites are thus made available near the core of the city and old, distinctive architecture is freed for new use.

Empty attics and former workspace and storage facilities in the yards of buildings are gradually being converted into dwellings. Defined by old structures and forms, these new homes make personal exceptions to the unsurprising formulas of industrialized housing development.

City development is also facing an increasing need to address issues of sustainability with regard to technology, planning and use of space. On the other hand, there is a growing desire for building and development on a small scale and at ground level.

City Home is an exhibition presenting recent residential architecture in the greater Helsinki area. The various scales of design are illustrated in pairs of exhibits reflecting the diverse and even conflicting challenges of residential architecture. The exhibits include an attic apartment in an Art Nouveau building and converted dwellings in a former public bath-house. There is a single-family house freely opening onto a wooded environment, and a courtyard building focused on itself and shielding its inhabitants. Also displayed are a prefabricated building masking its industrial construction technique with colourful individuality, along with an ecologically oriented block of flats encouraging communality. The redevelopment of an industrial site in an architecturally integrated yet vivid manner is paired with a former brewery block redeveloped in the traditional manner by different architects. In addition, *City Home* features the planning of a port zone drawing upon its maritime character, together with a compact, low-rise residential area of wooden houses in a rocky forest setting.

Roy Mänttäri

Finland

(Alvar Aalto Pavilion)

COMMISSIONERS
Severi Blomstedt
Roy Mänttäri

COORDINATOR
Hannu Hellman

WITH THE SUPPORT OF
The Museum of Finnish Architecture

EXHIBITORS
Arrak Arkkitehdit Kiiskilä, Rautiola, Rautiola Oy (Hannu Kiiskilä)
Arkkitehtistudio Elina Ahdeoja (Elina Ahdeoja)
Arkkitehtistudio Rauno Lehtinen (Rauno Lehtinen)
Arkkitehtistudio Susanna Pietikäinen (Susanna Pietikäinen)
Arkkitehtistudio Kimmo Friman (Kimmo Friman)
Arkkitehtitoimisto Brunow & Maunula (Anna Brunow)
Arkkitehtitoimisto Harris-Kijsik (Trevor Harris and Hennu Kjisik)
Arkkitehtitoimisto Olavi Koponen (Olavi Koponen)
Arkkitehtitoimisto Nurmela-Raimoranta-Tasa (Jyrki Tasa)
Arkkitehtitoimisto Juhani Pallasmaa (Juhani Pallasmaa)
Arkkitehtitoimisto Sarc Oy (Jan-Henrik Söderlund)
Arkkitehtityöhuone APRT Oy (Aaro Artto)

1

2

3

4

5

6

7

8

9

10

1
Arkkitehtistudio Elina Ahdeoja
(Elina Ahdeoja),
Loft Apartment,
refurbishing renovation, Punavuorenkatu 4 B 4, Helsinki, 2005.
PHOTO BY JUSSI TIAINEN.

2
Arkkitehtityöhuone APRT Oy (Aaro Artto),
Wooden Urban Village of Myllypuro,
Helsinki 2004.

3
Arkkitehtitoimisto Brunow & Maunula
(Anna Brunow),
Säterinkatu 8 Housing Company,
Espoo, 2002.
PHOTO BY JUSSI TIAINEN.

4
Arkkitehtitoimisto Harris-Kijsik (Trevor Harris and Hennu Kjisik),
Helsinki´s Eastern Harbour Residential Area, 2004.

5
Arrak Arkkitehdit Kiiskilä, Rautiola, Rautiola Oy
(Hannu Kiiskilä),
ATT Viikki SUNH-project Rental House,
Helsinki, 2000.
PHOTO BY MATTI KARJANOJA.

6
Arkkitehtistudio Kimmo Friman (Kimmo Friman),
Villa Hannus,
Helsinki, 2004.
PHOTO BY JARI JETSONEN.

7
Arkkitehtitoimisto Olavi Koponen
(Olavi Koponen),
Villa Lena,
Espoo, 2003.
PHOTO BY JUSSI TIAINEN.

8
Arkkitehtitoimisto Juhani Pallasmaa
(Juhani Pallasmaa),
Attic Apartment,
refurbishing renovation, Huvilakatu 2, Helsinki, 1991.
PHOTO BY RAUNO TRÄSKELIN.

9
Arkkitehtitoimisto Sarc Oy
(Jan-Henrik Söderlund),
Koff Block of Flats,
Helsinki, 1997-2003.
PHOTO SUOMEN BY ILMAKUVA OY.

10
Arkkitehtitoimisto Nurmela-Raimoranta-Tasa (Jyrki Tasa),
Pasila Engineering Works Site Residential Area,
Helsinki, 2004. Rendering.

Métavilla

A palace occupied by an exultant crowd is a common image of revolutionary excess. Each epoch plays its own variations on that image, in accord with the contingencies of history. Its persistence makes it a necessary or even ritual representation, constituting the very act of revolution. It embodies the hope for justice, by way of an equitable redistribution of space. The occupation is the architectural face of a social vision.

Métavilla tries to put this collective movement to work. The set-up is to the architectural exhibition what the act is to the idea. It offers a chance to experience the architectural concept, but, above all, to measure the ideal of life it upholds, not as a utopian speculation but as a gesture seeking fulfilment. The atypical occupation of the space and the opening of this foreclosed national pavilion to the public is an architectural act in its own right. Probably the only one that could be undertaken in this period of security panic and underlying war. To welcome the foreigner, the irreducibly other, is more urgent than ever. Fortunately, the joyful city that unfolds in the pavilion has its reality, here and elsewhere. This exhibition is merely a clue to its existence.

France

COMMISSIONER
Francis Lacloche

WITH THE SUPPORT OF
AFAA/
CULTURESFRANCE
Ministère des Affaires Étrangères
Direction de l'Architecture et du Patrimoine
Ministère de la Culture et de la Communication

Municipalities of
Calais
Marseille
Nantes
Roubaix
Regions of
Nord Pas de Calais
Poitou-Charentes
Rhône Alpes

SPONSOR
Groupe BPI
SIRC
Valeo

EXHIBITORS
Patrick Bouchain with Daniel Buren, Michel Onfray, Otar Iosseliani, Lucien Kroll, Igor Dromesko, Exyzt architecture, Pierre Giner, Liliana Motta, Jean Lautrey, Encore Heureux, Patrick Degeorges, Antoine Nochy, Cyrille Weiner, Gilles Clément, Pierre Guyotat, Arc en rêve, Villa Noailles, GAU:DI, Le channel

1

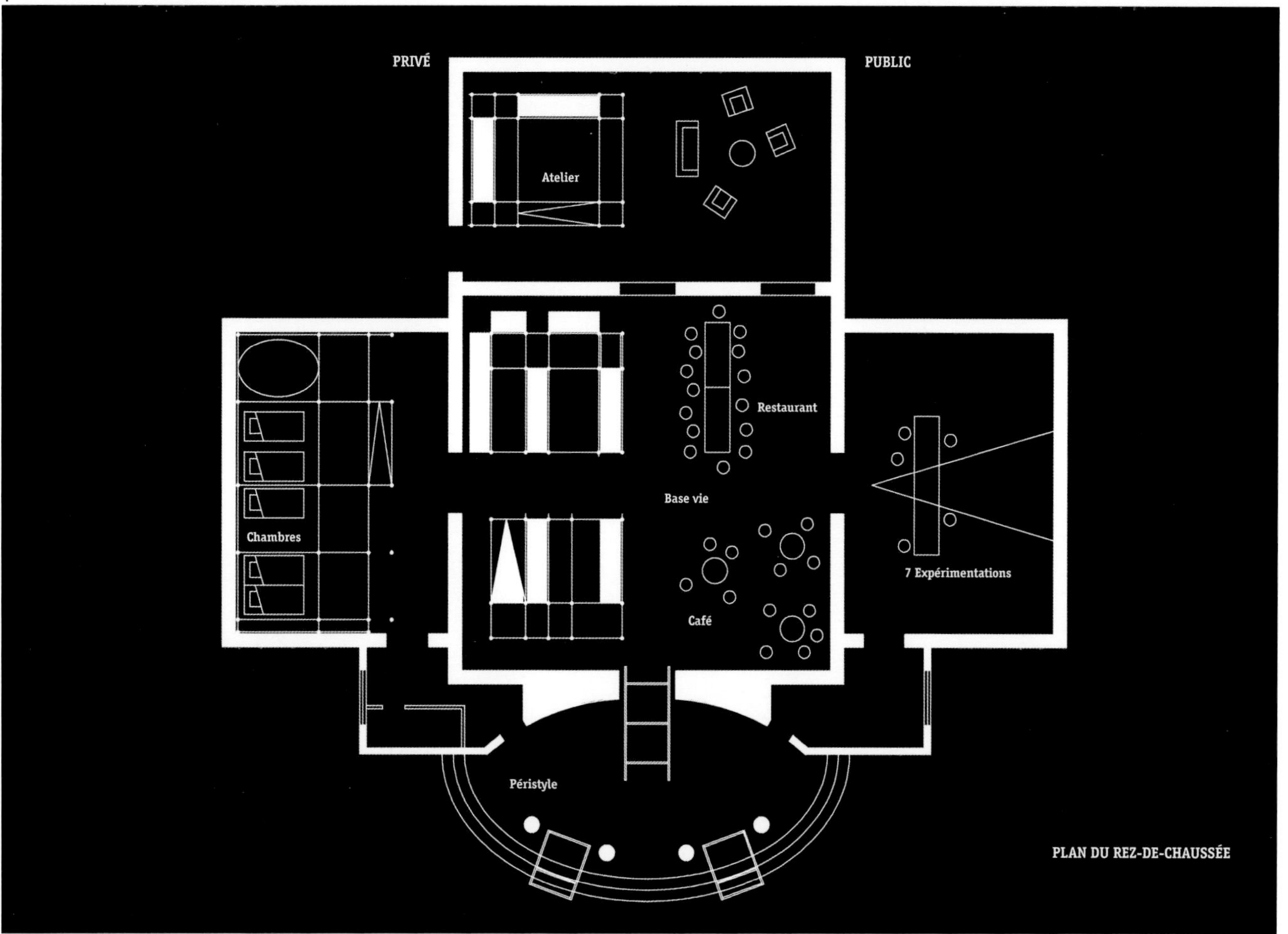

2

1
Métavilla-Métacité,
the French Pavilion.
2
The French Pavilion,
ground floor.

Past, Present and Future of the capital of Georgia - Tbilisi

The break-up of the communist regime gave rise to a new, post-Soviet stage of development in Georgian architecture and town-planning, which faced an entirely new political, economic, social and cultural context. The difficulties of adjusting the new realities to the 70 years of Soviet practices in architecture and town-planning have been apparent since the very beginning. The Georgian architectural society articulated its main goals as early as the 1900s, based on the need to overcome the inertia of these practices while taking into consideration the expected fundamental changes in the country's development (shifting to the principles of the market economy, private property, real estate privatization and self-governance), which would directly affect urban development. These goals can be formulated as follows:
- defining the strategy for integrating Georgian architecture and town-planning from an isolated area of totalitarian regime into a European space of democratic values;
- carrying out legislative and institutional reform as well as reform in planning and management in the sphere of architecture and town-planning, in full conformity with European standards.

There was no alternative to the system reforms as the main measure for overcoming the crisis in town-planning. Without these reforms, the above-mentioned changes would threaten turning urban processes into chaos and deforming town-planning structures countrywide.

The capital of Georgia-Tbilisi, as the central urban site where the main democratic and economic processes unfold, clearly reflects the main peculiarities of the controversial development of post-Soviet town-planning.

The main theme of our national exhibition at the 10th International Architecture Exhibition is retrospection of architecture and town-planning processes in Tbilisi.

23 architects from Georgia are participating in the exhibition.

Our projects will be submitted as posters (Photo prints).
David Abuladze

Georgia

COMMISSIONER
David Abuladze

CURATORS
Maka Memanishvili
Elisabed Giorgadze

DEPUTY COMMISSIONERS
Giorgi Beridze
Nino Tsomaia

EXHIBITORS
David Abuladze
Giorgi Beridze
Dimitri Mamatsashvili and Irakli Vacheishvili
George Giorgadze,
Archil Miqutchadze and Kirile Morchiladze
Gocha Mikiashvili,
Merab Bolkvadze,
Givi Shavdia,
David Chiqovani,
Beso Tatishvili,
Gela Kobiashvili and Zaza Matiashvili
Nino Tsomaia and Nodar Iremashvili
Nick Shavishvili,
George Mirianashvili,
Temur Kldiashvili and Sandro Mgaloblishvili
Vasil Kobulia and Givi Kobulia
George Kvitsinashvili
Tengiz Gogolashvili,
Zurab Matiashvili and Giorgi Tsanatsghkenashvili
Otar Vardanashvili,
Nikoloz Abashidze,
Otar Berianidze,
Levan Kvicaridze,
Ramaz Ramishvili and Avto Revazishvili
Merab Gagnidze,
Zaza Gagnidze,
Davit Kuprashvili and Amiran Patarqalashvili

1

2

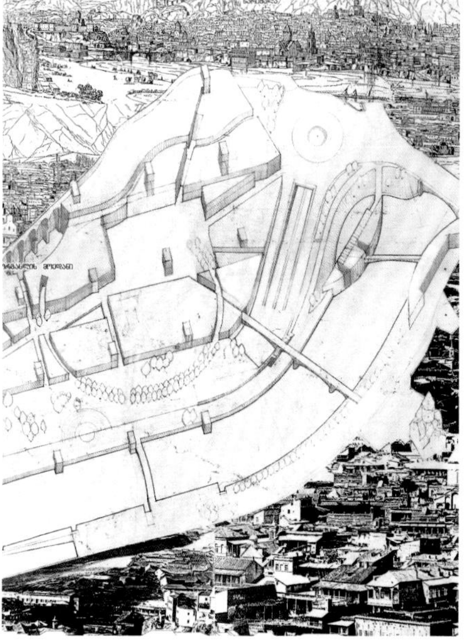
3

4

5

6

7

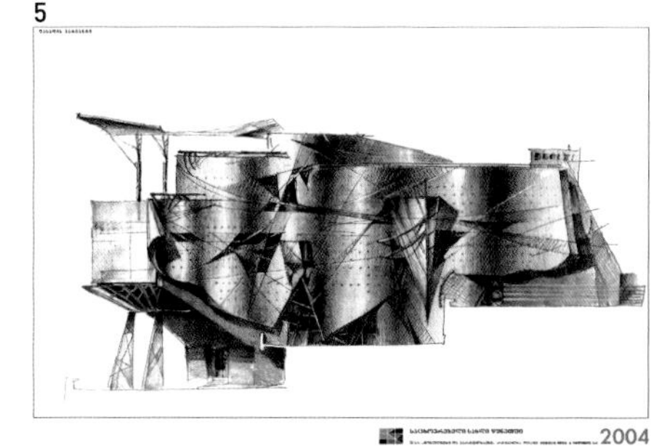

8

9

1
David Abuladze,
Residential house in Tbilisi-Paliashvili 16,
2000-2001. Organization: David & Company.
2
Giorgi Beridze (Graphic design team: Archil Ramishvili, Irakli Gharibashivili, Khatuna Mikaberidze),
Sport Palace for Tbilisi,
2006. Conceptual architectural Interventions. Organization: Paladi Invest.
COURTESY THE AUTHOR.

3
Irakli Vacheishvili, Dimitri Mamatsashvili (Graphic design team: Irakli Gharibashivili, Levan Dolidze),
Conception of urban design of Riqe quarter area in Tbilisi,
2006.
COURTESY THE AUTHORS.

4
George Giorgadze, Archil Miqutchadze, Kirile Morchiladze,
Rehabilitation Development Management Plan of adjacent to Bukhaidze Street territory,
District Chugureti, Tbilisi. Project implementation will start in the spring of 2006. Organization: Archimedia L.T.D.

5
Gocha Mikiashvili, Merab Bolkvadze, Givi Shavdia, David Chiqovani, Beso Tatishvili, Gela Kobiashvili, Zaza Matiashvili,
New housing block in Bagebi,
Tbilisi, 2005. Organization: IBERIA Real Estate L.T.D.
6
Nino Tsomaia, Nodar Iremashvili,
Secondary School in old district of Tbilisi,
2005.
COURTESY THE AUTHORS.

7
Nick Shavishvili, George Mirianashvili, Temur Kldiashvili, Sandro Mgaloblishvili (Design Team: CI&D Architects),
Theological Seminary for the Georgian Orthodox Church in Tbilisi,
Designed in 2003-2006, in construction. Anticipated completion 2008. Rendering.
COURTESY THE AUTHORS.

8
Vasil Kobulia, Givi Kobulia,
Residential house in Tskneti,
2004.
COURTESY THE AUTHORS.
9
George Kvitsinashvili,
The Georgian Football Federation office,
Tbilisi, 2004.
CLIENT: FIFA.

CONVERTIBLE CITY
Modes of densification and dissolving boundaries

Convertible City is an expression of the continuity and conversion of urban space
Convertible City is a call for maintaining the diversity of city life
Convertible City is a demand for the sustainable use of core cities
Convertible City is an alternative to urban sprawl encroaching on natural areas
Convertible City is the dissolution of boundaries in the urban habitat
Convertible City is a call for creative appropriation of metropolitan areas
Convertible City is the expression of a positive attitude to urban life
Convertible City is an inspiration and stimulation for new concepts of living

Concept

Urban life is marked by the varied interaction of economic, social, geographical, political, cultural and creative processes of transformation.

Contrary to the rapidly expanding new metropolises in Asia and Latin America, the form of the European city is still largely determined by tradition and history. The restructuring of industrial society, as well as demographic changes and an increasingly pluralistic society, present distinct challenges to architecture and urban planning in Germany, particularly with regard to existing urban structures. Meeting these challenges means discovering new opportunities for interaction between past, present and future.

The German contribution examines stimulating conversions in existing urban space situations that enrich the dynamics and creativity of city life. Exemplary projects illustrate the exciting tensions that densification and transformation exert on architecture and the urban fabric, as well as the sustainable use of the available potential of a 'vertically open' periphery for new working and living environments.

With an emphasis on transformation and conversion in the urban context, the exhibition reveals a shift in perception within the sphere of architecture. Focusing on the hitherto rather unattractive tasks of re-building and re-use contributes to their revaluation in terms of design and content not only amongst experts but also in the public consciousness.

Projects

The exhibition presents projects that are designed to meet the requirements of a constantly changing society and cultural landscape by change of use, transformation and re-projection. These include planned and completed projects by well-known and less well-known architects, urban planners, landscape architects and artists. The exhibits demonstrate new prospects for architecture through flexibility of thinking and concepts of sustainability. They also offer exhibition visitors interesting insights into the diversity of creative activity in Germany's urban space.

Design

Examples of urban vitality and architectural variety are displayed by way of large scale images in the main hall. In contrast to the bustling entrance, the side wings offer a calm and inviting atmosphere for a more in-depth contemplation of the individual projects. A temporary stairway construction leads from the main space up to the roof level and activates this area as a novel location with surprising perspectives. Thus the pavilion serves not only as casing or container to the exhibits, but becomes an exhibit in its own right.

Germany

COMMISSIONERS
Armand Grüntuch
Almut Ernst

SPONSORS/PARTNERS
ZUMTOBEL
Alfred Herrhausen Gesellschaft das internationale Forum der Deutschen Bank
Carpetconcept
Corian
Hasenkopf
Wilhelm Layher
Vitra

MEDIA
archplus
BauNetz

WEB SITE
www.convertiblecity.de

EXHIBITORS
Wiel Arets Architect and Associates
b & k+
Barkow Leibinger Architects
bb22 ı urbane projekte
blauraum architekten
Klaus Block Architekt
Bolles+Willson
BRT Architekten Bothe Richter Teherani
David Chipperfield Architects
Stefan Eberstadt
Olafur Elíasson
FloSundK
GRAFT
Hascher Jehle Architektur
Hoyer Schindele Hirschmüller + Partner
Hufnagel Pütz Rafaelian Architekten
INDEX Architekten
Ingenhoven Architekten
Kühn Malvezzi Architekten
L/B Lang Baumann
Lederer+Ragnarsdótt ir+Oei
Susanne Lorenz and AMP arquitectos with Gil Wilk, Gil Wilk Architekten with Thomas Freiwald
lüderwaldt verhoff architekten
Meixner Schlüter Wendt Architekten
mess (mobile einsatztruppe stadt und stil)
André Poitiers Architekt
Raumlabor + Partner
Realarchitektur
realities:united
sauerbruch hutton architekten
schneider+schumacher
Staab Architekten
Sissel Tolaas
TOPOTEK 1
Stadtsanierungsamt Tübingen
urban catalyst

CONVERTIBLE CITY
GERMANIA

Unknown Japanese Architecture and Cities – Surrealist Architecture and the City's Unconscious

Terunobu Fujimori's Architecture and the Roadway Observation Society (ROJO) are architecture and city-related movements that have been active for over a decade. Although well-known in Japan, they are still completely unknown elsewhere.

According to Kenjiro Okazaki, Fujimori is the world's only 'surreal architect'. He works with Genpei Akasegawa in the Roadway Observation Society, which searches out interesting urban scenes around the world that no-one has paid attention to before. The Roadway Observation Society regards these scenes as expressions of the city's unconscious.

Fujimori is a founder member of the Roadway Observation Society. Its other members also help to build Fujimori's architectural ideas, playing an essential role in the process and calling themselves the 'Jomon Kenchiku-dan' (Jomon Culture Construction Company).

Although it may not have been articulated as a coherent theory, there is clearly a common element running right through both Fujimori's Architecture and the Roadway Observation Society's activities. Exhibiting the two together creates a link between the architecture and the city, and is significant for bringing this new and still unknown direction out into the open for the first time.

What is ROJO? This word is an abbreviation of Rojo Kansatsugaku or 'Roadway Observation'. It is a field of study that takes in everything that can be observed on city streets. We go out, camera in hand, in search of things that are out of place, odd, unusual or mysterious. We focus on forms that are unconsciously created by people living in cities or traces left by natural phenomena. We find new beauty in the objects or structures discovered in this way and add our thoughts about what they might represent or stand for. Rather than an academic study, this is a new form of play for city dwellers that makes walking through the city more enjoyable.

Since the founding of the Roadway Observation Society in 1986, the members have made observation trips to places all over Japan with the cooperation of the Ministry of Land, Infrastructure, and Transport, local governments, railway companies, and private organizations. We have also carried out street observation in Asian countries such as China and Vietnam and European countries like Italy, France, England, and Germany. The large number of objects and structures discovered through this fieldwork and the thoughts stimulated by them have appeared in magazines, books, television programmes, and lectures, exerting a great deal of influence on urban planning, architecture, art, literature, and Japanese culture in general.

References

Eureka - Terunobu Fujimori edition, Seidosha, 2004

Rojo Kansatsu Nyumon (Introduction to Roadway Observation), Genpei Akasegawa, Terunobu Fujimori, Shinbo Minami eds., Chikuma Shobo, 1986

Exhibition details

1 The surrealism of architecture

1-1 Fujimori architecture

Models, sketches, drawings, photographs and videos

1-2 Examples from Japan and around the world

Photographs

2 Looking for a city's unconscious - roadway observation

2-1Examples from Japan

Slideshow

2-2 Venice, Paris, London, Shanghai, Hanoi and elsewhere (Slideshow)

Japan

COMMISSIONER
Terunobu Fujimori

DEPUTY COMMISSIONERS
Miki Okabe
Hiroshi Omori

EXHIBITORS
Terunobu Fujimori
Genpei Akasegawa
Joji Hayashi
Tetsuo Matsuda
Shinbo Minami
Hinako Sugiura

1

2

3

4

5

6

7

8

9

10

1
Terunobu Fujimori,
Nira-house + Atelier,
Dwelling Machida City, Tokyo, 1997.

2
Terunobu Fujimori,
Room of Charcoal - Tea room,
Arai City, Niigata, 1999.

3
Terunobu Fujimori,
Takasugi-an - Tea house,
Chino City, Nagano, 2004.

4
Rojo (Roadway Observation Society),
Ukiyoe Waves (Hokusai),
Miyagi.

5
Rojo (Roadway Observation Society),
Razor House,
Tokyo.

6
Rojo (Roadway Observation Society),
World's Best Slippery Slide,
Tokyo.

7
Rojo (Roadway Observation Society),
Plant Wiper,
Tokyo.

8
Rojo (Roadway Observation Society),
Green Dress,
Tokyo.

9
Rojo (Roadway Observation Society),
Chicken Television,
Tokyo.

10
Rojo (Roadway Observation Society),
Ascending and Descending,
Tokyo.

Echo City

Cities and Social Dynamics. That is a kind of big topic. Too big, I thought, for architecture alone. And so I turned to a team immersed in art, in music, in theatre, in design. The only rule in assembling the team was that they had to come from one city. This meant we could start discussions from the same point and work outwards. We had conversations about cities and social dynamics that simply bypassed architecture's normal obsessions with form and technique. Somehow issues that architects often privilege seemed rather limited, even irrelevant. Instead these architectural 'outsiders' developed a much richer discourse around cities – of stories, of sounds, of stuff, of memories.

The setting for this discourse is our own backyard: Sheffield. In the 1960s this city vaunted its architectural ambition on the international stage, but the buildings then produced turned round and bit the city back. It became a classic graveyard of failed modernist dreams. Fingers once burnt, it is a now a place of no great architectural distinction. but nonetheless it is a place that inspires enormous loyalty and affection. Our exhibition attempts to excavate the city to find out what produces an extraordinary urban quality almost *despite* architecture.

Of course in presenting the complexity of a city, the exhibition is inevitably partial (in both senses of the word); it offers a series of snapshots, echoes of a city that few of you will have visited. Our project will not speak of Sheffield but of 'Sheffields', of ghost and incomplete echoes of the city. We have organized these echoes according to scale, in an acknowledgment that one's understanding of cities operates across a range from the intimate to the global. Sheffield is thus registered at four different scales: 1:1, 1:100, 1:10,000, 1:10,000,000, using a different primary medium for each. In the end we admitted architecture but mixed it in with other urban hardware and software. These records of the city – dreamed, 'real', imagined, personalized, half remembered, mostly forgotten – are placed side by side and then – finally – interwoven. They tell a story of a city whose value exceeds the value of its architectural objects, and is none the worse for that.

Running through this urban register is a common thread of human experience. Exhibitions tend to reduce architecture to aesthetic object, and the visitor is equally diminished to passive observer. Distressingly, architectural exhibitions often reproduce, some might say even help produce, an architectural value system in which buildings are lifted out of time and the user dismissed as acquiescent and static. In contrast we have taken the role of people in the understanding – and by implication the making – of cities as a central concern, suggesting a more active and participatory model for urban engagement.

Our exhibition has Sheffield at its heart, but is about much more than Sheffield; it is about any city. Sheffield, once famous for its steel and cutlery, is now the archetypal post-industrial city, a global city, torn between its own identity and those of others. In this it is an echo of many cities, buffeted by the social and technological forces of modernity. We thus use Sheffield as the context to explore the present and future of all our cities. We do not make proposals for Sheffield, but give the context in which more empowering urban proposals may be developed for cities of all kinds.

Jeremy Till

Great Britain

COMMISSIONER
Emily Campbell

CURATOR
Jeremy Till

DEPUTY COMMISSIONER
Brendan Griggs

CONCEIVING AND PROJECT
Jeremy Till
Ian Anderson
Ruth Ben Tovim
Tim Etchells
Hugo Glendinning
Jim Prevett
Trish O'Shea
Martyn Ware
Sarah Wigglesworth

PROJECT MANAGER
Catherine Ince

PROJECT ASSISTANT
Will Sorrell

EXHIBITORS
The Designers Republic
Encounters
Martyn Ware & The Illustrious Company
Prevett & McArthur
Tim Etchells & Hugo Glendinning
Studio Egret West
Hawkins Brown
Sauerbruch Hutton
Mecanoo

1

2

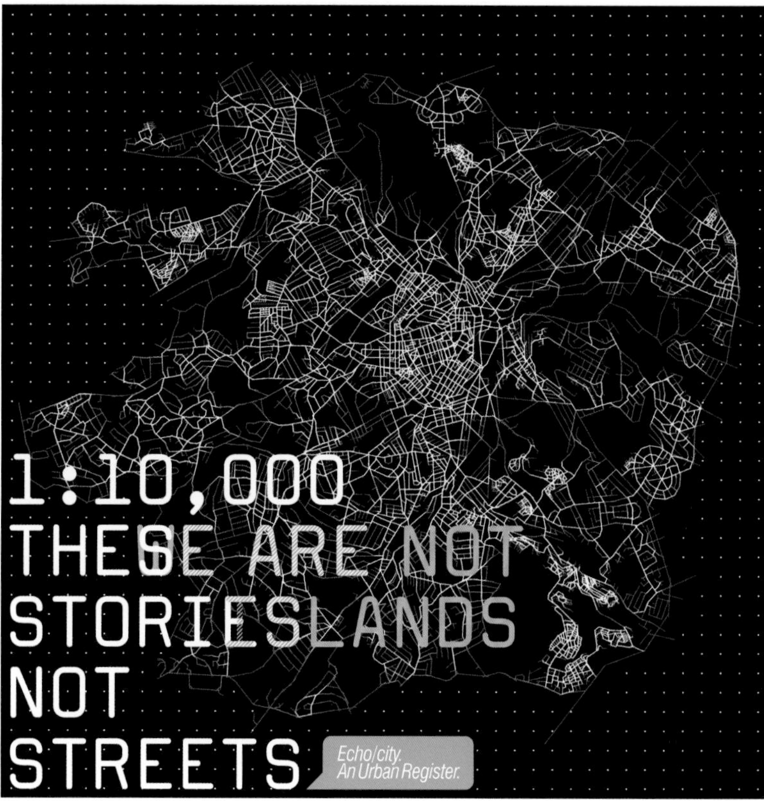

3

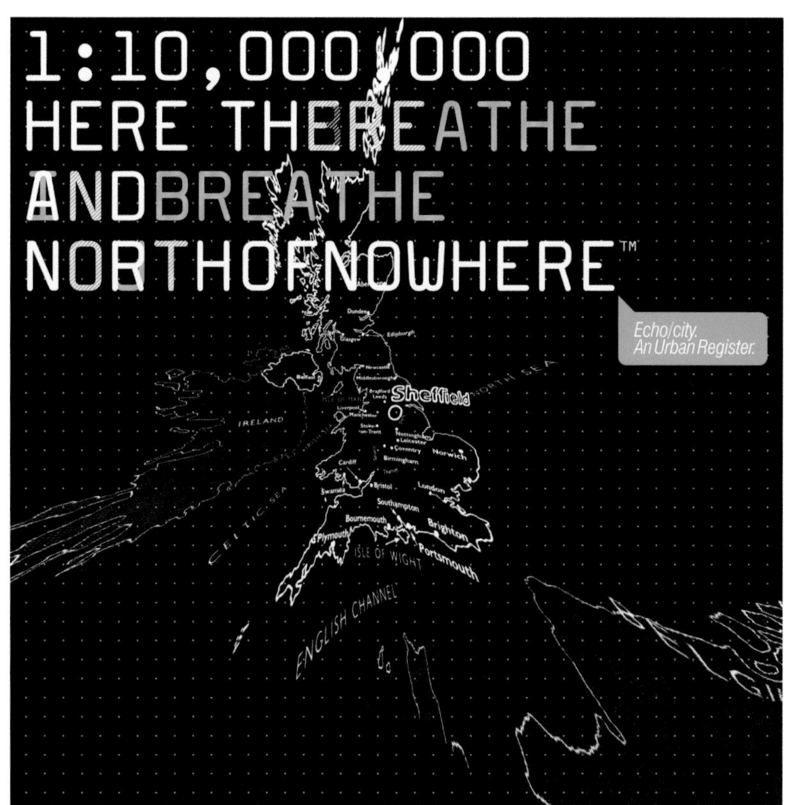

4

1
Designed by The Designers Republic, Sheffield.

2
1:100 Image.
Lewis Womerlsey, Sheffield City Architect, in front of Park Hill. Sheffield, 1962.
Designed by The Designers Republic, Sheffield.
PHOTO BY SAM LAMBERT, © ARCHITECTURAL PRESS.

3
1:10,000 Image,
A space syntax analysis of Sheffield.
Designed by The Designers Republic, Sheffield.
Credit: Professor Alan Penn, University College London, as part of the Vivacity 2020 project funded by the UK's Engineering and Physical Sciences Research Council.

4
1:10,000,000 Image,
Designed by The Designers Republic, Sheffield.
IMAGE BY GREG MOSS.

The Dispersed Urbanity of the Aegean Archipelago

1.
The Aegean Archipelago is a scattered city. The Aegean sea is not a void but a field which integrates the clusters of its 65 major islands into a *system of differences*: a complex network of social relations, economies, exchanges, symbolisms, infrastructures and the natural characteristics that constitute a city. The historians Romano and Asdrachas have argued that the Archipelago is not a theme park or a privileged resort, but a real community whose population of 1,300,000 inhabitants is tripled in the course of the year. Successive forced migrations and return journeys, tourist congestion and a multitude of economic migrants are exerting pressure on the human geography of this city and are shaping the islands' distinctive identities.

The peculiar physical geography and loose institutional protection of the urban fabric has prevented the settlements from gigantism, and the dispersion of the islands has discouraged their homogenization leading to the development of a *decentralized centrality*. The diversification in the relationship between built/unbuilt, in their models of habitation and in their rapidly changing architecture, generates island 'constellations' on the Archipelago map: they are the island utopias, the islands of prehistory, of hospitality, of rare products, of maritime shipping, of family tourism, of vanity, of liberality and tolerance, of anarchy, of exile and confinement, of shelter and of pilgrimage.

Greece

COMMISSIONERS
Elias Constantopoulos
Lois Papadopoulos

CURATORS
Elias Constantopoulos
Korina Filoxenidou
Katerina Kotzia
Lois Papadopoulos

WEBSITE
www.aegeancity.gr

2.
The endurance of the Archipelago – the fact that the Aegean city has not suffered any semantic impoverishment, that it has not been relegated to a state of alienation or to the non-space of alienated consumption – cannot be attributed to the diversified architectural physiognomy of the islands, nor to some transcendental resistance to change on the part of their historically shaped fabric. This endurance is rather due to the special way in which the Archipelago subscribes to the conditions of the metacity or to the features of its physical geography. Despite the predominance of aggressive models of tourism and local resource consumption, the pace in the Aegean is not set by mass tourism: visitors are absorbed into the residential folds of the existing villages, which retain the balance and rationale of their fabric. Also, the fact that the islands are surrounded by sea and exposed to light, sun and mighty winds, describes the unconditional relationship of the Archipelagic city with its nature, proposing not an anachronism but an alternative, *generic* and vibrant urbanity.

3.
Aquatic networks lie at the core of the Archipelago's perception as a city. The literary metaphor of the *journey* and the *sea routes* give the Aegean its shape. In the exhibition the Archipelago becomes a map of meanings, the Aegean experience of travelling from one place to another and the *ships* in the Aegean floating city squares, the public spaces of the city.

4.
Alongside the condition of freedom established by its physical geography and its architecture, the Archipelago, in the words of Cacciari, becomes the vital allegory of mutual social understanding, while according to Agamben it is identified with the world of outcasts, with the land of *exception*. In the context of contemporary urban discourse, the Archipelago introduces the example of an aquatic city as the land of desire. The allure of the Archipelago does not stem from nostalgia but from the endurance of a structure of habitation that contains the promise of a city that calls for freedom.

1

2

3

4

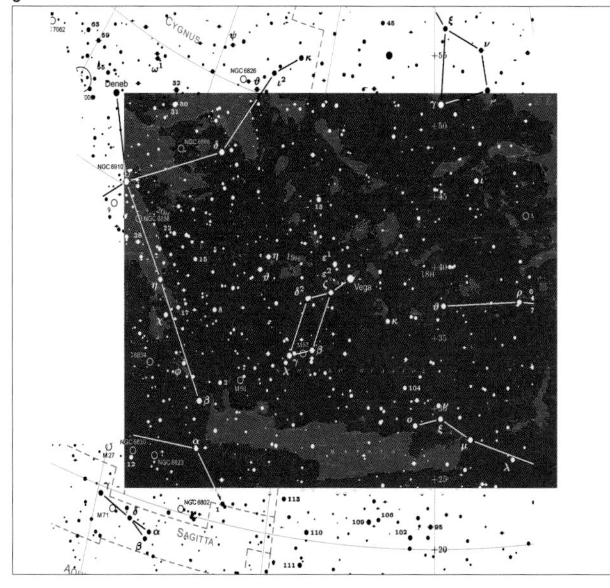

5

1-2-3-4
Journal 1998-2002.
PHOTO BY STRATOS KALAFATIS. COURTESY AGRA PUBLICATIONS, KALFAYAN GALLERIES.

5
The Aegean Islands Constellation.

SubUrban to SuperRural

One third of all the homes in Ireland have been built since 1995, 80% of them outside the major urban centres. Most of these homes sit on their own piece of land, with gardens to front and rear. Owning your own home is a reality for 80% of Irish citizens: the private house is an immensely successful, free-market consumer product, fuelled by our constitutional protection of the rights of private property, our innate desire to live on the land, our national obsession with the car and a deficit of infrastructure, integrated planning and political will unequalled in the developed world.

The singular solution to housing throughout the island has resulted in sub-urban sprawl - a vast, mono-functional organism that is choking our urban centres, devastating the countryside and atomizing our traditional sense of community. It is not uncommon to spend 15-20 hours per week commuting, inevitably by car. In little over a decade, the Emerald Isle, with the sixth lowest population density in the EU, has become a case study in extreme suburbanization.

Ireland's population is projected to grow by 25% by 2030 and the government's sole strategic infrastructural response has been to propose yet more roads. In the midst of this rush for more of the same, the absence of any accepted alternative expectations presents a rare freedom to re-imagine Ireland's future at a time of immense change and evolution within society. Are there new models for development that have been overlooked?

Accepting the reality of road-based infrastructure and low-density housing, can Ireland evolve new conditions in which to live? Conditions offering variety, social integration and environmental sustainability? Can we learn to value land again for its intrinsic qualities and not simply as a site for more houses? Can we create a new condition that is not a pale, less-than-urban condition but a ruddy hybrid of the rural and the urban, something more-than-rural - a SuperRural condition?

The emerging generation of Irish architects has been given the challenge to test this paradigm shift through research and the formulation of specific projects that imagine and illustrate a vision of how our SubUrban island can evolve into a SuperRural one between now and 2030.
Shane O'Toole, Michelle Fagan, Paul Kelly, Gary Lysaght and Ciaran O'Gaora

Ireland

COMMISSIONER
Shane O'Toole

CURATOR
FKL architects
(Michelle Fagan,
Paul Kelly,
Gary Lysaght)

DEPUTY COMMISSIONER
Ciaran O'Gaora

SPONSORS
Culture Ireland
The Arts Council /
An Chomhairle Ealaíon

EXHIBITORS
Boyd Cody Architects
Bucholz McEvoy Architects
de Paor Architects
FKL architects
Henchion+Reuter Architects
heneghan.peng.architects
MacGabhann Architects
ODOSarchitects
dominic stevens architect

1

1
Car Culture.
Produced
by FKL architects.

The Icelandic National Concert & Conference Centre
The East Harbour Project in Reykjavik

The Icelandic National Concert & Conference Centre in Reykjavik is publicly supported to build a centre for music, culture and tourism in the best location in the capital. It will create the best conditions for Iceland's continually expanding musical life and be the home of the Icelandic Symphony Orchestra. Furthermore, it will include a top-rate conference facility, closely connected to a five star, 300 room hotel. The estimated size of the CCC building is 25,000 m^2 and the hotel is of a similar size.

The prominent artist Ólafur Elíasson designed the building's outer shell and assisted in creating the connection between the building and its nearest surroundings, such as the Reykjatorg water plaza, which is a spectacular work of art by itself. One of Elíasson's key interests is the dialogue between the individual and his surroundings, and this project reflects his success, creating the potential for exchanges between the building and the people living in Reykjavik, the city itself, and the surrounding landscape and weather.

The main designer of the Icelandic National Concert & Conference Centre is the architectural firm Henning Larsen Tegnestue A/S of Copenhagen. The firm has gained a reputation for superb designs, such as The Opera in Copenhagen.

The world renowned US consultant company Artec is responsible for acoustics, sound insulation, and theatre and sound equipment design.

The Icelandic National Concert & Conference Centre will be constructed at the city centre harbour where the waterfront wharf and the old harbour wall meet on a striking coastal site embraced by the sea.

The building's design is influenced by the impressive and dramatic Icelandic landscape. Nature here is an endless source of colours: from glowing red to indigo blue, with variations from roaring ocean with white-foaming waves to a still, glassy sea.

The concept of the building is to create a crystalline form with a variety of colours dependent on the natural surroundings, giving the viewer a continuous feeling of sensuous change. The building stands alone as a monolith, reflecting the varying sky both in intensity and colour depending on the time of day, the weather and the season. The sun will accentuate the details in light and shadow, and the building will refer to the glowing lava when exploding in warm golden colours or to the glaciers when turning ice blue.

Iceland

COMMISSIONER
Thórhallur Vilhjálmsson

CLIENT
Austurhöfn-TR ehf (East Harbour Ltd), owned by The State of Iceland and the City of Reykjavik

PRIVATE PARTNER
Portus Ltd, private company owned by Nysir Ltd and Landsafl Ltd.
The project is a public private partnership (PPP) between Austurhöfn and Portus.

CONTRACTOR
Iceland Prime Contractor Ltd.

DESIGN
Henning Larsen Tegnestue A/S
Batteríið Architects.
Rambøll Danmark A/S
Hönnun Ltd.
Hnit Ltd.
Artec USA
Ólafur Elíasson

EXHIBITORS
Henning Larsen Tegnestue
Ólafur Elíasson

City planning

The plan strengthens the appearance of the city centre with the exceptional Concert and Conference building and a unique square where water is a major element.

A significant element in the proposal is a pedestrian street, proceeding from the old city square towards the Concert and Conference Centre. Pedestrians are protected by the curved design of the street and adjacent buildings. In addition to the Concert and Conference building, the private partner is responsible for development on adjacent sites with 50,000 m^2 of new building, taking the total City Centre addition up to 100,000 m^2, stretching from the old heart of the town to the East Harbour.

Three halls, three buildings, under one shell

The plan of the building is very simple with three halls side by side – a Concert Hall, a Rehearsal/Recital Hall and a Conference Hall, which will simplify flows within the building. Throughout the design process, emphasis has been placed on making it ideal for hosting bigger events and separating different conference halls from other areas of the building. This allows it to host different events simultaneously, without one interfering with the others.

Conference hall: 750 people
Rehearsal hall: 450 people
Concert hall: 1,800 people

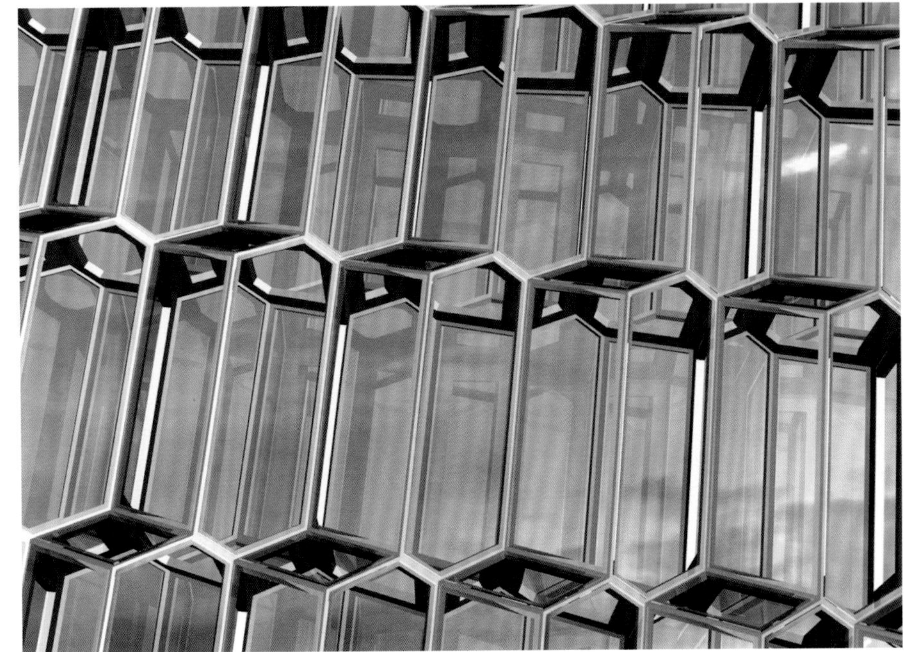

Life Saver
Typology of Commemoration in Israel
Architecture and Society
הרבחו תולכירדא - לארשיב החצנה לש היגולופיט -הלצה לגלג

Buildings of commemoration and memorial are edge structures: structures that harbour an emotionally charged issue, directed toward a large and diverse audience, and have a limited time framework in which to impress. These spaces represent an extreme example of architectural symbolism within society. This exhibition deals with buildings of commemoration and memorial in Israel, and the strong link between society and culture, and society and architecture.

The characteristic approach to such structures is that they mediate between the past and present toward the future. Commemoration and memorial spaces in Israel create the basis of legitimization for a society obliged to sacrifice life for its survival, as a means of justifying the hardships of daily existence, as well as paying the price for the future. Historic narrative – the past and its bereavement – isn't the entire story. The monuments and buildings in Israel tell another story, a story directly linked to a place. These places document history, death and pain, yet within this past representation, they form another viewpoint – looking forward, to the future.

There are two dominant anchors in Israeli history that form the accepted points of reference to this issue. The Holocaust represents the first and main point of convergence from which – the trauma, loss and pain – the state of Israel stemmed. The wars of the independent state represent the second keystone. They cultivated the notions of belonging and being part of the Israeli narrative and its fight for survival, this being the essence that arose from the cinders of the Holocaust.

This exhibition attempts to portray the unique nature of architecture in Israel. Commemorative architecture in Israel has created a dual vision via the rendition of opposites in the architectural space, representing two periods of time. This unique condition of dual vision: backward to past traumas, which must be remembered; forward: toward future life, is manifested within these architectural sites. The architects, being an integral part of Israeli society, portray this message by creating opposite experiences within the buildings.

The uniting factor of all these structures is that they are all characterized by a special 'order'. This 'order' is characteristic of commemorative and memorial buildings in Israel, but is not evident in other buildings. The essence of the 'order' lies in the reversal of space and almost all structures make use of more than one such opposition.

The three-dimensional representation of commemoration, looking backwards and forwards, is represented in the following manner: closed and open, dark and light, beneath and above, near and far. A variety of such oppositions are arranged in these structures, and almost all the structures take advantage of more than one such opposition.

Different kinds of oppositions are integrated into the structures. The oppositions allude to two contrasting conditions: conditions connected to the representation of time – in its wider context of past and future. Usually, the viewer is in the space at a certain time and leaves it to enter another time. The past and present exist while the viewer visits: he observes, stands, walks and, as he passes through, the transition occurs.

It is from here that the structures, in their form, place and architectural planning, give validity to the existing myths and social decree within the context of Israeli society.

Israel

COMMISSIONER
Michael Gov

CURATOR
Tula Amir

CO-CURATOR
Tal Zakut

DEPUTY COMMISSIONER
Arad Turgeman

ASSISTANT CURATOR
May Pundak

DESIGN
Sheri Arnon

SPONSORS
7VC
Ackerstein Industries
David Azrieli arc
Mifal Hapais Israel
National Lottery Council for the Arts
Israel Ministry of Defence Government of Israel
KKL Keren Kayemet
LeIsrael – Jewish National Fund
S.T.OR Lighting Design Center LTD
UPS
Israel Association of United Architects

EXHIBITORS
Tula Amir, architect
Erez Israeli, artist

LIFESAVER
SALVAGENTE

"Cantiere d'autore"
Architecture and photography for the MAXXI in progress

The exhibition being presented at the 10th Architecture Biennale by the DARC, the Direzione Generale per l'Architettura e l'Arte Contemporanee, proposes the theme of the building site; in particular, that of the MAXXI, the Museo Nazionale delle Arti del XXI Secolo in Rome, designed by Zaha Hadid.

The project entitled *'Cantiere d'autore. Architecture and photography for the MAXXI in progress'* is a photographic campaign commissioned by the DARC to increase the MAXXI architecture photo collections with a project centred on the construction of the new museum.

Launched to photograph the MAXXI building site in a non-conventional nor merely documentary way, the project involves photographers being invited to shoot the gradual construction of the work at varying stages. They were asked to capture the site from their own point of view with absolute freedom of choice and interpretation, in order to provide a multiple picture of the same place in continuous transformation.

The aim is to fix images of the building site from various points of view: a place of experimentation, a work place, a 'public' place, an object of curiosity and media attention.

The MAXXI building site is a public work with an international profile that demands constant attention to the technical and technological aspects and to the times and means of accomplishment in order to ensure excellent results. But the site is not only a construction and technological reality: it is also an evocative, constantly changing landscape that formerly was not there and will soon disappear to make room for the elegant volume of the museum. This transitory nature is one of the reasons that prompted the curators of the photographic project to 'fix' its nature as a variable, but at the same time concrete, 'in progress' place with the images of the photographers invited to date: Olivo Barbieri, Antonio Biasiucci, Giovanni Chiaramonte, Paola De Pietri, Ramak Fazel, Vittore Fossati, Moreno Gentili, Guido Guidi, Andrea Jemolo, Raffaela Mariniello and Luciano Romano.

Work on the MAXXI began in March 2003 with the 'laying of the first stone' and will finish in 2008. The stages of construction are also being documented by careful photographic monitoring – by the DARC architecture office – aimed at regularly capturing the progress of the building site, the experimentation and innovation that distinguish it, the techniques and materials used and the visible results.

The staging of the exhibition with an installation by Italo Rota introduces a critical perspective of the relationship between the reality, words and images of building.

Italy

Ministero per i Beni e le Attività Culturali
Dipartimento per i Beni Culturali e Paesaggistici
DARC - Direzione Generale per l'Architettura e l'Arte Contemporanee

COMMISSIONER
Pio Baldi

CURATORS
Margherita Guccione
Mario Lupano

COORDINATION
Francesca Fabiani

EXHIBITION DESIGN
Italo Rota

EXHIBITORS
Olivo Barbieri
Antonio Biasiucci
Giovanni Chiaramonte
Paola De Pietri
Ramak Fazel
Vittore Fossati
Moreno Gentili
Guido Guidi
Andrea Jemolo
Raffaela Mariniello
Luciano Romano

1

2

3

4

5

6

7

8

1
Luciano Romano,
Colour print on gloss photo paper, 51 x 71 cm, November 2004.
MAXXI architettura, Collezione di fotografia.

2
Andrea Jemolo,
Colour print on gloss photo paper, 25.3 x 37.9 cm, March 2005. MAXXI architettura, Collezione di fotografia.

3
Paola De Pietri,
Colour print on gloss photo paper, 70 x 48, April 2005. MAXXI architettura, Collezione di fotografia.

4
Antonio Biasiucci,
B/W print on photo paper, 41 x 41 cm, September 2005.
MAXXI architettura, Collezione di fotografia.

5
Guido Guidi,
Colour print on gloss photo paper, 30 x 24 cm, November 2005.
MAXXI architettura, Collezione di fotografia.

6
Vittore Fossati,
Colour print on gloss photo paper, 50 x 60 cm, February 2006.
MAXXI architettura, Collezione di fotografia.

7
Raffaela Mariniello,
Colour print on gloss photo paper, 60 x 50 cm, March 2006.
MAXXI architettura, Collezione di fotografia.

8
Ramak Fazel,
Colour print on gloss photo paper, 60 x 60 cm, April 2006.
MAXXI architettura, Collezione di fotografia.

Latvia

COMMISSIONER
Sergejs Nikiforovs
CURATOR
Ugis Senbergs in collaboration with Zigmars Jauja and Didzis Jaudzems
DEPUTY COMMISSIONERS
Edgars Treimanis Paivi Tirkkonen De Grandis
ORGANIZATION
Latvian Architects Association (Kristine Budze, Zanda Redberga)
PARTNER
Arte Communications Venezia
WITH THE SUPPORT OF
State Culture Capital Foundation Riga City Council

Urban Dice

So corrupted by work, that we don't know how to rest.
The die rolls and rolls and stops
On the five, the two, or the six
And we rest until the next toss.
Imants Ziedonis, poet

A dice-like home that the owner can transform to make the space serve various functions. The home is not bound to a particular place, though one is able to connect it to lines of communications in the designated places. Several homes may be mutually combined, thereby creating colonies of dice-like homes. The home is suited to various environments, and urges a person to undertake greater responsibility and initiative in the design of the surrounding space.

More than Compact

The transformations of a place, and the multifaceted, multi-functional possibilities for use. An economic utilization of resources, taking up only the minimum necessary land area, which is used exhaustively. Viewing resourcefulness and the small space not as a hindrance or as a mandatory provision, but rather as a way of organizing life whereby everything is only a short reach away and capable of being subjected to sudden changes, thus reducing the restrictions usually specified for a traditional piece of immovable property.

Unattached

A home that the owner is able to move and transform by him or herself, subjecting the home to his or her changing needs and desires. The home provides the opportunity to preserve one's own personal space, without taking into account the architectural traditions of a place.

Open Source

The self-organization of colonies of individual dice-like homes in the space and time designated for them, as well as the possibility for an owner to adapt a home to his or her own specific needs, becomes a unique type of architecture and environmental planning, equivalent to open source programming. In architecture, the open-source idea dispels the boundary between the regulator and the user of an environment. An architect and an environmental planner create a source code and construct an interchange system, which is supplemented, communicated with, and operated in by the user of the environment. The architect takes on a new social role, offering planning frameworks that urge a resident to work and apply him or herself in a creative manner; the architect effectively promotes communal responsibility toward the environment in which a resident lives.

The Game

The organization and transformation of space and the environment become a toy, removing the weight of seriousness and responsibility from these processes. This results in a joy in life, instead of a feeling of being resigned to fate. The game is a living space for the people of a post-capitalist society for whom the main things in life are not credit ratings, fancy entries in a C.V., regular visits to a psychologist or long lists of neuroses. The dice-like home offers frivolity in place of constant stress and tension; mobility in place of stability; free time in place of regulated working hours; and, instead of a passive observance of events, the chance to actively collaborate and express one's opinion, as well as a readiness to change the situation in architecture and environmental planning.
Ugis Senbergs

1

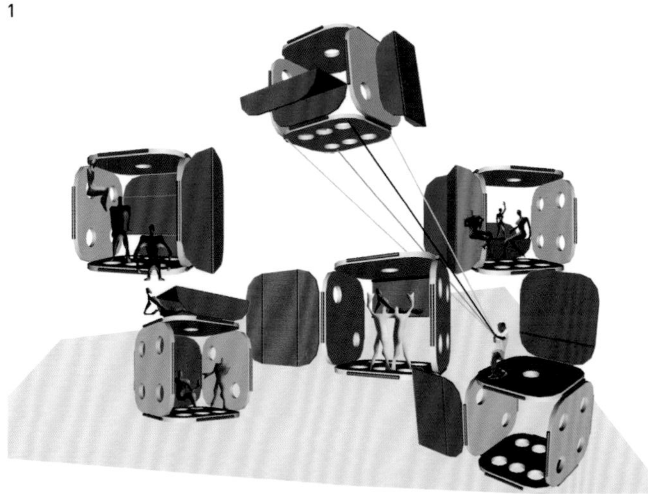

2

3

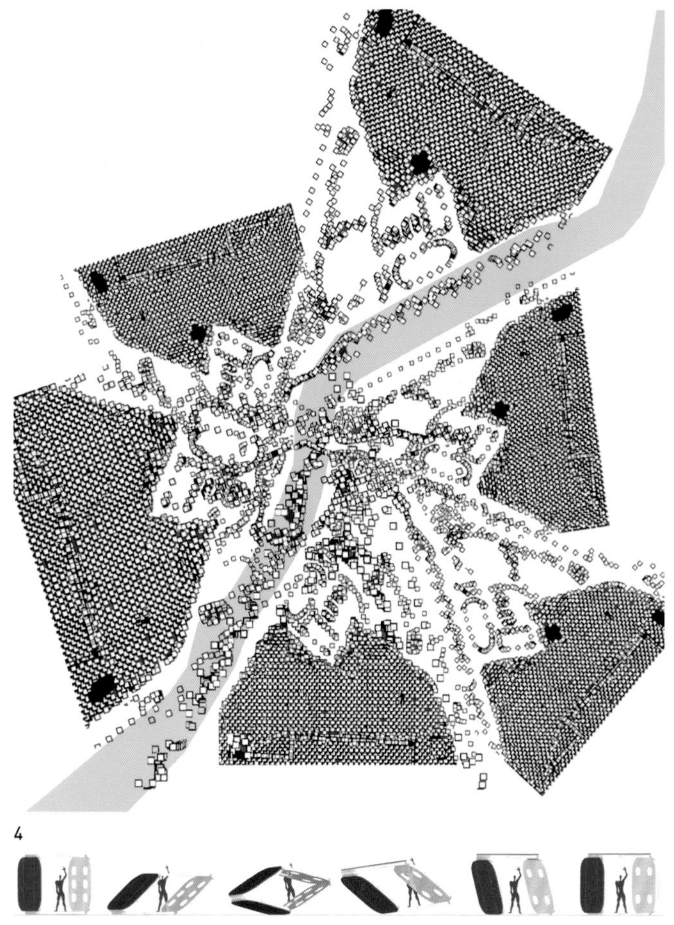

4

5

1
Ugis Senbergs,
Didzis Jaudzems,
Anna Kolesnikova,
Linda Leitane,
Urban dice can be located in Riga,
Latvia, 2006.

2
Ugis Senbergs,
Linda Leitane,
Didzis Jaudzems,
Urban dice can be transformed,
2006.

3
Ugis Senbergs,
Anna Kolesnikova,
Urban dice can be located in Venice,
Italy, 2006.

4
Didzis Jaudzems,
Urban dice can be used to set up self-organizing systems,
2006.

5
Ugis Senbergs,
Linda Leitane,
Urban dice can be re-located,
2006.

Welcome to Paradise

The Grand Duchy of Luxembourg is often referred to as 'paradise'. Benefiting from special fiscal treatment and low taxes, Luxembourg is one of Europe's first places to put or invest money. For close neighbours and commuters it is the place to find qualified employment and an inexhaustible supply of cheap gas. For tourists the Grand Duchy means green rolling hills and delightful valleys, medieval castles, vineyards and a quiet life.

The *Welcome to Paradise* project refers to a definition of Luxembourg as a socio-cultural paradise where the differences are balanced within a harmonious integration. Formed and governed by foreign powers for hundreds of years, Luxembourg was deeply influenced by labour migrants – particularly from Portugal and Italy – who came to Luxembourg in the heyday of the national iron industry at the end of the nineteenth century. Since the '60s, the arrival of financial institutes and European community organizations brought about new forms of residency and mobility. Today 40 to 50% of the people forming this country have complex migration experiences. They have a substantial impact on Luxembourg's history, economics, culture and the development of the city: a city of different identities, a metacity that is not simply structured by spatial realities, but in which social action provides societal existence.

During the Venice Biennale a multimedia installation will offer a taste of this 'paradise', using a bus on its way through the city of Luxembourg as a simplified but strong metaphor. The bus is seen as a micro-cosmos of urban reality: a place of fortuitous encounters, enforced closeness and mixed identities forming transitory communities, unchosen but heading for a collective destination. But as paradise does not exist without hell, this paradisiacal means of transport carries its demons...

Within this context the objective of the installation is to question the relevancy and the metaphorical truth of the paradisiacal reputation of Luxembourg as a European model society for cultural and social integration. The approach taken by the curators is to look at:
- food for urban thinking: images provided by bus travel affecting the perception and conception of the physical and social urban landscape;
- paradise by bus: terminal destination Paradise?;
- sonic voyeurism: voices of urban experience/ consciousness.

Promoting broader, deeper ways of perceiving the issues involved in the co-existence of different cultures and identities, the project aims to give the visitor insight into the emotions associated with it and to bring a part of everyday Luxembourg city-life to the Venice Biennale by means of a conceptual installation. The opening will be accompanied by a performance exploring and discussing the current and the future dynamics emerging from the interplay of cultures and identities (absence of dialogue, comprehension and solidarity; fear and loneliness) on the basis of Othello.

Luxembourg

COMMISSIONER
François Valentiny

CURATOR
Fondation
de l'Architecture
et de l'Ingénierie,
Luxembourg

DEPUTY CURATORS
Christian Bauer
Tatiana Fabeck
Shaaf Milani-Nia
Stefano Moreno
Andrea Rumpf
Nico Steinmetz
Lisi Teisen

SCIENTIFIC COMMITTEE
Jacques Brauch
Alain Linster
Bohdan Paczowski

COORDINATOR
Anouk Bernard

CO-ORGANIZATION
Arte Communications
Venezia

Seeing is Knowing: The Dutch Urban Perspective

Good architects don't just plan cities; they imagine them. They see them in their mind's eye, from the great heights or from the vantage point of an imagined future viewer. In the Netherlands in particular, architects have long seen the city as a complete environment in which each element is the result of complex negotiations over the precious amount of space available and the whole has to be calibrated by the architect to maximum effect. The Dutch do not just let cities happen or control them with planning instruments, they make them as concrete, coherent artefacts – a 'makeable society'. This year the Netherlands presents a survey of perspectives on the city, drawn from its comprehensive collections in the Rietveld Pavilion.

Perspective has long been a key element in Dutch art and architecture. Much of the charm of seventeenth-century Dutch art is the result of its explicit organization of otherwise everyday objects in a carefully composed spatial environment. With the help of treatises on perspective drawing, painters produced both interiors and city views that represent reality in a refined, carefully mapped and seemingly complete manner. Through the painter's art, we gain control over reality.

When Dutch architecture began to develop as an independent discipline, late nineteenth-century perspectives helped designers imagine the fast-growing metropolis, as well as design completely coordinated interiors. The best example was the plan for Amsterdam South, which H.P. Berlage saw as a coherent new urban area in which public space was defined and controlled through the manipulation of building masses. He used perspective drawings that showed how the city would look.

In subsequent years, Dutch architects became more ambitious and more abstract in their methods, imagining whole new towns and even new land. City planners gained more power and their perspectives moved from eye level to God's eye, as they took on the role of scientific interpreters of everyday. They sketched the urban ensemble as it would be seen from an aeroplane (J.J.P. Oud) or as a series of building blocks strewn around on the ground (C. van Eesteren).

The reaction to this elevated viewpoint came in the '70s, when architects began arguing for a more human scale. They drew fragments of cities and moments of transition, focused on details and proposed familiar elements. The perspective became fragmented and informal, taking on the quality of an illustration of elements of daily life that may not have an overall coherence. Recently, the computer has let architects meld eye level, God's eye and collage perspective into the seamless swoops and pans of animation. These methods, again, trace and reinforce design attitudes. Architects like Rem Koolhaas imagine their buildings as spirals unfolding out of the present in a continuous sequence of highly differentiated spaces; UNStudio believes that they can amalgamate form from data into unfolding shapes; MVRDV assembles elements into conceptual unities.

Taken together, these magnificent drawings from two centuries of Dutch architecture history will show how architecture can imagine the city as a place to be inhabited, understood and perhaps controlled. They show the tools we have for making sense of the messy metropolis while letting us delight in the craft of design. Instead of planning for the future, they offer us views on what the future could and perhaps should look like.

Aaron Betsky

The Netherlands

COMMISSIONER
Netherlands Architecture Institute

CURATORS
Aaron Betsky
Martien de Vletter

DEPUTY CURATORS
Mieke Dings
Clara Stille

EXHIBITION DESIGN
Eventarchitectuur / Herman Verkerk

SPONSOR
Ministry of Cultural Affairs

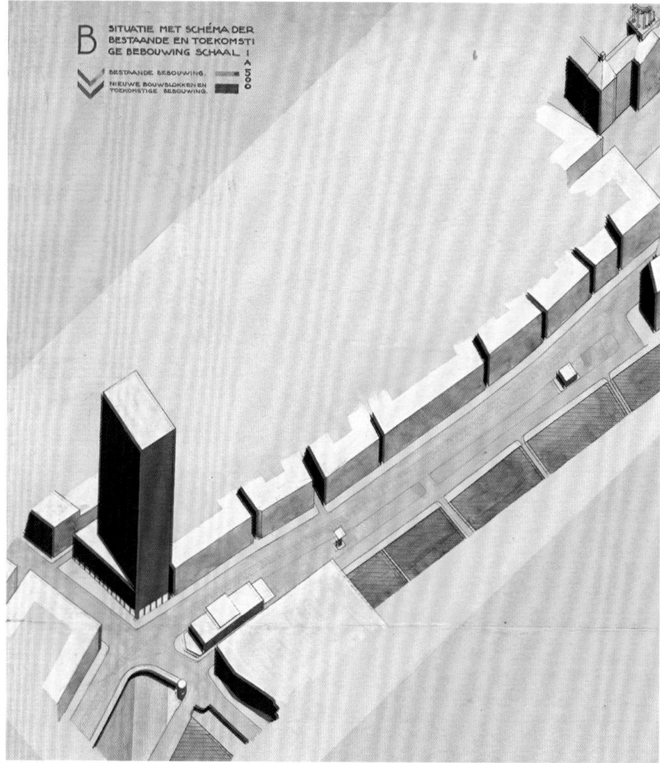

1

2

3

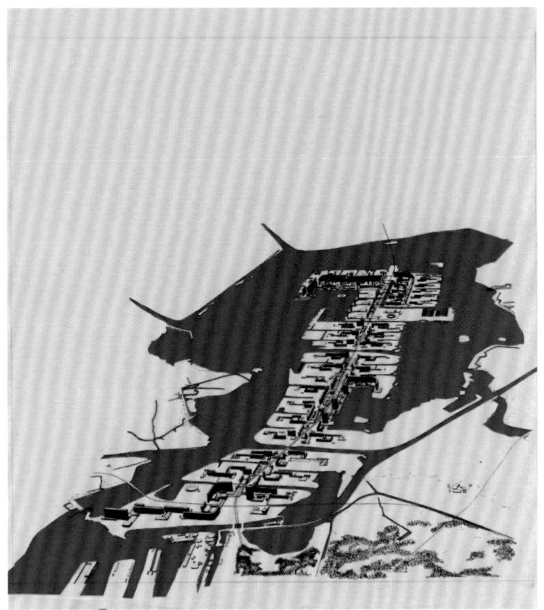

4

5

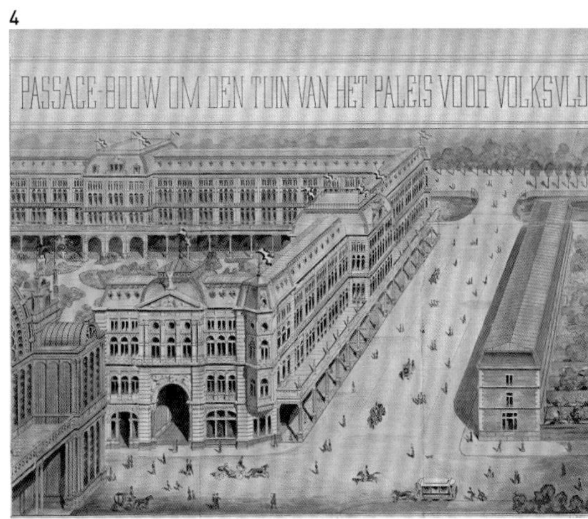

6

7

8

1
C. van Eesteren,
Competition design for the Rokin,
Amsterdam, 1925.
COLLECTION NAI.

2
C. van Eesteren,
Design for a business quarter, 1926.
COLLECTION NAI.

3
J.C. van Epen,
Housing for the Hendrik Jacobszstraat,
Amsterdam, 1918.
COLLECTION NAI.

4
J.B. Bakema,
Plan for city on the island Pampus, 1964.
COLLECTION NAI.

5
M. de Klerk,
Housing Eigen Haard,
Amsterdam, 1927.
COLLECTION NAI.

6
A.L. van Gendt,
Palace for "Volksvlijt", Amsterdam, 1881.
COLLECTION NAI.

7
M.A. van Nieukerken,
Images for a new city,
1939.
COLLECTION NAI.

8
P.J.H. Cuypers,
Rijksmuseum Amsterdam, 1875.
COLLECTION NAI.

Arctic cities: Kiruna, Oulu, Tromsø

Kiruna, Oulu and Tromsø are among Europe's northernmost cities. In their own ways they have each developed under demanding climatic conditions to become international operating environments that also serve their inhabitants. People near the Arctic Circle live on the global margins but in the midst of the good life.

Cities of Water, Snow and Ice
Kiruna in Sweden, Oulu in Finland and Tromsø in Norway are in different parts of the Nordic region. The coastal city of Tromsø is the westernmost and northernmost one, Kiruna is in the inland part of Lapland and Oulu is located furthest to the south on the shore of the northern reaches of the Gulf of Bothnia. Their location and climate make them all cities of water, snow and ice.

These cities are of different ages: Oulu is 400, Tromsø ca. 200 and Kiruna over 100 years old. They are a mix of international currents and the local cultures of their surrounding regions. The Sámi heritage has a special role alongside the Nordic cultures in the area. The traditional livelihoods are still important, although the economy of the cities is now largely based on high technology and is being developed into new, growing sectors while relying on the prominent specialist skills of the areas concerned.

International and national currents are present in urban planning and architecture, as well as local reactions and interpretations of them. Architecture and development in the region reflect the northern landscape and way of life, even where internationally renowned architects have been involved. The main changes in the urban environment in the future will be seen at Kiruna, where preparations are under way for moving the city centre to a new location. In the growing cities of Oulu and Tromsø there is an emphasis on a continuing process of intellectual renewal in urban planning and resulting changes in the urban environment.

Kiruna – Living on the Edge
With a population of roughly 20,000, Kiruna is Sweden's northernmost city. It is an important European mining location and a centre of space research while also attracting tourists and visitors. It is known for its interesting history of town planning, beautiful buildings and innovation related to its role as a winter city.

A city to be relocated
At Kiruna, major parts of the city have to be relocated as mining will extend to beneath the present city centre. At this stage, there is naturally a great deal of discussion on the Kiruna of the future. Local authorities have chosen two main alternatives for the direction of relocation as the basis of continued work. The alternatives will have different long and short-term effects, which will be compared.

The land of the Sámi
Sámi culture is prominent in Kiruna, being also reflected in local architecture. The most recent project for the city will be the construction of the Sámi Parliament building on the basis of the winning entry chosen by the Sámi Parliament of Sweden. Facing east, this crescent-shaped building will be of major symbolic importance for the Sámi people, and is already regarded as the new landmark of the city.

Nordic Countries: Finland, Norway, Sweden

COMMISSIONERS-COORDINATORS
Roy Mänttäri
Eija Salmi

FINLAND/DEPUTY COMMISSIONER
Severi Blomstedt

NORWAY/COMMISSIONER
Eva Madshus

NORWAY/DEPUTY COMMISSIONERS
Ulf Grønvold
Knut Eirik Dahl
Hege Pålsrud

SWEDEN/COMMISSIONER
Karin Åberg Waern

SWEDEN/DEPUTY COMMISSIONERS
Bitte Nygren
Mats Winsa

EXHIBITORS
Finland:
Oulun Kaupunki
Norway:
Tromsø Kommune
Sweden:
Kiruna Kommun

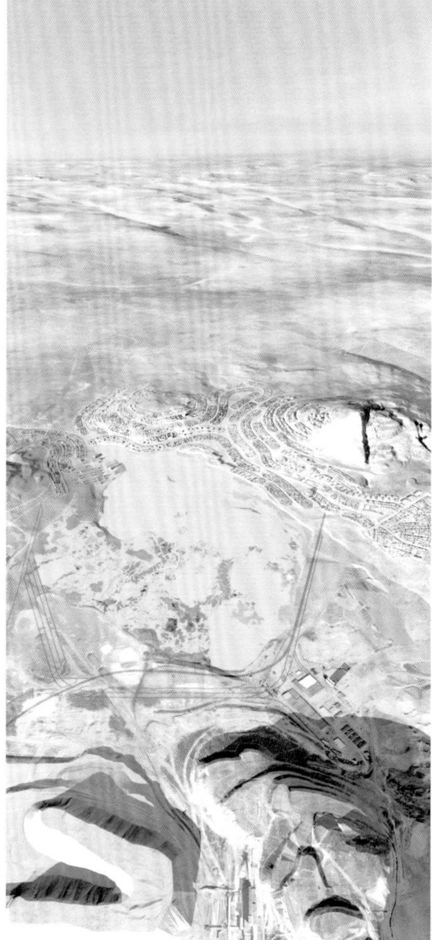

1

Oulu – Venice of the North

Oulu is the largest city in the northern part of the Nordic region. This coastal city has some 130,000 inhabitants and its economic zone has a population of over 200,000. Oulu is an international centre of high-technology industries with a long history of administration and education. It is also the location of a school of architecture. Urban planning in Oulu is supported by the city's own programme of architectural policy.

The architectural policy programme of Oulu

In keeping with European objectives, Finland has adopted a national architectural policy programme. In accordance with its recommendations, several regions and cities have begun to prepare their own architectural policy programmes. The Oulu programme involved urban architectural policy and is already being monitored by other localities.

According to the programme, the built environment is a recognized and central aspect of the cultural and welfare society and the programme tells how the residents of the city feel their shared environment should be planned and built. It gives planners, architects, developers and decision-makers instructions on how the future of the city should be developed. The challenge is to make Oulu a residential and living environment promoting cultural diversity, a light-spirited atmosphere and a creative urban spirit. The preparation of the programme includes a large number of expert residents of the city and it has been officially approved by the municipal government. There has been commitment to the programme and it has been followed in the media. It is felt in Oulu that the city cannot afford to be without an environment and architecture of high standard.

Tromsø - The City of the Arctic Sea

Tromsø is the largest city on the northern coast of Norway. With a population of over 60,000, its development has been based on high-level skills and international interaction. Tromsø is a centre for research in climate and energy safety and sustainable development. The effects of global climatic change on sea levels and environmental conditions are important for Tromsø as a city on the Arctic Sea. A central concern for the city is to be active in issues of environmental cooperation concerning the production of oil and gas, which is significant for Norway and neighbouring Russia, and the extensive fishing industry in this maritime region. The development of the city is based on the preservation of unpolluted natural conditions and a high standard of living with attention to issues regarding development of the urban environment. Tromsø reflects the growing international role of the northern regions and the emerging activity of citizens in taking part in the development of the city.

A programme of urban development open to inhabitants

Tromsø is involved in realizing a programme of urban development in which the local inhabitants have a central role. The year 2005 was designated as a special year for urban development and it included open civic debate on all projects concerning the city centre. The issues were addressed through a specially developed method, with seminars and walking tours of the city. Focusing primarily on the role of the city centre, urban architecture and public space, strategies and information, the programme has led to reappraisals concerning the development of the city.

2

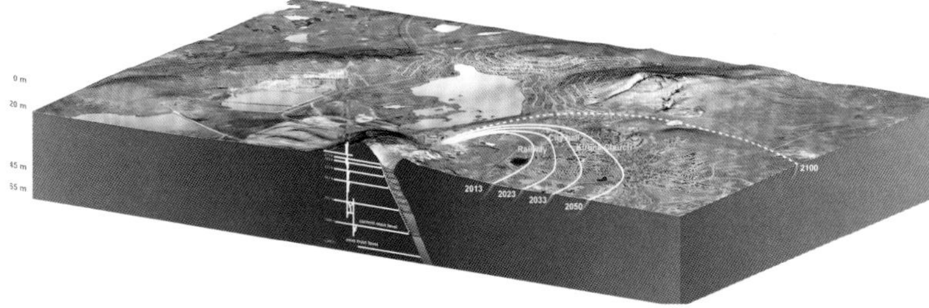

3

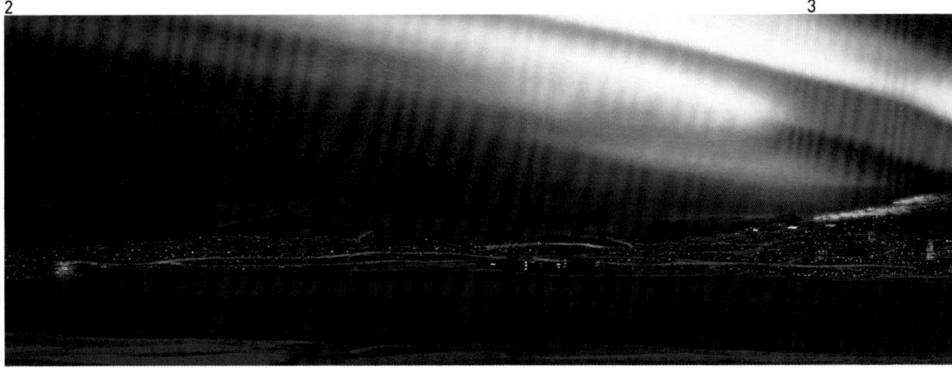

4

5

6

1
New Kiruna from south with the LKAB mine in the foreground.

2
Birdseye view of the new Kiruna growing seamlessly from the existing city. The deserted mine to the right and the Luossavaara mine to the left and the lake Luossajärvi in the centre.

3
Section showing the ore body penetrating under the present city of Kiruna forcing its relocation.

4
Simulated view of New Kiruna from lake Luossajärvi. The new position of Kiruna church to the left.

5
Kiruna Townplan conceived as an environmental grid structure consisting of 90 meter wide blocks meandering across the landscape. Netscape meets landscape.

6
Estuary of the Oulujoki River, Oulu townplan by Alvar Aalto.
PHOTO BY ILPO OKKONEN / STUDIO ILPO OKKONEN OY.

7

8

9

Impacts of a warming Arctic

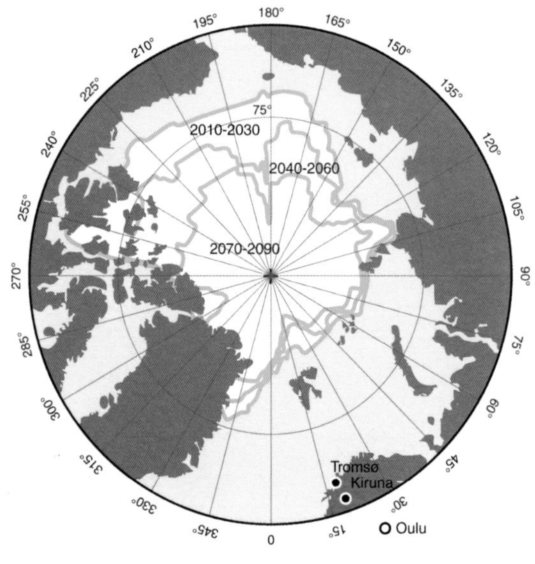

10

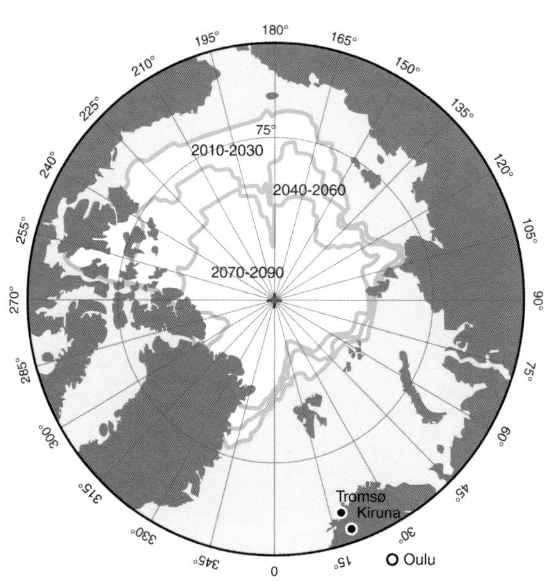

11

12

13

14

7
Midsummer night in wooden city, Oulu.
PHOTO BY ILPO OKKONEN / STUDIO ILPO OKKONEN OY.

8
Oulu city center waterfront.
PHOTO BY ILPO OKKONEN / STUDIO ILPO OKKONEN OY.

9
New one family housing at the seaside in Oulu.
PHOTO BY ILPO OKKONEN / STUDIO ILPO OKKONEN OY.

10-11
Impacts of a warming Arctic. Graphics: Audun Igesund, Norwegian Polar Institute Polarmiljøsenteret.
SOURCE: AMAP, WWW.AMAP.NO.

12
Tromsø: gateway to the Arctic sea.
PHOTO BY YNGVE OLSEN.

13
Tromsø citizens involved in urban development.
PHOTO BY JON TERJE EITERÅ.

14
Tromsø: Paul Bjørviks Brygge - Multifunctional urban transformation. Knut Eirik Dahl (Dahl& Uhre Arkitekter).
PHOTO BY LAURITZEN&WESTH.

Transfer

Transfer, the title of Jarosław Kozakiewicz's conceptual-architectural project at the Polish Pavilion, denotes the act of transporting something or someone from one place to another, the transfer of people, information, money and technology, but also the conveyance of an image from one surface to another, such as by tracing. 'Transfer function' is a term known to sociologists (a statistical method) as well as to architects designing, for instance, airport terminals.

The guiding theme of Kozakiewicz's project – the author is a sculptor and designer of architectural projects – is Warsaw as an example of the contemporary culture of congestion, a city on which the post-1989 political, economic and social transformation has left a powerful, unique imprint. Warsaw is a city that is constantly subject to criticism, a city of great construction projects, but at the same time of architectural and planning failures.

Transfer is inspired by Warsaw's historical and cultural spatial axes, its lost architectural values, such as the Saxon axis, the King Stanislaw axis or the Prague axis. Kozakiewicz proposes a new organic transfer network for Warsaw, partly overlapping existing thoroughfares, but at the same time creating new connections and bringing the historical axes back from oblivion. The transfer network consists of a system of overpasses and performs three main functions:

1. it connects green areas (city parks, suburban wooded areas), facilitating alternative communication routes for pedestrians and cyclists without the need to use modern transit facilities;
2. it connects places of particular interest, creating specific trails, e.g. of memory, art, education, entertainment or leisure;
3. it improves the transfer function of existing communication routes.

The planned overpass network symbolically overlaps the city's existing networks: with its transfer (bus, tram, train, metro), power, telephone, water or gas networks. Short animated films present fragments of the selected routes, e.g. a memory trail referring to the historical Saxon axis, leading toward the suburban Kampinoska Forest through historical sites, forgotten monuments and cemeteries; an art trail connecting Warsaw's museums, galleries and theatres, or a leisure trail connecting green areas.

The transfer network changes its form as it moves through the city, alternating, depending on local conditions, between open overpasses modelled on park alleys; tube-like roofed overpasses, encouraging transfer in adverse weather conditions; and ground pedestrian trails, i.e. streets closed to vehicular traffic. The elevation of the overpasses varies according to, for instance, the presence of tram cabling or the height of nearby buildings. Either open or roofed, from the bottom the overpasses reflect views of the city and ground traffic, making it possible to partly 'dematerialise' them.

As Michel de Certeau points out in his *Practice of Everyday Life*, the mass transit facilities in contemporary Athens are called *metaphorai*. To get to work or go home, the city's inhabitants use 'metaphors,' or transfer means, such as the bus, car or metro. Kozakiewicz's project offers criticism of the specific situation of a congested city, while retaining the ambiguity of a metaphor. The overpass network isn't an immediately executable architectural project, but rather a proposition suggesting that we change our 'means of transport', and thus also our viewing angles and the ways we experience the city; that we transfer not only from place to place but also in time.

Gabriela Świtek

Poland

COMMISSIONER
Agnieszka Morawińska

CURATOR
Gabriela Świtek

DEPUTY COMMISSIONER
Ewa Wojciechowska

EXHIBITOR
Jarosław Kozakiewicz

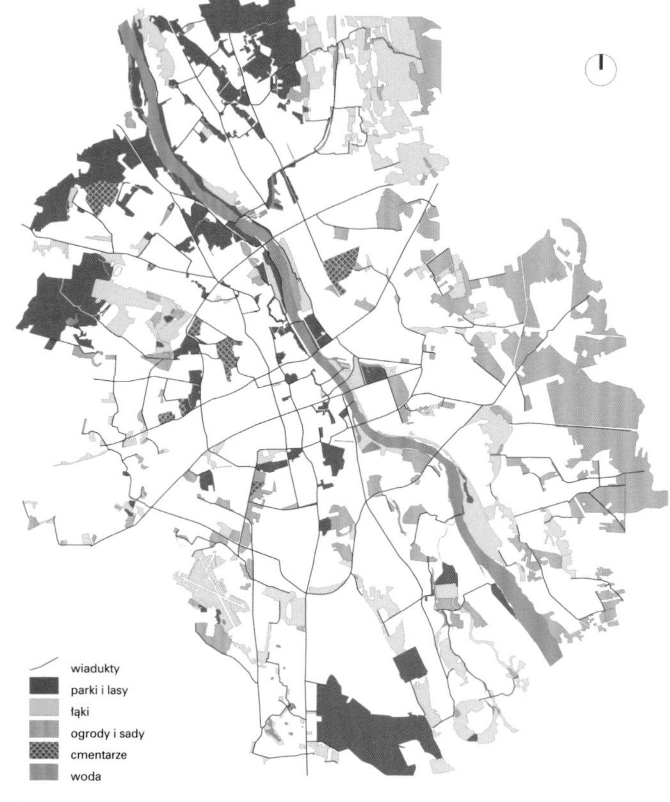

1

2

3

4

5

6

7

8

1
Jarosław Kozakiewicz,
Transfer,
2006. Plan for the organic transfer network in Warsaw, drawing.
COURTESY THE AUTHOR.

2-3-4
Jarosław Kozakiewicz,
Transfer (project, Warsaw),
2006. Closed viaduct, rendering.
COURTESY THE AUTHOR.

5
Jarosław Kozakiewicz,
Interior geometry II - Cinema (project, Warsaw),
2005. Rendering.
COURTESY THE AUTHOR.

6
Jarosław Kozakiewicz,
Love Tower (project, New York),
2004. Rendering.
COURTESY THE AUTHOR.

7
Jarosław Kozakiewicz,
Oxygen Towers (project, Rome),
2005. Rendering.
COURTESY THE AUTHOR.

8
Jarosław Kozakiewicz (with Ewa Kosiacka, Karolina Tunajek, Piotr Twardo),
Souls' Bridge,
Park of the Reconciliation between Nations - Gardens of Europe, close to the Auschwitz - Birkenau Museum, Oświęcim, Poland, 2005 (under construction). Rendering.
COURTESY THE AUTHOR.

Lisboscopio

The city of Lisbon has an estimated population of 400,000 inhabitants.

Greater Metropolitan Lisbon, which encompasses 3.3% of Portugal's surface, has a population of 2.7 million inhabitants, i.e. 27.1% of the country's population. Everyday, up to two million people arrive in Lisbon to work and to engage in multiple dwelling dynamics that add one million cars to the city.

The public transport system is fragmented and dispersed. The design of the 'new city' is interdependent with the design of auto mobility. The road systems have bulked up and polarized the city's sense of inhabitation, and built new centralities within the expanded new city. It appears that what used to be the centre has become peripheral, and the periphery has created its own centres as self-organized entities and systems. These are places that create a new possibility for the city, considering it is in their midst that new cultural expressions are being manifested, recreating themselves and becoming active. The city grows and spreads out with no specific geography as an expression of multiple processes and becomes a place for dwelling and experimentation. Its geographic borders are both plastically and temporally expandable, which allows for the emergence of contact and transference surfaces.

The exhibition project consists of a spatial construct as an open possibility to the dwelling experience, evoking the city of Lisbon. It conceptualizes openness as an architecture of space. The installation can become a place through the individual experience of inhabiting and dwelling.

The work is ephemeral and mobile. It can dwell in other places, in other cities. Its construction acknowledges the re-use of specific matter-elements, which are but codes of a city's fabrication. It is architecture that adapts itself to the surrounding placement, so it can reinvent the experience of the Biennale's garden, without destroying an inch of its physical actuality. The transformation process occurs solely in the self-experienced sphere of the inhabitability of this space.

The project by Amâncio (Pancho) Guedes and Ricardo Jacinto consists of a device-container of ideas on the city, constructed as a unique piece that opens up to reveal itself and folds up in order to travel. The container holds both the structure and the content. The latter, consisting of text and image, is inscribed in its 'skin' and in the structure. This can simultaneously be a fragmented and continuous space to amplify the experience of the dweller.

Amâncio (Pancho) Guedes (Lisbon, 1925) and Ricardo Jacinto (Lisbon, 1975) are architects who began their architectural and artistic practice in different epochs. In the Portuguese and international architecture and art contexts their work has contributed to a different conception of space, underlining the fact that architecture is a timeless process of free creation for the space to live in.

Portugal

COMMISSIONER
Claudia Taborda

EXHIBITORS
Amâncio (Pancho) Guedes
Ricardo Jacinto

ORGANIZATION
Instituto das Artes / Ministério da Cultura de Portugal

LOCAL PARTNER
Arte Communications Venezia

1

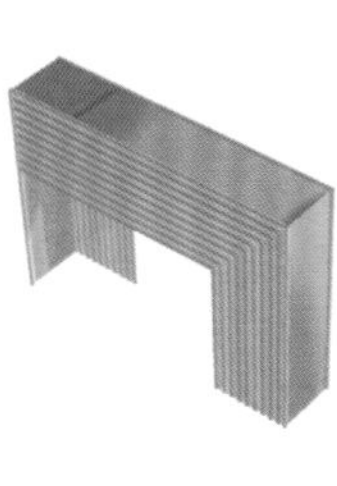

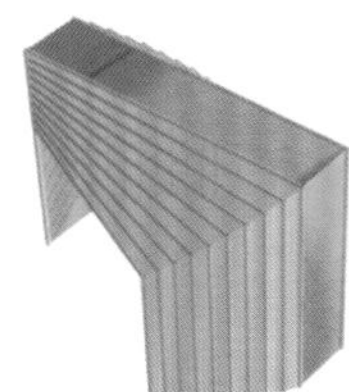

2

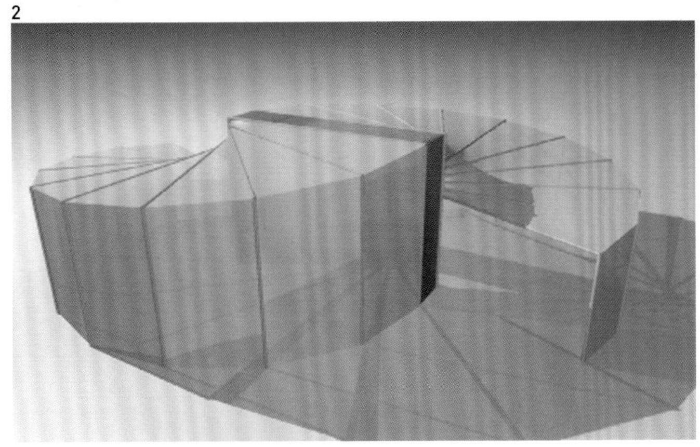

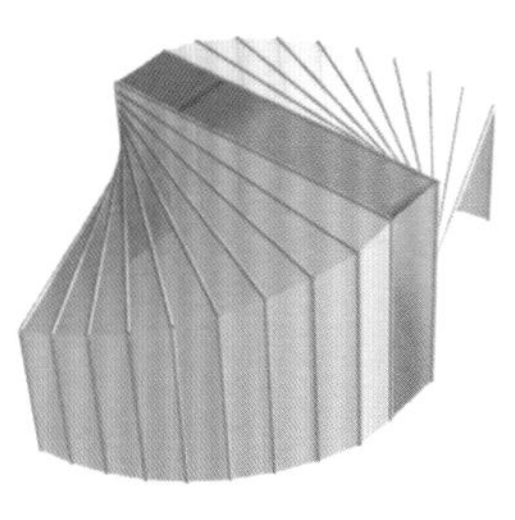

3

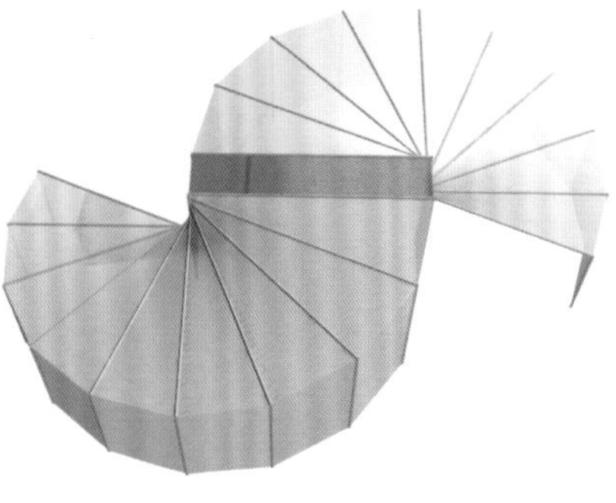

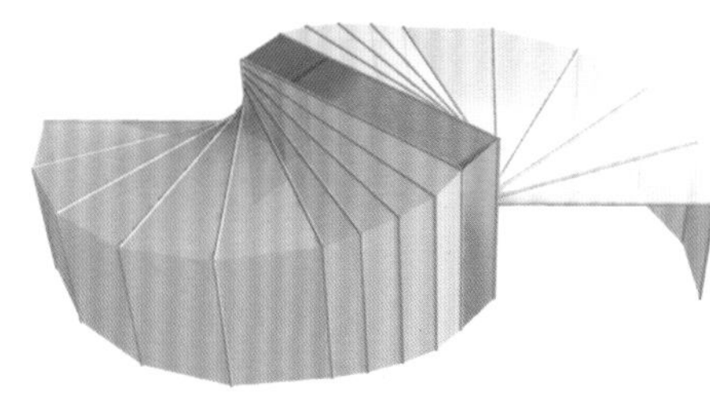

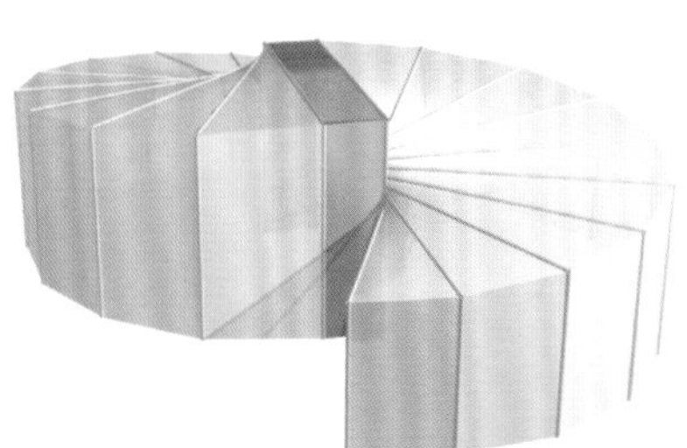

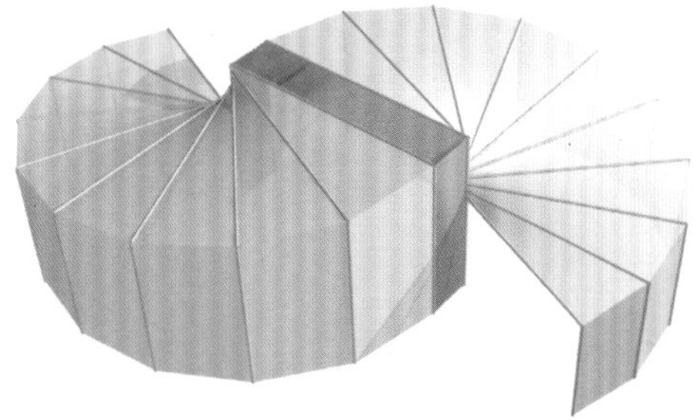

4

5

1
Amâncio (Pancho) Guedes, Ricardo Jacinto, **Lisboscopio,** photomontage by Ricardo Jacinto, April 2006.

2
Amâncio (Pancho) Guedes, Ricardo Jacinto, **Preliminary model.**

3
Amâncio (Pancho) Guedes, Ricardo Jacinto, **Sidetopview.**

4
Amâncio (Pancho) Guedes, Ricardo Jacinto, **Exhibition container.**

5
Amâncio (Pancho) Guedes, Ricardo Jacinto, **Exhibition container,** concept drawing.

MetaCity

The initial subject was *MetaCity*, i.e. a large city, a metropolis, to which people flock in ever growing numbers. Architecture is unable to keep abreast of this by constantly creating a high-quality environment throughout the city for all inhabitants. The lifestyle and functions of the city are changing, disintegrating into smaller entities; the city is turning into a cluster of different parts, whose interdependence in practical life is becoming looser. True, there is still a large centre (historical, social, political, cultural) somewhere, but ordinary people almost never go there – they increasingly tend to be interested in the outlying suburbs where the shopping centres are located.

So what is the role of architecture in such a city? And what about the role of the architect? There is the contemporary one, who views things distinctly and is in a way already anchored somewhere in the past (whether recent or distant), and the future one, who is still maturing, collecting ideas and, to a varying degree, both cooperating and competing with the person preparing him for the job. The subject is thus the architect and his students, his disciples, and the view they share of today's large city, the *MetaCity*.

One such *MetaCity* is the Czech Republic itself, with its population of 10 million. It has one large city, many smaller ones and even more towns and villages. The countryside between these built-up areas is really just the park. It is not important any more where these areas begin and end, the boundaries are less clear now that people's mobility is speeding up and distances are becoming shorter. The *MetaCity* theme therefore relates to an entire country, not just a selected region. This is not about the future, because we already live in such a *MetaCity*.

Ivan Kroupa has been systematically focusing on the city from different aspects and with various possible solutions for the past 15 years. The city and its conversions, the concentration in terms of architecture; the individual parts of the city, the suburbs, the urban landscape and the city's expansion into the countryside have all been the subject of his own work, but also something he has been systematically tackling with his students in the Faculty of Architecture at the Czech Technical University in Prague.

Information on what we think architecture is today, and what it will be in 10-20 years time. A search for answers to contemporary issues in the Czech Republic, seeking modern solutions. A solution in which we prefer drawing inspiration from our own development, a transcription of our own work or indirect inspiration, with all kinds of influences.

We are not designing a *metacity*, we already live in one. The Czech Republic itself is a *metacity*, a single location with its own specific concerns.

We don't want to construct and cut into nature, we don't want to expand and extend the existing urban structures. The natural setting for architectural development is the city with its historical central core /theme 1/. Periphery /theme 2/. Architecture under extreme conditions, the re-integration of devastated land into the system /theme 3/. Infrastructure, connection, flows, roads, highways, waters /theme 4/. The scenery, architecture in the countryside, presentation of architecture via scenery, presentation of scenery via architecture /theme 5/.
Radomíra Sedláková

Czech Republic and Slovak Republic

COMMISSIONER
Radomíra Sedláková

WITH THE COLLABORATION OF
Pavel Piekar

ORGANIZATION
National Gallery in Prague

IN COLLABORATION WITH
Slovak National Gallery in Bratislava

WITH THE SUPPORT OF
Ministries of Culture in Czech and Slovak Republics

EXHIBITORS
Ivan Kroupa Architects and Ivan Kroupa Studio at the Faculty of Architecture, Czech Technical University

1

1
Ivan Kroupa,
Gallery of Contemporary Art,
Prague, open in September 2006.

South Africa › Trans-formations:
Between **ownership** and **belonging**, transitional space in the post-apartheid metropolis

South Africa's liberation and peaceful transition to democracy is widely known and admired throughout the world. The transition has particular resonance internationally due to the successful resolution of a seemingly intractable racial conflict.

The apartheid system was notorious for the way in which it institutionalized racial separation and discrimination and also for how it successfully enlisted architecture and planning in its grand socio-spatial project. Racial segregation and unequal development were designed into all spheres of life - from farms and rural towns, to cities and townships, from streets and public spaces to the workplace and public buildings.

For observers and practitioners in city planning the question raised is: how have South African cities transformed in the aftermath of apartheid?

The South African exhibition at the Venice Biennale 2006 will be a reflection (twelve years after the demise of apartheid) on how, and by what agencies South African cities are or continue to be transformed out of their racially segregated past. The central question is that of integration: where and how is it happening and what are the aesthetics and material nature of these patterns of social movement and change? How are the disciplines of architecture, planning and urban design responding to the emerging, African indeterminacy, provisionality and contingency that accompany rapid change?

South Africa's decision to participate at the 10 International Architecture Exhibition is motivated by the desire to promote discussions and debate around the transformation of our cities. In particular, it is hoped that the debate will contribute to the process of bringing together the previously separate communities of our young democracy.

The notion of 'trans-formation' (beyond or across form) extends the area of interest of the exhibition beyond the purely formal and physical. It is intended to include a re-imagination and re-presentation of the emerging city.

The exhibition focuses on specific sites where possibilities of a new public culture and a transforming (South) African urban identity are emerging out of an apartheid past. *Ownership* refers to interventions that contribute to social inclusion and recognition of the citizenship and creative practices of the previously disenfranchised. *Belonging* deals with nation building and the symbolic representation of the new *polis* where the emerging heritage and memory are enlisted as 'urban generators.'

Urban projects falling within these two categories will be exhibited through various forms of architectural representation, drawings, models, photographs etc., bringing into relief the transitional terrain between 'ownership' and 'belonging.'

These will be augmented by other cultural readings (through art, film, texts etc.) that attempt to expose the forms and aesthetics, and the social and racial tensions of the post-apartheid city. These tensions are explored through the themes of 'identity' and the extent to which it determines socio-spatial power relations, urban experience and 'mobility' (the means of accessing and overcoming the dislocated nature of the apartheid city).
Lenin Shope

Republic of South Africa

COMMISSIONER
Lenin Shope

CURATOR
Mphethi Morojele

DEPUTY COMMISSIONER
Alwyn Figgins

PATRON
Lindiwe Mabuza

PROJECT BY
Department of Foreign Affairs and Department of Arts and Culture of the South African Government and the South African National Heritage Resource Agency

COLLABORATORS
Zwakala productions (Multimedia)
Faculties of Architecture, Universities of Witwatersrand and Pretoria (Research)
MMA and ASM architects (Exhibition Design)
Associazione EDNET (Technical Support)

1

2

3

4

5

6

7

8

9

1
Lucien le Grange Architects,
District 6 destruction,
ca. 1980.
COURTESY THE DISTRICT 6 MUSEUM, CAPE TOWN.

2
ASM Architects with MMA Architects,
Faraday Transport Interchange,
2004.
PHOTO BY WIM BOTHA AND ALBONICO SACK MZUMARA.

3
Herbalist at Faraday market.
PHOTO BY ZWELETHU MTHETHWA, 2004.

4
Jozi colors - Johannesburg inner city skyline,
2006.
PHOTO BY SOLAM MKHABELA.

5
Jozi colors - Noord Street, Johannesburg inner city,
2006.
PHOTO BY SOLAM MKHABELA.

6
Noero Wolff Architects,
Red location Museum: Context Red Location,
2005.
PHOTO BY ROB DUKER.

7
Noero Wolff Architects,
Red location Museum: Memory Boxes,
2005.
PHOTO BY ROB DUKER.

8
Noero Wolff Architects,
Red location Museum: Projection Screen,
2005.
PHOTO BY ROB DUKER.

9
Noero Wolff Architects,
Red location Museum: Resident,
2005.
PHOTO BY ROB DUKER.

Porous Borders

The Green Line of Nicosia
- 1191: 815 years ago. Richard Lion heart, Knights, Guy de Lusignan.
- 1489: 517 years ago. Venetian period. Fortress walls surround Nicosia. A defensive system encircles the city while the river that crosses it from East to West cuts it in two. A strip of water, a bridge for reciprocal crossings.
- 1882: 124 years ago. The strip of water turns to earth, it becomes a road lane that divides and unites.
- 1963: 43 years ago. The road lane across the centre of the city becomes the border that keeps the two communities apart. The 'green line' gains length and width. Along its path, a dead zone grows and divides the city.
- 1974: 32 years ago. A border and a neutral zone made of empty shells, the fossils of houses and streets. An enforced separation, a frozen boundary, surfaces of concrete and sandbags, barrels and barbed wire, a labyrinth of rooms and staircases, balconies and gardens, streets and shops, memory and oblivion, hostility and hope, sound and silence, voices and pauses, light and shadow.
- 1979: 27 years ago. Two communities, two languages, two religions begin to study the master plan of the city.
- 2003: 3 years ago. The border acquires a control gate, a passage to the other side. The boundary, similar to a wall, can be viewed from either side. However, the in-between space remains inaccessible.

Programme

A labyrinth, a different spatial structure is revealed. The soldiers cut holes that penetrate building after building, exposing spaces, yards, dead-ends, and blocked facades. Parallel courses, parallel stories, condensation and inflation. The boundaries are diffused. New passages are opened, leading from one building to the other, overturning what used to be. If public is the space that we share with others, where we become conscious of their presence, a dead zone is at the same time a public and a private place. What used to be public is now forbidden, what used to be private is now public. A labyrinth, a new spatial structure that intersects the existing one, suggests that this structure can be permeated, can be porous.

The dead zone, folding matter, space and time, creates a desert land. Can architecture reveal what is hidden, bring to light the obscure, invent mechanisms and form links among the various contradictions: yesterday/tomorrow, two communities, presence/absence, city as a living reality/ memory land, subjective/objective?

Ten groups of architects are asked to read the place and interpret it through their projects. Two threads are followed at the same time: the interpretation of the complex nature of the 'no-place', and the proposal/experiment that intends to transform it into a real place. The projects aim to investigate the interface and to restore the porosity between the perceived and the actual space, between the living city and the dead zone.

The memory of the place; the osmosis between the public and the private realm; the complexity of the spatial structure; the idiosyncrasy of a non-existing place, a place of porous nature with elements of instability and volatility in time, a space built with surfaces and volumes, woven with matter and light, shadows and sounds, recollections and myths, tensions and pauses, trajectories and impossible escapes; concepts and themes that unite or divide, (communities, activities, urban tissue), can become some of the themes to be explored.

Morfo Papanikolaou, Irena Sakellaridou, Memos Filippidis

Republic of Cyprus

COMMISSIONER
Petros Dymiotis

CURATORS
Morpho Papanikolaou
Irena Sakellaridou

GUEST CURATOR
Memos Filippidis

EXHIBITORS
Marios Christodoulides and Christos Christodoulou
Chrysanthos Chrysanthou
Margarita Danou
Epi tessera Architects (George Georgiou, George Paroutis, Elena Parouti, Maria Charalambidou)
Christos Hadjichristou
Yiorgos Hadjichristou, Petros Kwnstantinou and Veronica Antwniou
Eraklis Papachristou and Irwin Dickon
Gregoris Patsalosavvis
Paris Philippou, Antwis Antwniou and Alessandra Swiny
Socrates Stratis and Maria Loizidou

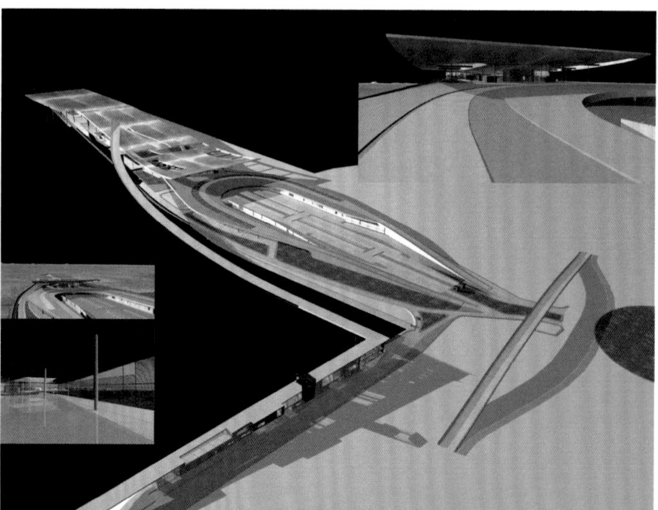

1

2

3

4

7

5

6

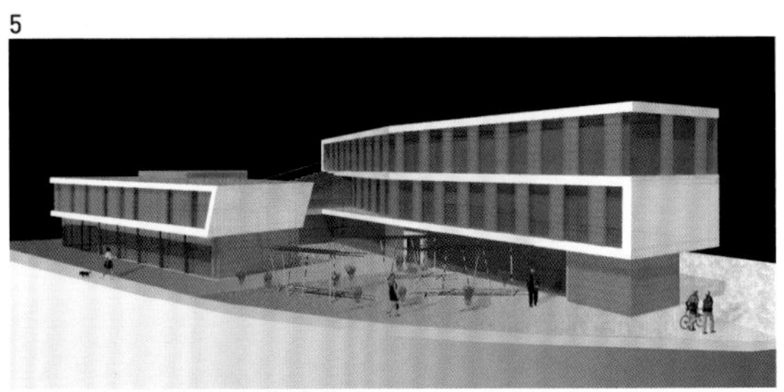

8

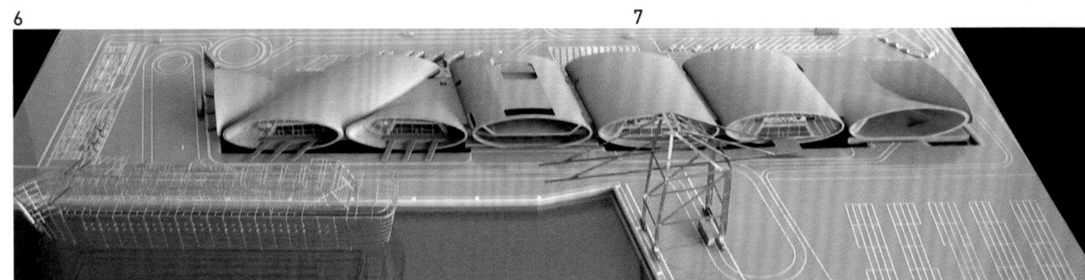

9

1
Marios Christodoulides, Christos Christodoulou (Design team: Zenonas Sierepeklis, Marios Christodoulides, Christina Sierepeklis, Christos Christodoulou, Tereza Tourva), **Limassol Port - Architectural competition entry,** design 2004.
RENDERING: MARIOS CHRISTODOULIDES.

2
Chrysanthos Chrysanthou, Eraclis Papachristou, **Student's residence - University of Cyprus,** design 1999, construction 2001-2004.
PHOTO BY CRISTOS PAPANTWNIOU.

3
Danou Margarita (Design team: Margarita Danou, Sevina Flwridou; Civil engineers Hyperstatic Engінerring Ltd; Electrical engineers Aspelo Consulting Ltd), **Pedestrian Coastal Promenade at Voroklini,** Cyprus, design 1997-2001, construction 2001-2003.
PHOTO BY THEODOROS FRANGINOS, M.P.L. MODERN PRODUCTIONS, LTD.

4
Epi tessera Architects (Design team: George Georgiou, George Paroutis, Elena Parouti, Maria Charalambidou), **Residential Building in Nicosia - Apollonos street,** Commission 2004, construction 2006.
RENDERING: CLP COMPUDESIGN LTD.

5
Socrates Stratis, Christos Hadjichristou (Design team: Socrates Stratis, Christos Hadjichristou; Assistant architects: Riccardo Urbano, Erchim Ulug; Civil Engineer: Andros Achillews (Hyperstatic); Electrical Engineer: George Chari; Mechanical Engineer Thoma Gregory), **European Architectural competition for the redevelopment of Eleftheria Square and its surrounding area (2nd prize),** design 2004-2005.
PHOTO BY WORK TEAM.

6
Yiorgos Hadjichristou (Design team: Yiorgos Hadjichristou; Civil engineer: Yiannakis Antwniou), **House and workshop of a sculptor in Dali,** design 1997, construction 2000-2004.
PHOTO BY YIORGOS HADJICHRISTOU.

7
Grigoris Patsalosavvis (Design team: Gregoris Patsalosavvis, Tereza Tourva, Iwanna Kwnstantinidou), **Nice Day Imperial,** design 2001, construction 2002-2005.
PHOTO BY AGISILAOU & SPIROU PHOTOGRAPHY.

8
Paris Philippou (Office: I + A Philippou; Design team: Paris Philippou, Pavlos Philippou; Work team: Andreas Philippou, Paris Philippou, Pavlos Philippou, Giannos Orfanos; Help from: Elena Tsolaki, Giwrgos Grigoriou), **Regional Headquarters building of Cyprus Workers Confederation, in Pafos,** Commission 2004, realization 2006.
RENDERING: I + A PHILIPPOU.

9
Irwin Dickon (Office: irwinkritioti. architecture; Design team: irwinkritioti. architecture, Margarita Kritioti, George Marcou; Structural Engineer EPS Nicos Kalathas & Giorgios Demetriades; Mechanical Electrical Engineers Eliophotou Zineris Stasis MELTEC), **Competition - The new Limassol Cruise Terminal (1st prize),** design 2004, realization 2007.
MODEL AND PHOTO BY IRWINKRITIOTI ARCHITECTURE.

Perma n stant

The practices of architecture and urbanism in Korea, as is the case with any other typical contemporary society, are engaging more and more closely with reality, in a much more complicated way than before. In this regard, we find that *Cities. Architecture and Society*, the theme of 10th International Architecture Exhibition La Biennale di Venezia, parallels our particular concerns to summarize the ways current architectural and urban issues involve our society. This year's participating architects took part in numerous debates and sessions before extracting the following thematic phrase for the show: 'cumulated time, and instant events in the old places'; or in other words, *'perma n stant'* (possibly, permanent + instant). As one of the oldest modern metropolitan areas with more than 600 years of history, Seoul still energetically thrives as a huge buffer where the old ideas and substances collide every hour with the most updated ones. This city with its self-conflicting nature should consequently integrate largely unpredictable, unexpected patterns of townscapes and lifestyles. So here one could not help but witness all the mutated, temporary versions of urban scenes and events, and how intriguingly the recognitions and emotions of its occupants work.
The city exposes its marginal layer of time-cumulated strata when the innumerable thin layers of instant events incessantly tints its surface. The first part of the theme, *perma* supposedly epitomizes all the characteristics and fundamental geographic elements the city has with relatively constant nature, while the latter part, *n stant* could suggest all its present momentary and adaptable images and shifts. The content of this year's exhibition in the Korean Pavilion mainly reflects the 'less critical' views or perceptions of the participating architects on what is in progress in the city. They maintain a fair distance from those phenomena and reserve any judgment in this multi-dimensional showcase, depicting them with more calm and a neutral atmosphere. The teamed-up project is a combined display of large scale sectional models and moving pictures taken from five different sectors of the city. Its size and population have provided numerous documents of how its extreme topographies have been overcome. In one of the five individual projects, a modernist architect shows how he perceives a traditional district and has painstakingly adapted his works to it over the decade[1]; the second one, with the theme of 'city in a city', diagnoses insecure alterations deriving from the fringe of the city[2]. The third interprets volatile properties of urban surfaces[3], while the fourth, with the theme of 'catalog city', makes various indications about futuristic housing based on the ways today's commercial housing suppliers acutely interact with their customers[4]. The last one takes on the intricate urban web of artificial nerves and sensory devices and their everyday data, being accumulated and analysed through its dwellers who can never avoid being constantly exposed to the systems[5].
Joh Sung-yong

[1] Choi Wook, *New Phenomena in Aging Land.*
[2] Kim Seung-hoy, *Constellation_time_city*
[3] Kim Chanjoong, *Surgical Machine for Urban Surface.*
[4] Shin Haewon, *Catalog City.*
[5] Kim Hun, *Monitor City.*

Republic of Korea

COMMISSIONER
Joh Sung-yong

DEPUTY COMMISSIONERS
Yi Jong-ho
Choi Moongyu

CONSULTANT
Francisco Sanin

ART DIRECTOR
Ahn Sang-soo

COORDINATORS
Lee Jae-jun
Kim Seunghui

COORDINATOR IN VENICE
Kim Eun-jeong

WITH THE SUPPORT OF
The Arts Council Korea

EXHIBITORS
Choi Wook
Kim Chanjoong
Kim Hun
Kim Seung-hoy
Shin Haewon

1

3

2

4

5

1
Kim Chanjoong,
Urban dwelling pod linked to subway station.
Year of realization: 2008. Prefabricated three dimensional panel component and its application on existing building surface.

2
Kim Hun (with Wha Sur-yeon),
Ocular City.
Composite images and motion pictures from images taken from the city of Seoul and architectural works of the exhibitor.

3
Kim Seung-hoy,
Constallation_time_layer.
PHOTO BY II MIN KANG.

4
Choi Wook,
Studio small,
2003. 2,4 x 8 x 8 m. Palpan-dong, a street across from Samchung-dong - a reservation for Han-Ok (Korean traditional House), has been changing unnoticed rather ignored as it is excluded from the reservation due to administrative reasons. City grows and changes, which is quite natural, however when such a change comes from developmental conveniences and economic reasons accompanied by thoughtless planning, our city wears a gloomy, sad look.

5
Shin Haewon,
Catalog City.
AVI file format.

Formula New Ljubljana

Ljubljana became the capital of a new country 15 years ago. But despite this change, it has clearly remained the same in size, historical sediment and financial potential. It is, of course, also the same in terms of its potential to transform itself into a city of the third millennium. All the parameters are essentially small, manageable and pleasant for a short time, a short visit. Over the last 100 years Ljubljana has seen the post-earthquake redesign of the city centre, based on late nineteenth-century and early twentieth-century ideas. It has seen interventions that we have come to call the 'Plecnik Ljubljana', and fragmentary realization of the late '60s' modernist vision. But none of these periods were realized in their full or planned scope, so what we see may be called a sum of icons that today make up the architectural landscape of Ljubljana.

The *Formula New Ljubljana* is based on iconography and atmosphere. Co-opting and considering old icons and creating new ones are the more permanent elements of the formula, whereas the creation of atmospheres is the more fleeting, personal part of the process. Iconography and atmosphere in turn create the groundwork for the branding of the city, a newly created layer of city that also allows for interpretation of the urban organism as a market product. The *Formula New Ljubljana* is not a finished product, it is an dynamic, ongoing process that should include investors, urban planners, designers of new spaces and other stakeholders.

The Sadar Vuga Arhitekti office creates new city layers that are part of the *Formula New Ljubljana*. This is primarily the creation of ambiences with the potential for at least some of the architecture to become iconic. It is impossible to talk about either consistency of architectural language as it was understood in the '80s, or about aesthetic doctrine, much less about typology or topology. Instead, the Sadar Vuga Arhitekti architects explore the ways a certain ambience communicates in a certain project – how it communicates with users, visitors, the city. The experience of the communicative architectural blueprint generates new concepts and, potentially, new icons. The vision of the end-effect of communication is the beginning of the creation of ambience, which in turn represents the skeleton of the architectural form; this skeleton is a potential generator of iconography. The communicating ambience and the emerging icon represent the groundwork layer of the city's brand.

The *Formula New Ljubljana* is a potential generic model for the development of cities, for which it makes no sense to begin with a certain historical style, the dimensional fact of a world metropolis or an autonomous architectural fact. Instead, the *Formula New Ljubljana* offers an example of a new city layer, a layer whose architectural forms are not organic heirs of the past, but which by communicating ambiences allow for a spectre of individual experiences, interpretations and icons, all of which create a city brand. After all, this is the ultimate purpose of the *Formula*.
Tomaž Brate

Republic of Slovenia

COMMISSIONER
Tomaž Brate

CURATORIAL TEAM
Tomaž Brate
Sadar Vuga Arhitekti (Jurij Sadar, Boštjan Vuga)
Actar (Albert Ferre, Ramon Prat)
Aurora Fonda

EXHIBITOR
Sadar Vuga Arhitekti

1

2

3

4

1-2
Sadar Vuga Arhitekti,
Trnovski Pristan Residential building,
Lubljana, 2002-2004.
PHOTO BY RAMON PRAT.

3-4
Sadar Vuga Arhitekti,
Gradaska Flats Block,
Lubljana, 2003-2005.
PHOTO BY RAMON PRAT.

The exhibition in the China Pavilion this year is in two sections. The exterior section is about 1.600 square metres. The exhibition plan considers the application of traditional Chinese culture in the development of modern cities. Recycled clay tiles are used on the outdoor surface, based on the layout of the 'virgin garden'.

A simple prefab structure of steel or bamboo supports a large roof that is half flat and half sloped. It is a roof or a slope site, or a different type of garden. It is a garden of clay tiles, a place of contemplation, meditation and reflection. The interior will display five years of research and development since 2001 by the architect Wang Shu, which informs and contextualizes the outside work, including the finished half campus and the half still under construction. It will also show the whole process of the architect's five-year study being applied, his analysis of Ci Cheng, a traditional town, and the almost completed experimental construction of five public buildings (namely the Five-scattered Houses).

The other part of the interior installation will feature drawings and paintings by another artist, Xu Jiang, on the same subject taken up by the architect. A similar slope site as the exterior one is used for the indoor floor, where models and drawings construct a space for dialogue between artist and architect. Traditional Chinese architectural drawings employ a low angle bird's-eye view that is transcendental. Recycled clay tiles, continuing a traditional practice of reusing old material and opening a new sustainable method, are used both in the new campus of the China Academy of Art, Hang Zhou, and the Tile Garden in Giardino delle Vergini, Venice. Rise up, stand on the roof platform, the view is transcendental and inspires contemplation. It is an abstracted expression of a concept, an emphasis of the sharp conflict between modernization and tradition in China and a shock to the contemporary mind.
Fan Di'an, Wang Mingxian

People's Republic of China

COMMISSIONER
Fan Di'an

CURATOR
Wang Mingxian

CURATORIAL TEAM
Fan Di'an
Xu Jiang
Wang Mingxian
Cai Guoqiang

COORDINATOR
Jennifer Ma

EXHIBITORS
Wang Shu
Xu Jiang

1

2

3

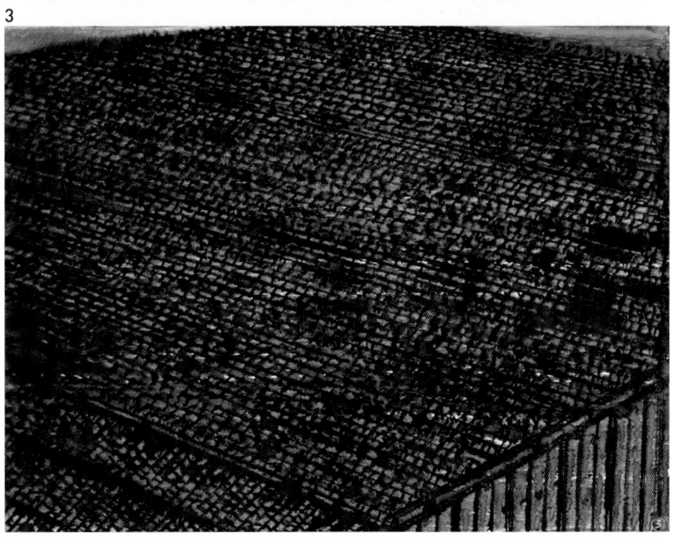

4

1
Wang Shu,
The tiles garden,
2006. Timber frame + recycled traditional tiles construction, 1680 sq. m.
Horizontal perspective. Rendering.

2
Wang Shu,
China Academy of Art, New campus of Xiangshan School,
2004. Concrete frame + steel frame + recycled traditional tiles construction, 67,000 sq. m.
Overlook at the small stadium from the management office and art studio tower.

3-4
Xu Jiang,
Overlooking a tile garden,
2005. Oil-painting. details of the painting, 500 x 1000 cm.
PHOTO BY FAN LI.

Remix! Urban drama for nine cubes and many players

We would like you to take part in a game with pieces of urban identity. Every visitor becomes a player, making choices and proposing his own project for a region.

Urban development is actually a game, with overlapping and changing teams, taking on a series of actions, reactions and negotiations between individual and collective interests. During the totalitarian period there was only one team of 22 million players in Romania and one absolute leader, with strict but arbitrary rules and individual survival and resistance strategies. Its development involved the total authority of the State in public spaces, while private space was a refuge in which to protect individuality. Nowadays it seems that there are 22 million teams, each playing by its own rules. In fact, the game spun out of control, leading to a logic by which space was savagely retrieved and appropriated, in a collision of various individual energies. Prison-like public space has not changed into one of negotiation, but into a no-man's land patched with numerous private, protected, interior territories. The urban reality has become a disjointed archipelago of places.

Is this an inevitable transition period or a new spatial paradigm? As development has finally started, the insatiable desire to build and arrange space can only be matched by the rapid destruction of the natural and built heritage, and the possible failure of efficient and balanced growth.

The arrangement of the pavilion is guided by two main ideas: the presentation of reality with its fragmentary nature, and an installation – the game - inviting involvement. A first step to assuming responsibility would be to express your own opinions about development. That is followed by dialogue and then by negotiated and accepted development.

The exhibition encapsulates nine fundamental categories out of the infinity of personal fragments, thus describing models or, should we say, 'myths' of Romania's urban reality: the ideal house, monuments, dwelling myths (from the idealized village to imported suburbia), the image of nature, the relationship with the totalitarian past, spaces for socializing etc. It also shows how small alternative approaches try to counterbalance global mechanisms.

Secondly, we propose that visitors join in a game with simple rules. The pieces are represented by the nine categories of the exhibition. The game consists of remixing the given collection of fragments: by choosing one element from each category, the player will emphasize one or the other tendency, and try to compose his own image of future urban development in Romania. The sum of the selected pieces will be decoded by a computer program and the player told the result. The sum of these individual games (played by both professionals and non-professionals) will render the image of a shared project, a model of how to shape future urban identity in Romania; or, rather, it will show the main unbalanced areas, the ones that most need negotiation and community involvement.

We'd like you to play, remix, react and be involved.
Justin Baroncea, Ana Bleahu, Ștefan Ghenciulescu, Constantin Goagea, Cosmina Goagea, Carmen Popescu

Romania

COMMISSIONER
Marius Marcu-Lapadat

DEPUTY COMMISSIONER
Constantin Goagea

COLLABORATORS
Ștefan Tuchilă
Liviu Chelcea
Georgiana Toth
Victor Vulpe
Iulian Tălpigă
Alexe Traian Popescu

CONCEPT
Union of Architects of Romania

IN COLLABORATION WITH
Ministry of Culture and Religious Affairs
Romanian Cultural Institute

WITH THE SUPPORT OF
Carpatcement

WEBSITE
www.arhitectura1906.ro

EXHIBITORS
Justin Baroncea
Ana Bleahu
Ștefan Ghenciulescu
Constantin Goagea
Cosmina Goagea
Carmen Popescu

1

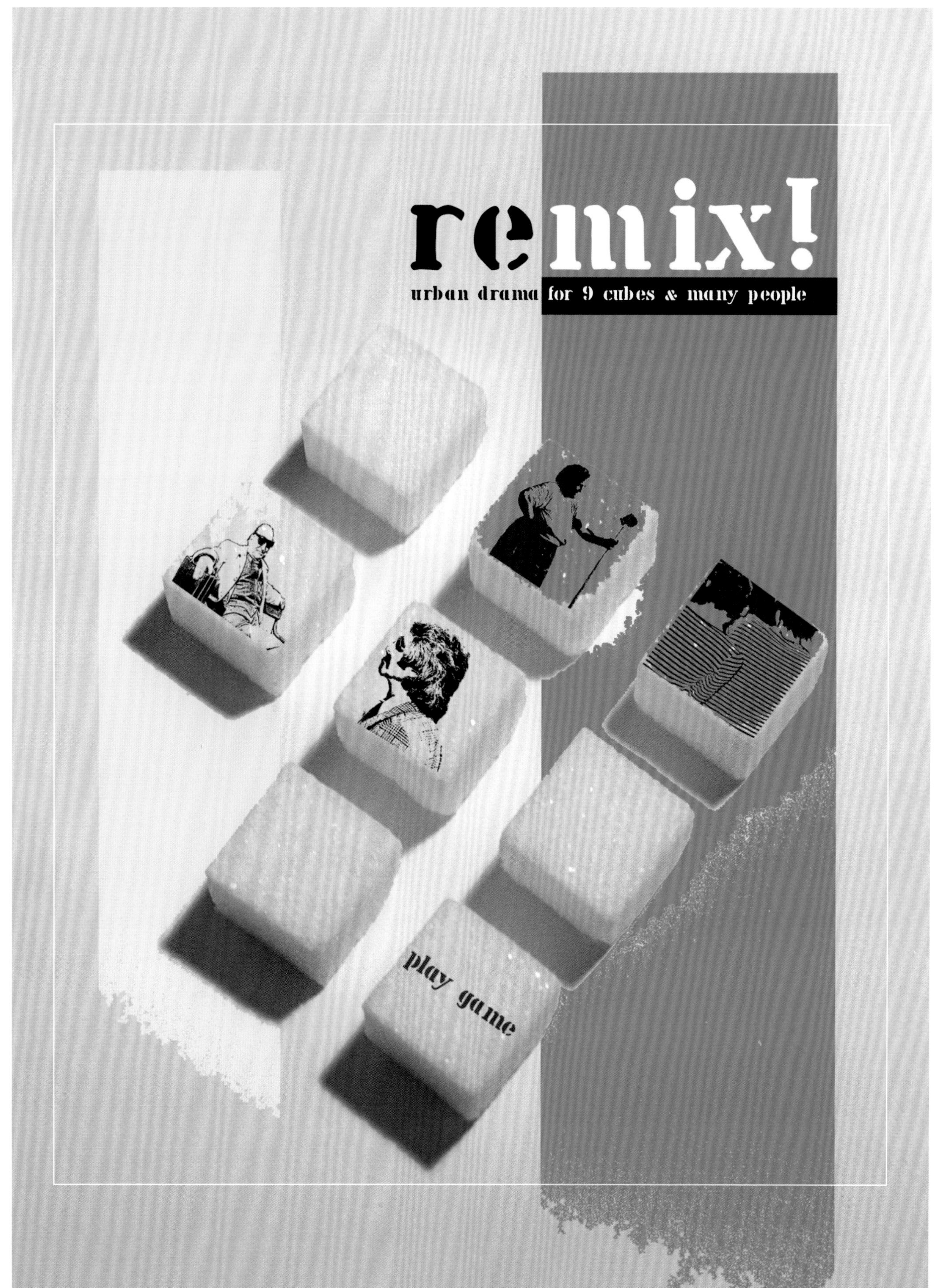

1
An archipelago of private fragments.
Bucharest, 2005.
PHOTO BY ȘTEFAN TUCHILĂ.

Inhabited Locality

The inhabited localities of Alexander Brodsky

An exhibition of Alexander Brodsky's work is being shown in the Russian Pavilion at the Architecture Biennale. He could just as easily take part in the Art Biennale. Brodsky came to art as an architect and returned to architecture as an artist. This is his creative credo as well as a biographical fact.
From virtuoso engravings as a 'paper architect', he went into sculpture and multi-media installations that were exhibited in the world's great galleries and museums. Having achieved prominence in this field in New York and Milan, he changed his role and opened an architectural office in Moscow.
For the majority of architects, creating art is a subsidiary activity or a side-product of their work. The Brodsky phenomenon forces one to reconsider the correlation between architecture and art. Today, Brodsky the architect is indivisible from Brodsky the artist. Just as his architectural roots are a constant presence in all his artistic works, so Brodsky's architectural projects are full of the intuition and sensitivity of an artist.

The main theme of Brodsky's art is memory. But this is not the professional memory of an architect, which normally goes no further than the recollection of historical styles. It is personal human memory, where childhood, books, friends, life's happenings, places and many other things co-exist. In a world fixated on commerce and technical innovations, there is little room left for poetry in architecture. In this sense, the Brodsky's poetical gift is unique. It allows him to metaphorically interpret memories in architectural language and transform non-architectural subjects into 3D forms and details. Looking at Brodsky's work one feels that these spaces already have a history and were inhabited even before his visitors and residents appeared in them. He always creates certain kinds of *Inhabited Localities* – whether it is a modest interior or city complex. Happily, his irony helps him avoid any importunate theatricality or sentimental narratives.

The city is the instrument of memory and its condenser is Alexander Brodsky's favourite object of reflection. His urban installations are not projects in the usual meaning of the word. In contrast with traditional town-planning projects, Brodsky's models and objects treat the city first and foremost as a special existential space, the space of everyday life. The project presented in the pavilion, *Inhabited Locality*, naively, joyously and ironically interprets the individual's living environment within the structured associations of the city, with its uniform spaces and rituals of everyday life.

An expose of Alexander Brodsky's architectural work is simultaneously on display on the ground floor, in the form of original sketches and architectural drawings, as well as slides of his completed buildings.
Evgeny Asse

Russia

COMMISSIONER
Evgeny Zyablov

CURATOR
Evgeny Asse

COORDINATORS
Olga Nestertzeva
Sergey Serebrennikov
Natalia Milovzorova

EXHIBITOR
Alexander Brodsky

1

1
Alexander Brodsky,
Vodka ceremony pavilion,
Klyazma Vacation Center, Moscow region, 2003.
PHOTO BY YURY PALMIN

New efforts

The traditional definition of the theory of architecture states that it is a written system of architecture, either all-encompassing or partial, which is based on aesthetic categories. Nevertheless, some of the cult exhibitions organized during the past few decades have shown that there are other media, besides the written word, through which theoretical thought can be expressed. This can also be done through architectural and town planning projects, the idea and aim of which was at no time their construction, but which were rather, from the very outset, intended to deliver a certain message. Following this line of thought, the Serbian participation in the 10th International Architecture Exhibition is based on the transmission of the views of Serbian architects on the values of architectural space expressed through the widest possible variety of creative media. Serbian architecture is presented through images, words, sounds and movements. The exhibition is based on a synthesis of architecture, music, the spoken word, film and design and consist of two parts; one toward the architectural past – earlier efforts – and the second turned towards the future – new efforts. In this last section a group of young architects present their works and express their point of view about the architecture of the future.
Miloš R. Perović

Serbia and Montenegro

COMMISSIONER
Spasoje Krunić

CURATOR
Miloš R. Perović

CONSULTANT
Marina Djurdjević

PROJECT DIRECTOR
Dragan Sakan

ART DIRECTORS
Zoran Lazović
Dejan Miljković

TECHNICAL AND EXECUTIVE DIRECTOR
Maja Gavric
Bluoostudio

CREATIVE CONCEPT, PR, DESIGN
New Moment New Ideas Company

EXHIBITORS
Arhitekt P.T.
Dušan Babić
Bogdan Bogdanović
Milutin Borisavljević
Đurđe Bošković
Aleksej Brkić
Nikola Dobrović
Aleksandar Đorđević
Jan Dubovy
Dejan Ećimović
Milutin Glavički
Ivan Goll
Branislav Jovin
Branislav Kojić
Spasoje Krunić
Dimitrije T. Leko
Sveta Lukić
Stojan Maksimović
Stanko Mandić
Dušan Matić
Ljubomir Micić
Dejan Miljković
Mihajlo Mitrović
Mustafa Musić
Božidar Obradović
Milorad Pantović
Duška Pavlović
Branko Ve Poljanski
Prvoslav Popović
Zoran Radojčić
Marko Ristić
Predrag Ristić
Leonid Šejka
Andra Stevanović
Bratislav Stojanović
Josip Svoboda
Branko Tanazević
Boško Tokin
Lazar Trifunović
Mihailo Valtrović
Aleksandar Vučo
Vane Živadinović-Bor
Radojica Živanović-Noe
Milan Zloković

1

2

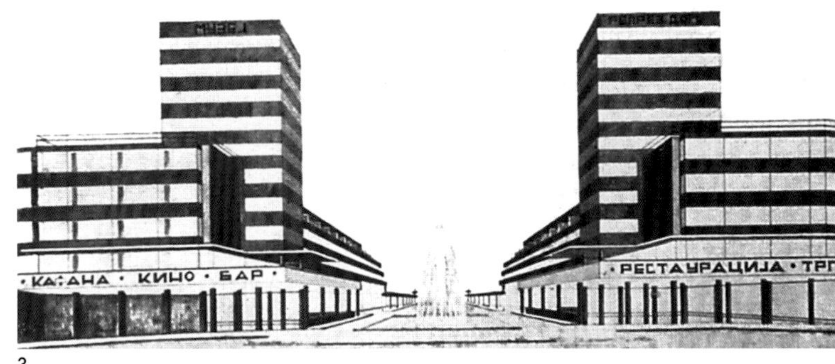

3

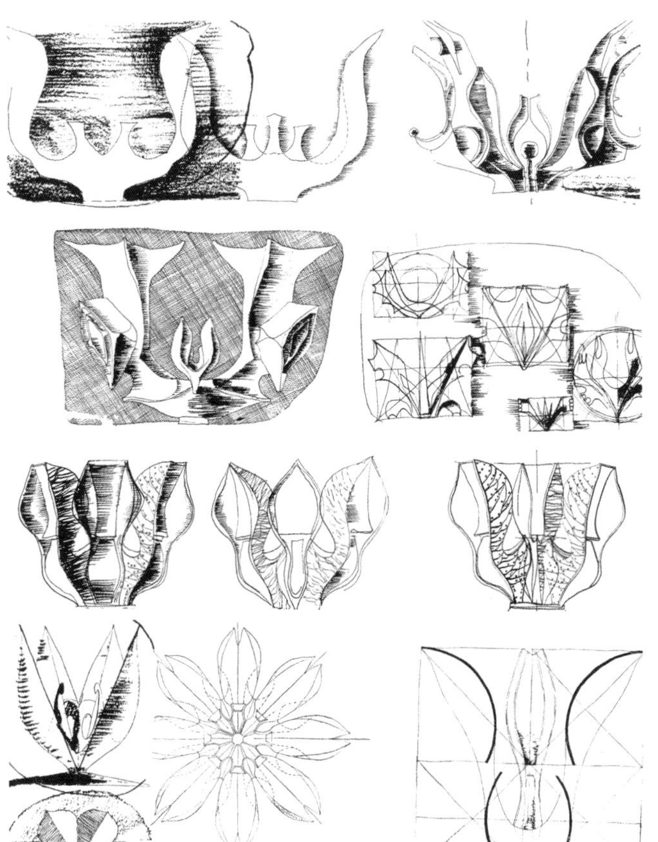

4

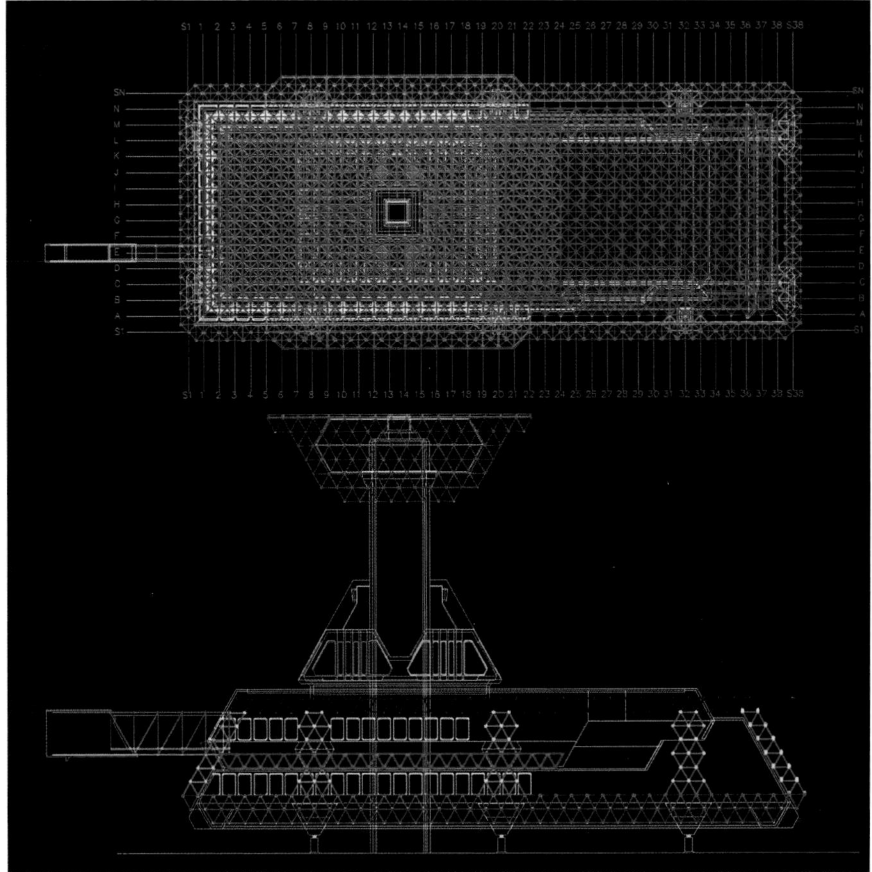

5

1
Momir Korunović,
Post I,
Belgrade, 1914.
Pencil, ink, watercolour and guache on paper.
138,7 x 146,5 cm.
Unaccomplished work.
Private collection.

2
Branislav Kojić,
Villa on the Topcider Hill,
Belgrade, 1929.
Graphite and charcoal on transparency.
45 x 55,5 cm.
Unaccomplished work.
COURTESY MUSEUM OF SCIENCE AND TECHNOLOGY, DEPARTMENT OF ARCHITECTURE, BELGRADE.

3
Nikola Dobrović,
Terrace in Terazije,
Belgrade, 1930.
View from Terazije and from the interior street. International competition (1st prize).
Unaccomplished work.

4
Bogdan Bogdanović,
Jasenovac monumental area,
1966. Design of the main theme.

5
Spasoje Krunić,
Headquarters of Belgrade Center of Interior Affairs,
Belgrade, 1984.
The plan of the main floor and the longitudinal section.

Singapore Shopping

Shopping is fun.
Shopping is art.
Shopping is strategic.
Shopping is lifestyle.
Shopping is identity.
Shopping is culture.

Shopping is an inescapable process. Perfecting the art of shopping is a carefully well-informed process. It is pleasurable, exciting and cutting edge. Shopping is the device to meet the urgent need of cities to buy ideas, labour and objects to push urban development. Global competition precludes the time for inventing from zero; acquired assets are installed, tested, reconfigured to make them uniquely a city's own. Shopping is an instrument towards economic building. Shopping is driven by the strong vision to do better, to create a global city that is the best place to be, a home in which to live work and play. Shopping is a continuous cycle to replace the old and unsuitable. One cannot stop shopping. Life is not complete without shopping. Life is not possible without shopping.

Singapore Shopping is a new attitude to shopping beyond mere consumption. Shopping is a process. Shopping is urban planning, architecture making and the economics of city building. Shopping is a carefully thought out means to an end.

Singapore Shopping is a celebration of shopping, an unforgettable sensorial experience; it is an operation to understand phenomena that are affecting the transformation of the city, society and architecture. It is an investigation aimed at understanding our selves, our condition, our society and our city. The Singapore Pavilion is its flagship store.

Singapore Shopping is the text of a city, the story of a city. It is contemporary Singapore as a manifestation of the abstract idea of the City State being part of a global process determined to become the best it could be. It is the metaphor of Singapore.

Singapore Shopping will feature: *Newater - a life and death issue of the city*; *Greening Singapore* a habitat eco-system; workforce compositions; physical transformations of vital industries (biotechnology, finance, education, creative, service, tourism); and the DesignSingapore – Toyo Ito Design Studio exploration to rethink public amenities of the city. *Singapore Shopping* will show the story of the committed process for Singapore to be a global city, the best place to be.
Budi Wijaya, Christopher Lee, I-Lin Tay, Randy Chan and Erwin Viray

Singapore

COMMISSIONER
Milton Tan

ADVISOR
Toyo Ito

COMMISSIONING PANEL
Lucas Chow
Chua Beng Huat
Geoffrey Eu
Fun Siew Leng
Lee Tzu Yang

WORKING GROUP
Yeo Piah Choo
Jacks Yeo
Elaine Khoo
Eunice Hong
M + B Studio
Troels Bruun

1

2

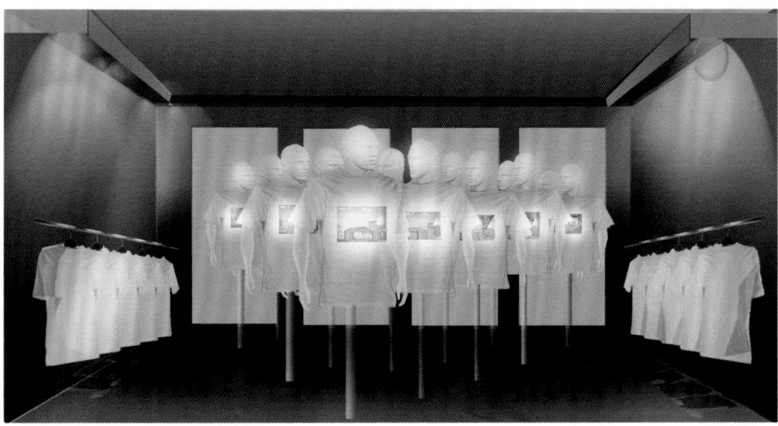

3

4

5

6

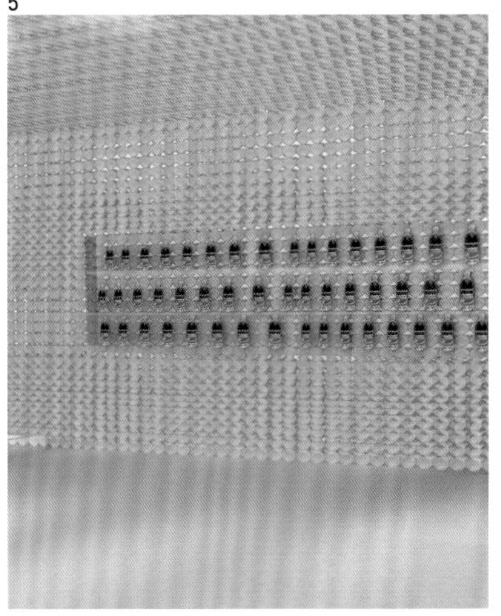

7

8

1
Visions,
Singapore Pavilion 2006.
2
Plain Outside,
Colourful Inside by Christopher Lee, Singapore Pavilion 2006.

3
Workforce,
Singapore Pavilion 2006.
4
Opening Soon,
by Christopher Lee, Singapore Pavilion 2006.

5
Green Singapore,
Singapore Pavilion 2006.
6
Composition,
by Budi Wijaya, Singapore Pavilion 2006.

7
Newater,
by Randy Chan, Singapore Pavilion 2006.
8
Water Box,
by Randy Chan, Singapore Pavilion 2006.

Spain [f.] we, the cities

We, the cities, the protagonists, the avatars, the incarnation of society, are the nodes of a real and virtual territory confused in the hazy terrain between perception and knowledge. The installation reveals part of the plot of today's city, of the complexity of features and actors that make up its structure, of the dialogues exchanged and its perpetual monologues of voices, allowing us to come face-to-face with its performers, to hear their discourse, understand its works and its problems.

Spain offers a pavilion with feminine faces, embodying the gender of the country's very name, embodying the very gender of its cities. They are figures in the symbolic space of the Biennale, acting agent roles in its cities and, at the same time, actresses and spectators, weaving contemporary city life. It is a Spain, a Europe, in which gender still means difference, the makeup of which gradually shifts, composed of more and more distinct components.

There is no Lorcan chorus this time, but rather voices representing the living characters in the city, those who live here and build here, those who are the managers, designers, those who make and maintain their cities. It is a city of female performers, speaking on behalf of their own work, their colleagues' and their very lives. They are a living part of their cities, making up a heterodox ensemble within the space of the Biennale. People, personas, faces and masks overlap and gaze at us with a uniformity of gender, with a diversity of roles, somehow made even more visible by their apparent symmetry.

It is a structure of multi-faceted, complex, intermingling relationships, of voices melding into a single murmur, tense monologues overlaid, building a dialogue amongst its elements, amongst the administrators, builders and users. It builds a choral work with the voices we no longer hear, deafened by our own collective noise.

A small microcosm reflects being another inside society's structure; the singularity caused by origin, age or the diffused anonymity of the urban tribe, the biased and complementary perspective produced by a job, a particular profile. Faces and voices join together to construct a simulated fabric of urban relations. Building types fulfilling different social needs, so varied yet at the same time so structurally limited, follow the flows that operate within the complex structure.

They are the inhabitants of an interlinked world where many already belong to a digitally born generation, where knowledge is now spread in a different way. A world which, paradoxically, by creating global information mechanisms, has raised local-level awareness, allowing us to access the images of our city, our neighborhood or our home, re-defining the conscience of our personal territory in which consumption and information feed off of each other, creating a new communication network that overlaps urban territory, a new virtual space.

We, the cities features anonymous and prestigious figures, choral voices and solo artists; intermediaries who reflect the reality in which the architecture of our cities moves through human protagonists.
Manuel Blanco

Spain

COMMISSIONER/CURATOR
Manuel Blanco

WITH THE SUPPORT OF
Ministerio de Vivienda
Ministerio de Asuntos Exteriores y Cooperation

EXHIBITORS
1
Acebo x Alonso (Victoria Acebo and Ángel Alonso)
2
ARANGUREN & GALLEGOS (Mª José Aranguren López and José González Gallegos)
3
BB&GG (Beth Galí)
4
Carme Pinós
5
Carmen Calvo
6
EMBT (Enric Miralles, Benedetta Tagliabue)
7
ESTUDIO ENTRESITIO (María Hurtado de Mendoza Wahrolén, César Jiménez de Tejada Benavides and José María Hurtado de Mendoza Wahrolén)
8
Imma Jansana (Imma Jansana, Robert de Paauw, Conchita de la Villa)
9
Izaskun Chinchilla
10
Josep Llinàs Carmona
11
MGM Morales+Giles+Mariscal (José Morales Sánchez, Sara de Giles Dubois, Juan González Mariscal)
12
MVRDV + Blanca Lleó (Winy Maas, Jacob van Rijs, Nathalie de Vries and Blanca Lleó Fernández)
13
NIETO SOBEJANO ARQUITECTOS (Fuensanta Nieto and Enrique Sobejano)
14
Plaza Europa (Hospitalet de Llobregat)
15
P02-Arquitectos (Marcos Parga + Idoia Otegui)
16
RCR ARQUITECTES (Rafael Aranda, Carme Pigem and Ramon Vilalta)
17
RGR+Teresa Galí (Ignacio Rubiño, Pura García, Luis Rubiño and Teresa Galí)
18
Sancho-Madridejos (Mª Soledad Madridejos and Juan Carlos Sancho Osinaga)
19
Santiago Calatrava
20
SELGASCANO (Jose Selgas e Lucía Cano Pintos)
Rojo/Fernández-Shaw Arquitectos (Luis Rojo, Begoña Fernández-Shaw)

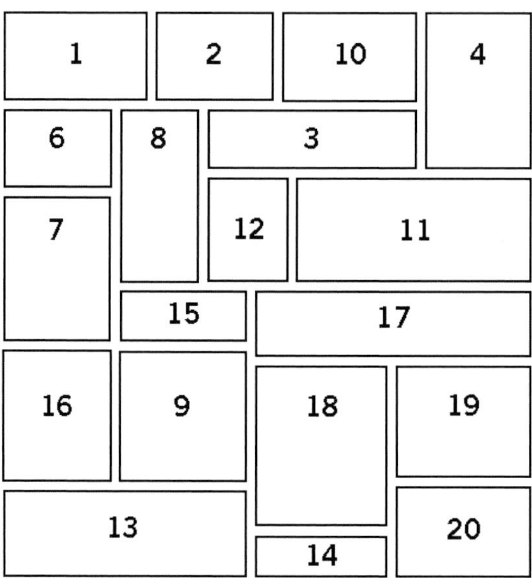

España [f.] nosotras, las ciudades

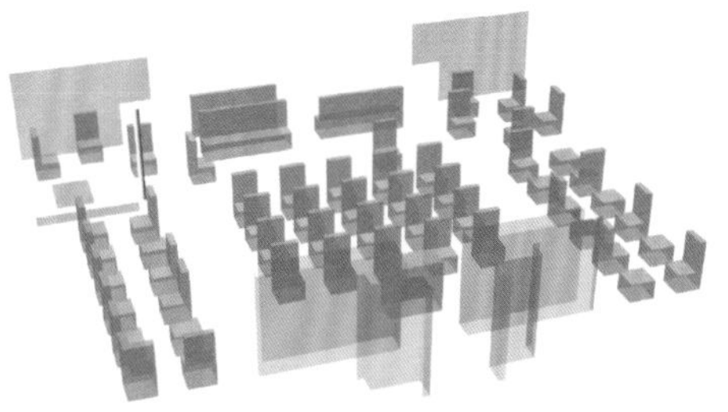

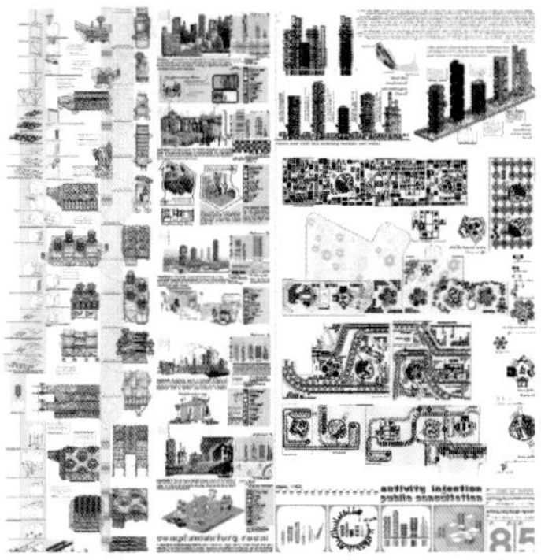

After the Flood: Building on Higher Ground
An overview of the devastating effects of hurricane Katrina on New Orleans and the Gulf Coast, with modern responses to new forms of regionally appropriate housing.

The official US Participation at the 2006 Venice Architecture Biennale will showcase innovative architectural proposals for rebuilding New Orleans and the Gulf Coast of the United States in the wake of hurricane Katrina. The exhibition presents the winning designs of an international competition for replacement housing initiated by Architectural Record, with the participation of the Tulane School of Architecture. For the competition, Architectural Record solicited proposals from architects and designers for multifamily housing in New Orleans, and designs from students for single-family houses. The winning entries of these two competitions, which comprise the major sections of the exhibition, explore meaningful contexts for rebuilding the areas devastated by the storms of 2005.

After the Flood: Building on Higher Ground examines the larger picture of rebuilding New Orleans and the Gulf Coast through inventive designs that recapture the distinctive cultures of the area and respond to the environmental needs of the region. The exhibition includes drawings, physical models, displays of computer modelling, and mock-ups of winning houses and housing designs. It also features a film by documentary filmmaker Neil Alexander and photographs by Michael Goodman. Additional sections will include contextual/historical material on New Orleans and the Gulf Coast, including vintage photos, contemporary photos, satellite images and explanatory texts depicting the character of the places and people. A separate section, *What next?*, organized by Tulane University's Architecture School under the leadership of its dean, Reed Kroloff, will outline some of the planning issues that must be addressed in rebuilding New Orleans and the Gulf Coast. A portion of the Public Broadcasting Service television series, 'Design:e2' on sustainable architecture, and produced by kontentreal of New York City, will also be shown in this section.

United States of America

COMMISSIONER
Robert Ivy

CURATOR
Christian Bruun

DEPUTY COMMISSIONERS
Clifford Pearson
Suzanne Stephens

ORGANIZATION
Architectural Record

WITH THE SUPPORT OF
Bureau of Educational and Cultural Affairs of the U.S. Department of State
American Institute of Architects

IN COLLABORATION WITH
The Peggy Guggenheim Collection, Venezia
The U.S. Consulate General, Milano

PATRON
Autodesk

1

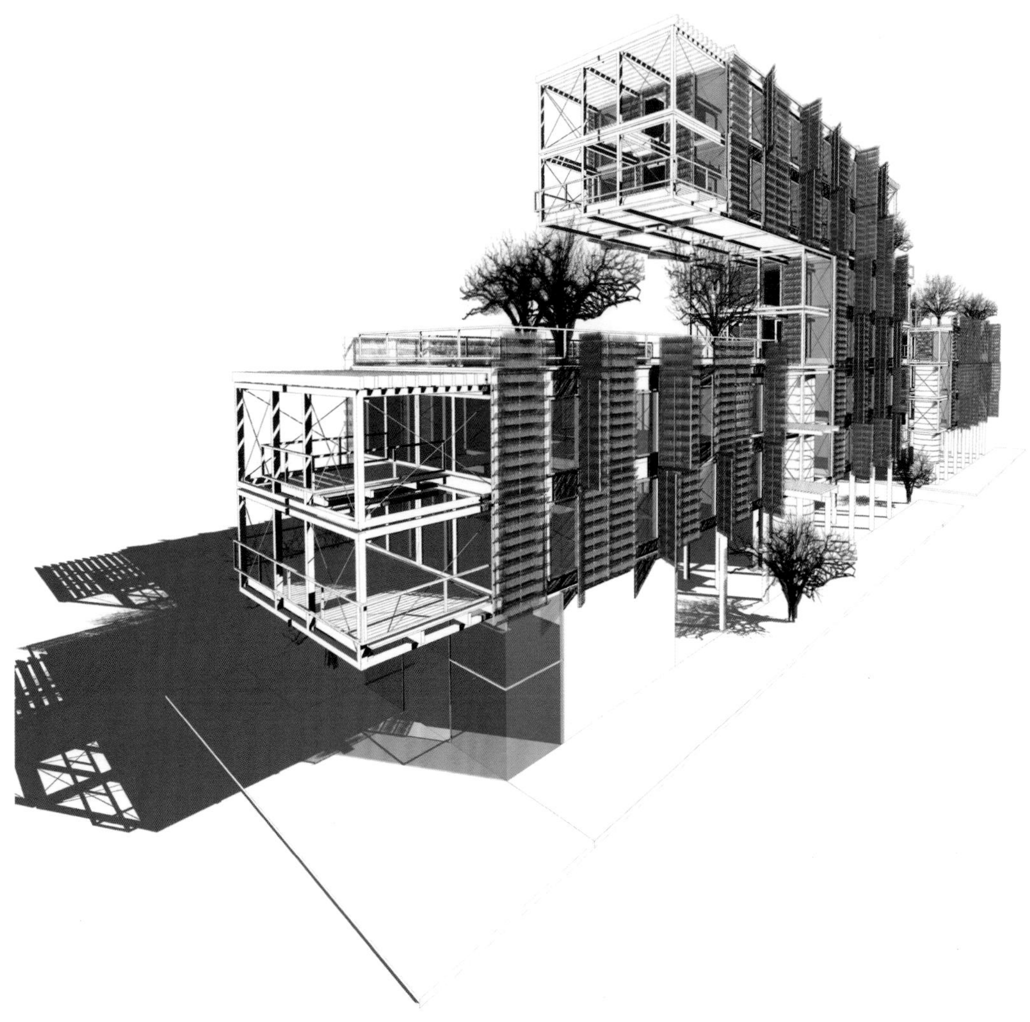

2

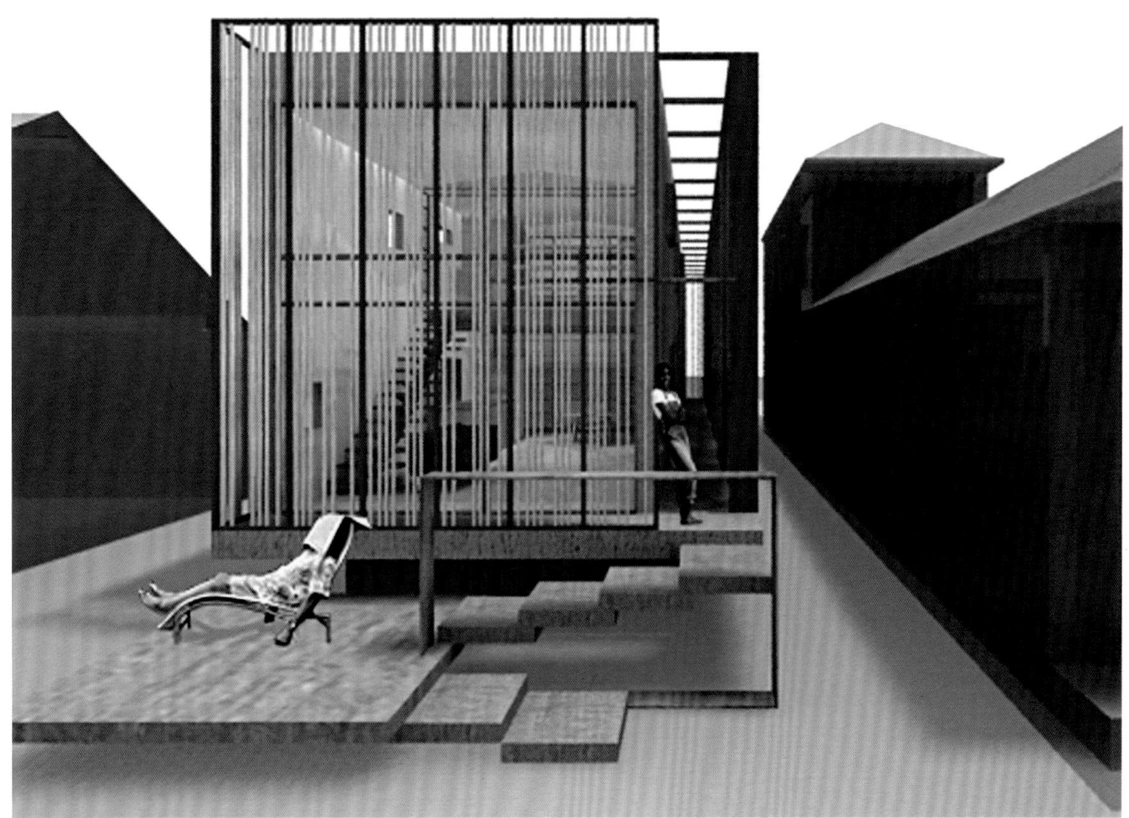

3

1
Eight Inc.
San Francisco, California
(Tim Kobe, principal, with Doo Ho Lee, Ryoji Karube, Jeff Straesser, Jie Siang Yong, David Herman, BJ Siegel),
High Density Housing.
Honour Award.
2
Anderson Anderson Architecture
San Francisco, California
(Mark Anderson, Peter Anderson, Kylie Moss, Aaron Brumo, Alan Owings, Brent Sumida, Dennis Oshiro, Ji Young Chung , Rita Sio),
High Density Housing.
Honour Award.
3
Michelle Jellison
Montana State University, Bozeman
(John Brittingham, instructor),
Prototype House.
Honour Award.

1

2

Switzerland

COMMISSIONER
Urs Staub

DESIGN TEAM
Kim Starr
Dominic Leong
Angie Co
Christopher Lee
Yang Yang

EXHIBITOR
Bernard Tschumi

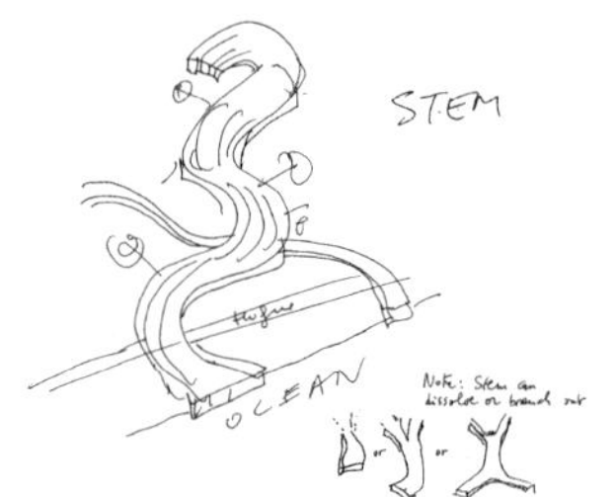

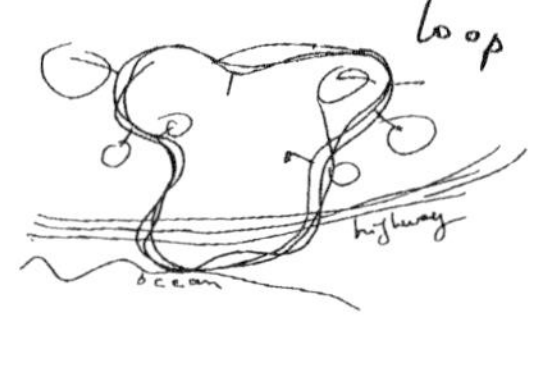

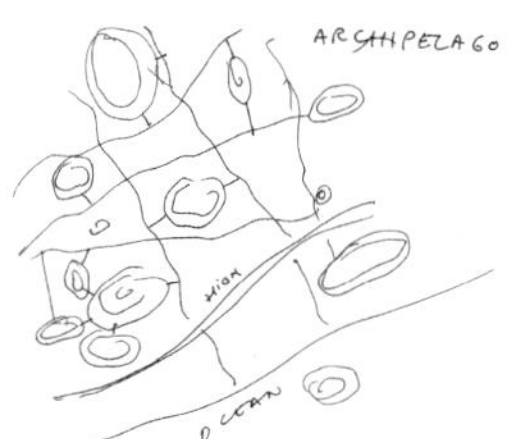

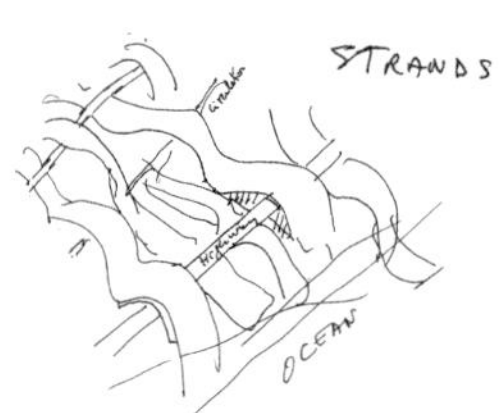

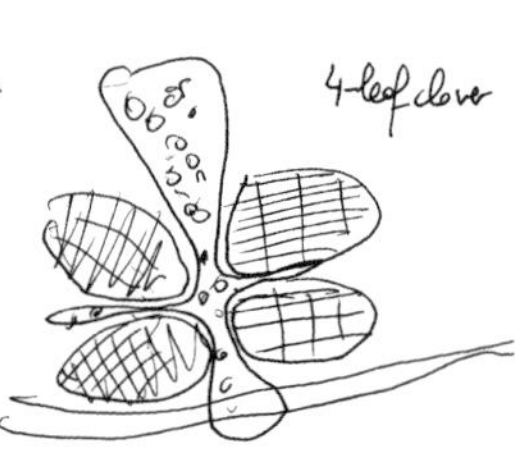

3

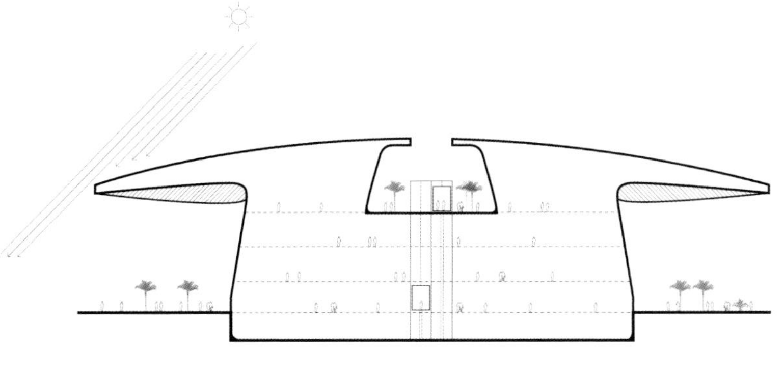

4

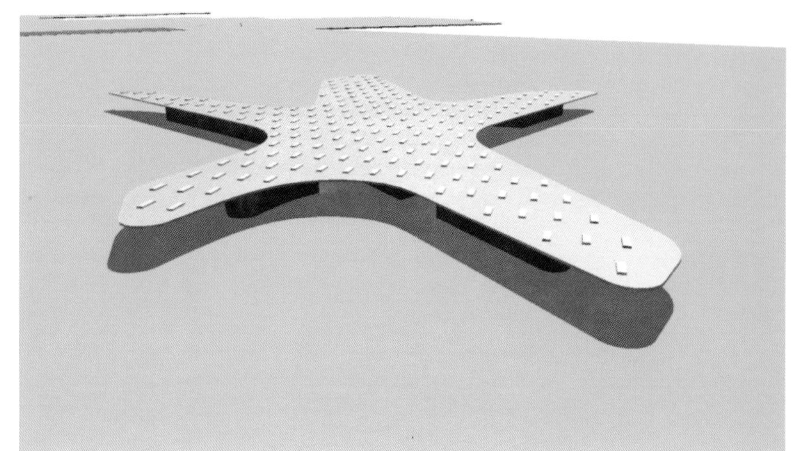

5

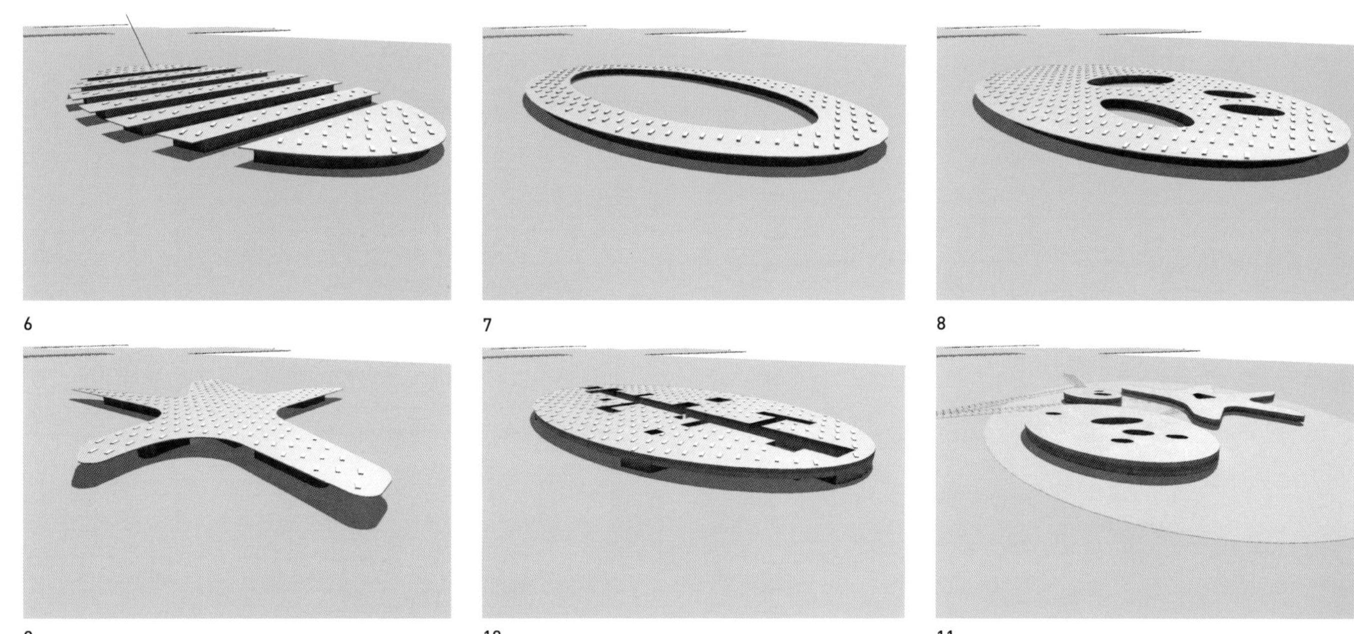

6 7 8

9 10 11

1
Butterfly,
Main road stem flanked by programmatic "islands".
RENDERING. COURTESY BERNARD TSCHUMI ARCHITECTS

2
Leaf,
A series of parallel roadways with programmatic "islands".
RENDERING. COURTESY BERNARD TSCHUMI ARCHITECTS

3
Sketch,
COURTESY BERNARD TSCHUMI ARCHITECTS

4
Hypothetical office section,
Each building has a large swing.
RENDERING. COURTESY BERNARD TSCHUMI ARCHITECTS

5
Perspective,
We also looked at the possibility of walking within a climate controlled environments, without having to go out in the hot and humid air.
RENDERING. COURTESY BERNARD TSCHUMI ARCHITECTS

6-11
Solar panels,
6. Strips + individual canopies.
7. Ring + canopy.
8. Courtyards + canopy.
9. Star cluster + shared canopy.
10. Liner courtyard + canopy.
11. Archipelago of different office types.
RENDERING. COURTESY BERNARD TSCHUMI ARCHITECTS

re:orient – migrating architectures

The exhibition material will be created in the dialogue of a reflexive research work group, a designer installation team and the public, through continuous translation and feedback, following an iterative model of development.

The work of the first team, one of social scientists, media researchers and anthropologists, will be more intensive in the first part of the project, producing statements that are coherent in the given disciplines and are logical in an interdisciplinary context, and which will be presented in their entirety in the publication accompanying the exhibition.

The second group, of architects and artists, will also pursue parallel lines of thought, partly doing its own research (surveying scenes, analysing, collecting), and partly making spatial/architectural interpretations of the first team's results, presenting them in non-textual media. The end result of this process is the installation that will be presented in the exhibition space.

Through regular, public and documented presentations, the dialogue will try to include critical views and ideas/suggestions from anyone interested, even by enlarging the team if necessary, in the hope that the result will be rich and widely accessible like the cultural product of a community. We also think the project should initiate a dialogue within the profession in Hungary, as well as between the various professions.

We would like to emphasize that the presentations are public. We invite interest and suggestions from the profession and the press. The dates of the presentations are to be announced later.

The immigration process that has made Hungary the European bridgehead of Far Eastern countries began at the time of the political transition that brought about fundamental changes in Hungarian urban culture. It did not take long for the 'Chinese' – the common shorthand for the many different groups of East-Asian immigrants – to set up the ubiquitous outlets of their commercial networks in an architectural context of constantly changing ownership and functions, creating a new environment that is present in almost every inhabited place in the country, and has a practically uniform, characteristic and easily recognisable design. For large portions of society, the 'Chinese' restaurants, discount stores, supermarkets and markets have become an important source of goods, and they have transformed the Hungarian environment through the objects, clothing and technology that have found their way into individual households.

The 'Chinese' immigrants are present everywhere in the country, even in the smallest villages, and the strategies of their appearance are remarkably similar. If we look at the concept of the 'meta-city' from the perspective of the immigrants, the structure and boundaries of our cities will obviously not be identical with our own concepts: you can consider the entire country a single meta-city, you can identify zones and territories that are different from the known administrative districts etc. Learning their town planning and architectural characteristics may help us define the nature of our cities. Budapest (or any other Hungarian town) is no longer imaginable without these phenomena, even though city policies ignore them.

Does Chinese architecture, the new Chinese boom, appear in Hungarian architecture? What happens to the immigrants, many of whom are also refugees, when the Chinese state officially declares Hungary its European centre of logistics? How do the two groups, living in spatial and economic symbiosis, connect to global processes? What can we learn from the emerging town planning and architectural solutions? How does this connect to what has been considered an almost linear history of architecture and the cities? These are the questions that can stimulate research and creative work in the coming half year.

Hungary

COMMISSIONER
Zsolt Petrányi

CURATOR
Attila Nemes

DEPUTY CURATORS
Adam Somlai-Fischer
Samu Szemerey

ASSISTANT
Júlia Gáspár

WEBSITE
www.reorient.hu

1

2

3

4

5

6

7

8

9

1-9
Éva Horvát
Architecture of invisible Networks (Józsefváros Market, Budapest, 8th District),
2006. Photo series.
COURTESY THE AUTOR.

The Montevideo Seminars, spaces for collective reflection and proposals through the urban projects

The Montevideo Seminars are annual meetings that provide a forum for academic work and discussions on urban and land planning issues. These are approached through a project, which brings together contributions from various disciplines and institutions.

Since they were first presented in 1998, the Montevideo Seminars have had the following general objectives:
- to contribute to the training of the School of Architecture's students, teachers and graduates and people from other academic fields, and to be actively involved in issues related to urban and land management work through the contributions of national and foreign lecturers and professionals and, especially, using collective work as a project workshop;
- to broaden the view of stressful issues that could trigger social, environmental and territorial mutations;
- to make progress in an inter-disciplinary reflection on alternatives for the contemporary city and territory;
- to propose ideas for setting performance guidelines.

Year after year, various topics and areas are identified and selected during each seminar, in an attempt to make progress in community construction with regard to specific issues, always guided by the above-mentioned general objectives.

The seminars are jointly organized by the Universidad de la República's School of Architecture and various public institutions. The Montevideo city council has had a leading role, seeking to bring together the most authoritative experts on the topic and area selected each year. Furthermore, the seminars have received academic, organizational and/or material support from public and private institutions. We wish to highlight the permanent commitment of the Society of Architects of Uruguay and the Centre for Architecture Students, the latter playing a decisive role in the creation and consolidation of the event through its travelling Groups.

Participants include Uruguayan and foreign university departments, students, professionals and public and private bodies and at times the general public.

Activities are organized at exhibition venues, while debate of the topics is related to the theme and to subjects of a general interest (talks, lectures, panels, exhibitions) and project Workshops, which are the very core of the process of discussing, developing and drafting the proposals. Several project Workshops are organized every year under the guidance of a director (usually a foreign guest) with a team from the national faculty and contributions from advisors. Workshop participants spend almost two weeks drafting a proposal, which is subsequently presented and debated at plenary meetings with presentations by invited lecturers. The plurality of the workshops elaborates on common topics and/or areas, and provides a forum for various contributions, often contrasting, thereby enriching the debate and collective reflection.

A substantial part of the working processes and the main products are recorded, filed and published to build a long-lasting base for university teaching and for formulating proposals on things to do in the region and city.

Some proposals have been adopted and incorporated as a basis for concrete proposals and actions by public bodies.

Uruguay

COMMISSIONER
Cristina Bausero

DEPUTY COMMISSIONERS
Ricardo Cordero
Flavio Morán

WEBSITE
www.farq.edu.uy
www.seminariomontevideo.edu.uy

EXHIBITOR
Facultad de Arquitectura - Universidad de la República

HOMAGE TO ELADIO DIESTE

PROMOTERS
IILA Istituto Italo-Latino Americano
Embassy of Uruguay at the Quirinale

ORGANIZING COMMITTEE
IILA Cultural Secretary
Irma Arestizábal
Alessandra Bonanni
Paola Pisanelli

Tribute to Eladio Dieste. Talent, architecture and a sense of place

Eladio Dieste was educated at the École des Ponts et Chaussées in Uruguay, and was an engineer, architect, builder and man of exceptional talent.

The cultural environment of his education in the first half of the twentieth century was liberal and open to foreign, especially European, trends. In 1929 Le Corbusier's visit to Uruguay signalled a change, as did the Dutch influences of the 'Wendingen' magazine, as is evident in much of the local architecture. The works of Eladio Dieste appeared in this scenario: projects infused with thoughtful reflection and a strong sense of the Latin American context where the master exercised his profession: Uruguay.

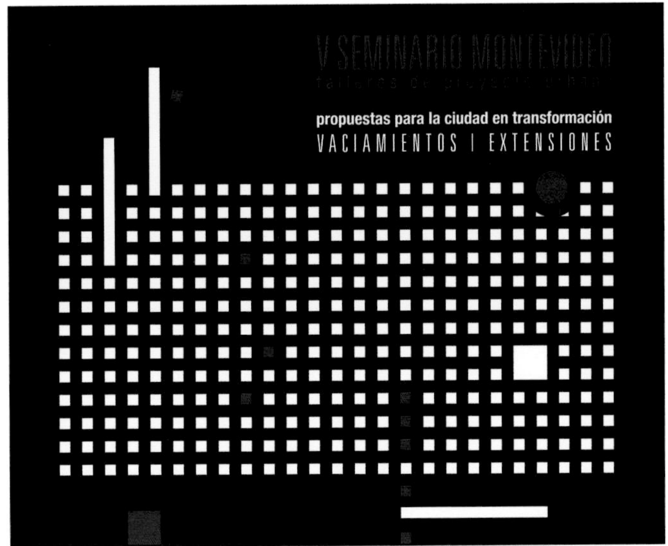

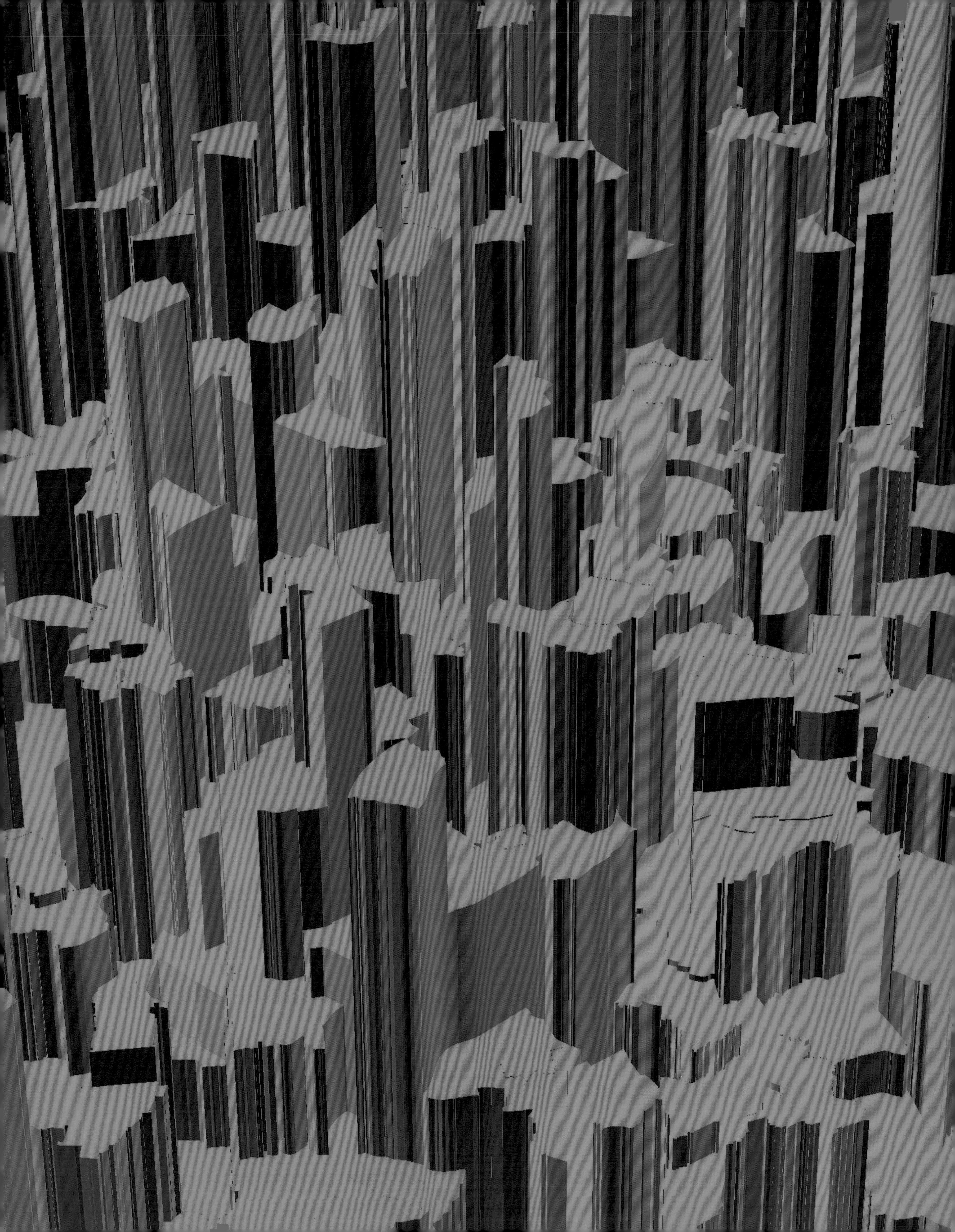

Partners' Initiatives

Risanamento Initiatives:

Ex Area Falck and Milano Santa Giulia

Ex Area Falck (Former Falck Area)

Sesto San Giovanni was the city of factories.

Factories of technology and modernity, but also of democratic and social growth.

You can see all this in its planning, but also in its culture and the dignity of its people. The transformation project under way cannot ignore this.

I would like it to remain a factory: a factory of ideas.

I envisage research centres, a university, young people at work and a seedbed of companies, in a context of new jobs.

There will certainly be shops, houses, offices, places of trade and of culture, and a big park, on the basis of the only city model we have (a model that combines thousands of activities that make it live).

But its real soul must continue to be that of the factory.

From city of factories to factory of ideas.

The project cannot be anything but an open system: the walls of Falck come down and suddenly the entire community takes possession of a big park.

The roads link up, green areas invade the old and new, and bridges are built between the existing city and the industrial area, above and below the river of railway lines.

The big park, even bigger than could be imagined, is a whole world in which fragments of the factory flourish again here and there, the living and noble memory of a mighty past.

But the green is not just that of the park, it is also that which invades the streets, the avenues and keeps everything together.

Of course the subject of energy and sustainability, consumption and public transport must be very important, the worthy heir of the modernity that is part of the history of Sesto San Giovanni.

Now let us talk about architecture: I like the idea of constructing tall buildings for living, working and studying; not tower blocks, which are often symbols of arrogance and power, but Tall Houses that only touch the ground with their framework.

All the other buildings would also connect with the earth by way of big porticoes and open spaces: not a fortress city but a city that communicates.

This also means that the mass of green passes near it and creates an effect of lightness and transparency, which I would like to nominate as the poetic style of the whole project.

The Tall Houses do not touch the earth, and on their roofs there are only gardens (not technical equipment) and their vibrant, coloured skin bears a surprising message of life.

We are only at the beginning, but it is the beginning of a wonderful adventure.

Renzo Piano

1

2

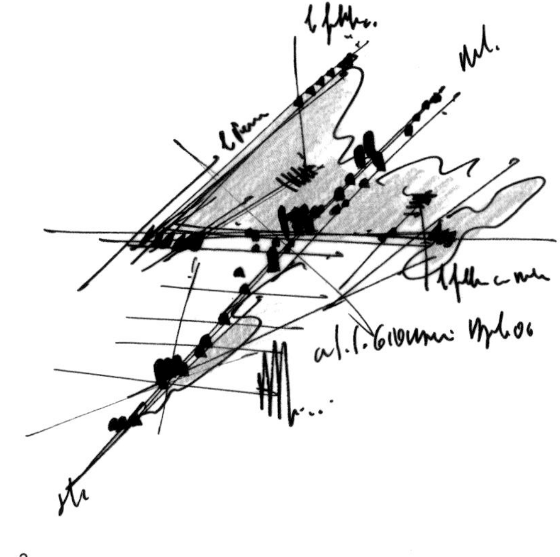

3

1
T3 Rolling-mill.
PHOTO BY MAURITS VAN DER STAAY. © RPBW.

2
Old Falk Area.
PHOTO BY GIANNI BERENGO GARDIN. © RPBW.

3
General view. Sketch by Renzo Piano.
© RPBW.

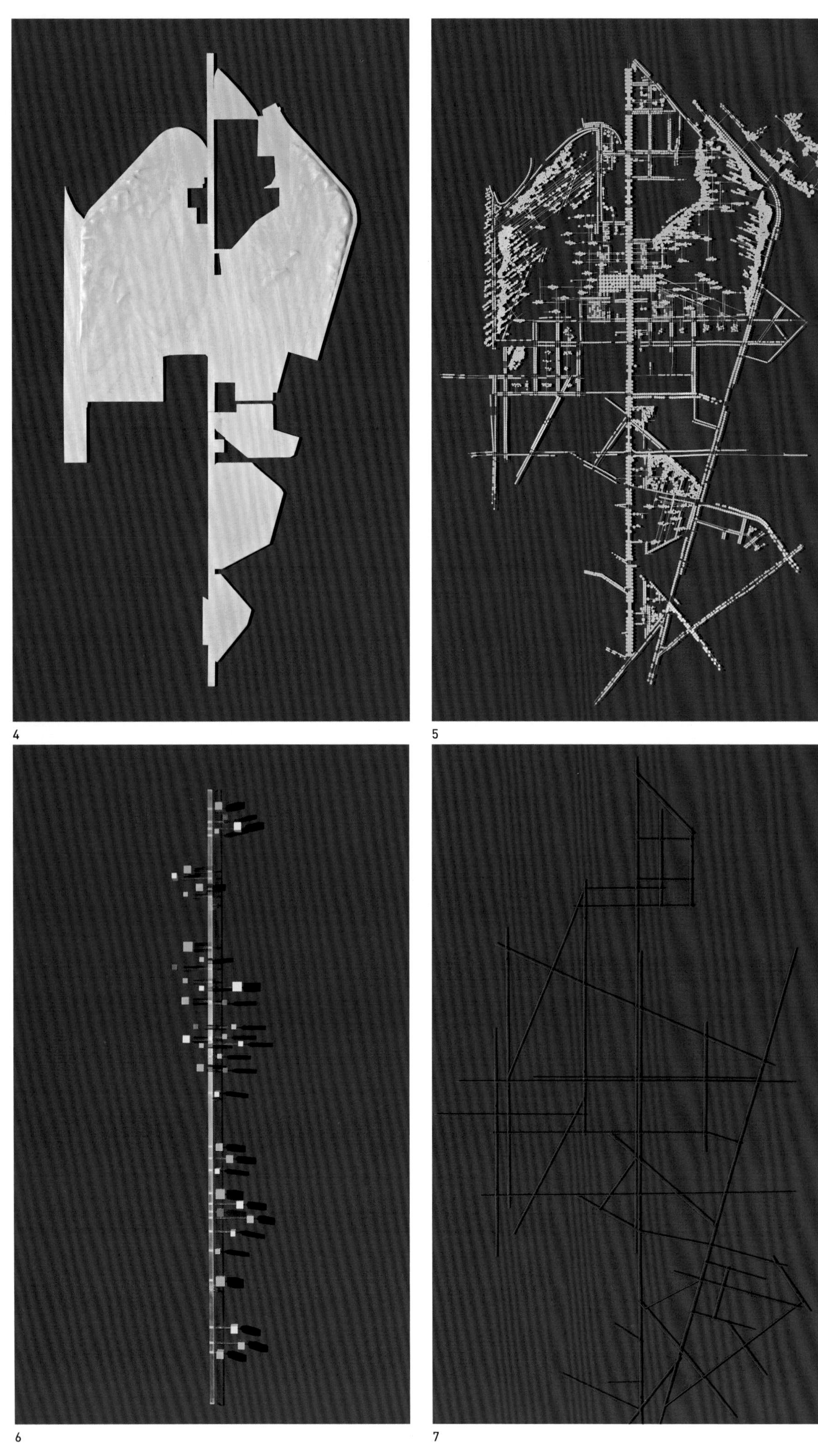

4
The Park.
PHOTO BY STEFANO GOLDBERG.
© RPBW.
5
Garden connection axis.
PHOTO BY STEFANO GOLDBERG.
© RPBW.
6
North-South axis on Viale Italia: the "Case Alte".
PHOTO BY STEFANO GOLDBERG.
© RPBW.
7
The pattern of the urban re-establishment.
PHOTO BY STEFANO GOLDBERG.
© RPBW.
8
General plan.
PHOTO BY MICHEL DENANCÉ.
© RPBW.

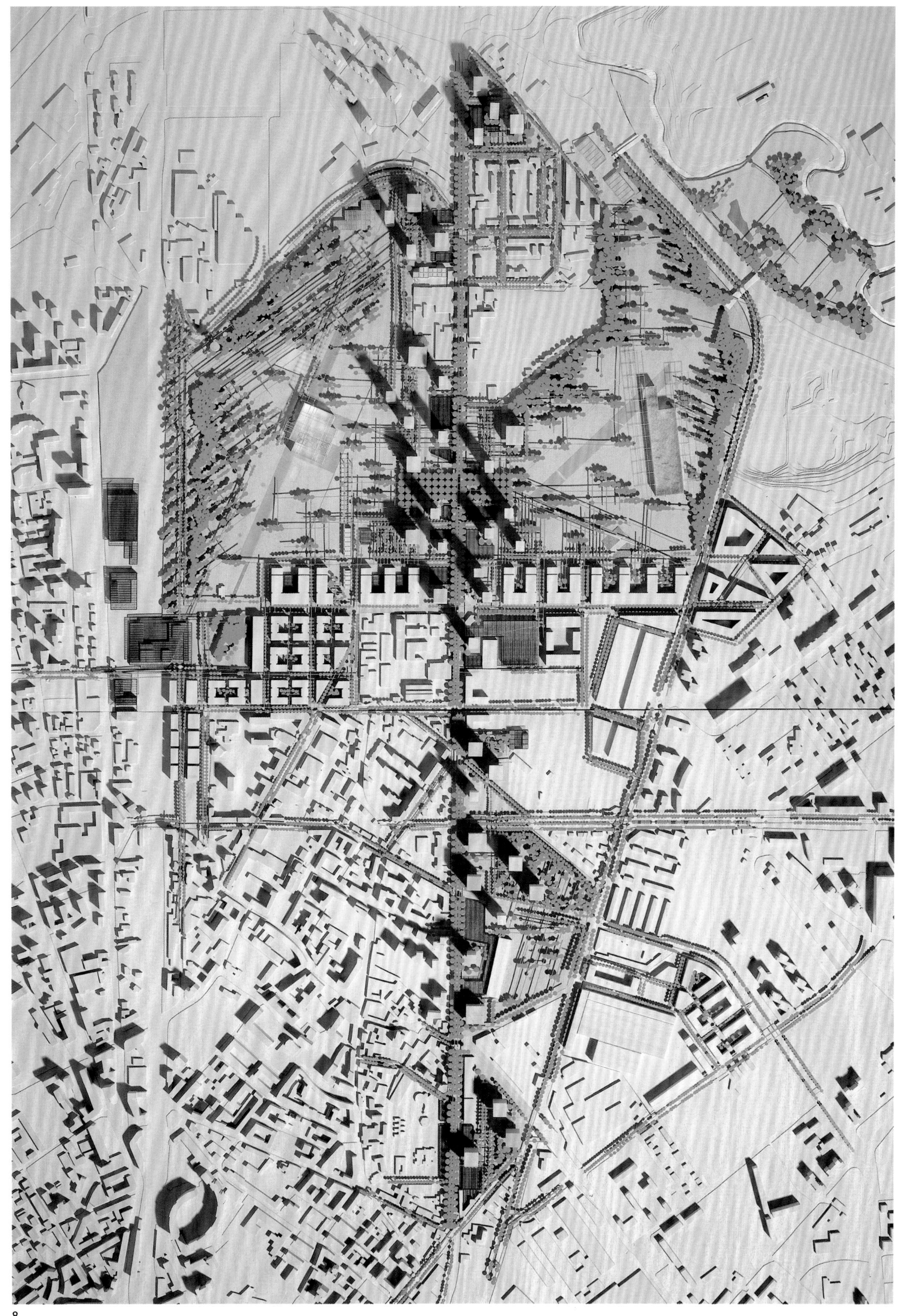

8

9

10

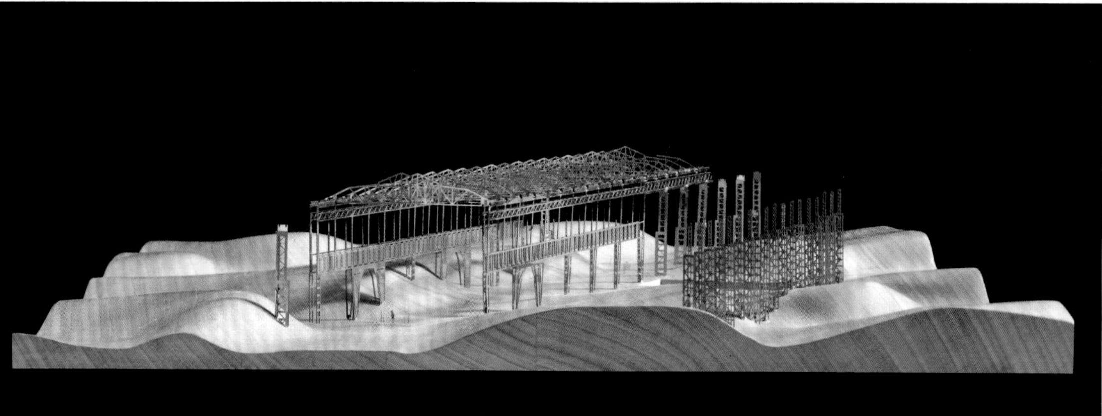

11

9
View on the Rambla.
© RPBW.

10
The "Case Alte", type 20x20x100 m.
PHOTO BY STEFANO GOLDBERG. © RPBW.

11
Extant building: "Le Rovine".
PHOTO BY MICHEL DENANCÉ. © RPBW.

12
The Children's Town. Sketch by Renzo Piano.
© RPBW.

13
The "Case Alte". Sketch by Renzo Piano.
© RPBW.

14
"La Rambla". Sketch by Renzo Piano.
© RPBW.

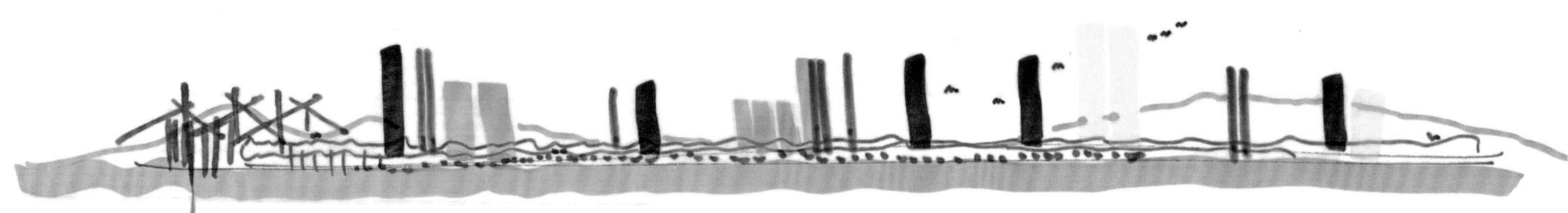

12

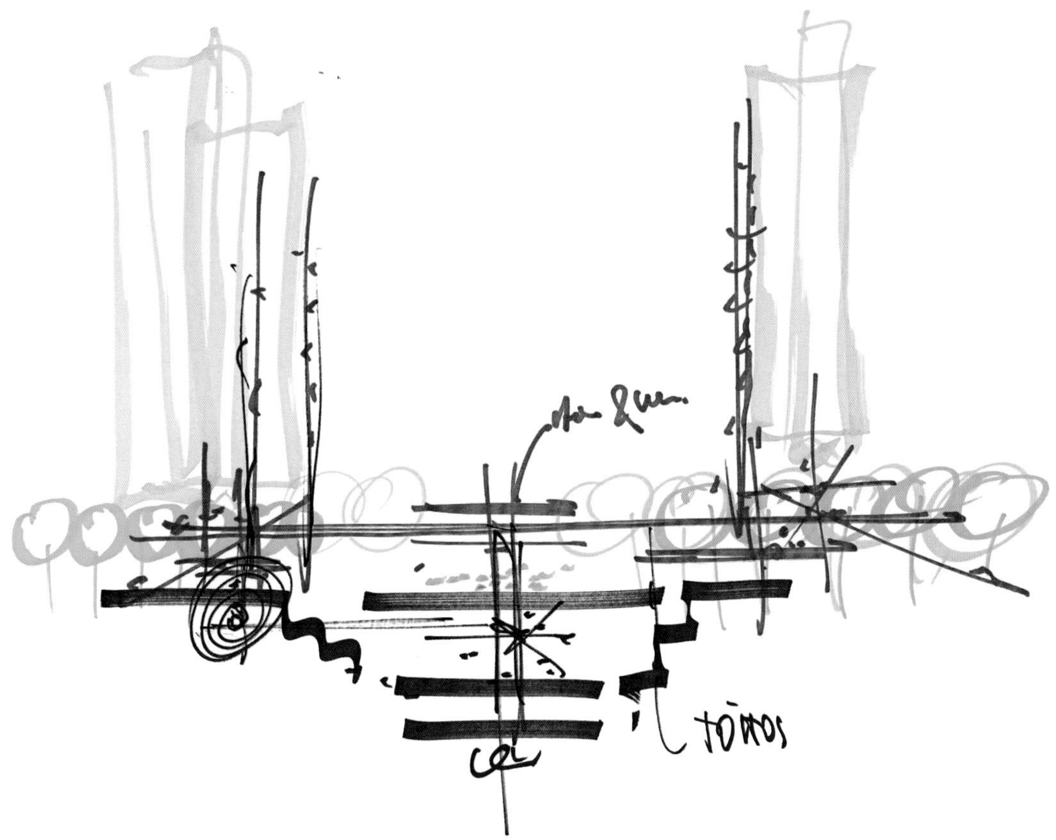

13

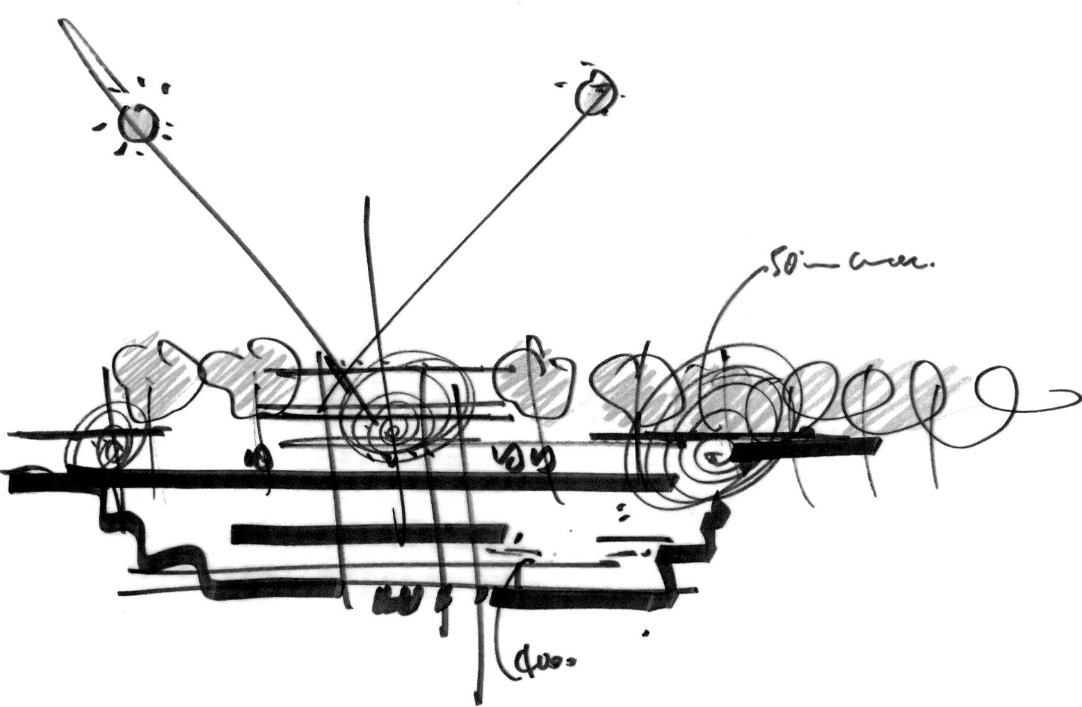

14

Risanamento Initiatives:
Ex Area Falck and Milano Santa Giulia

Milano Santa Giulia
The ideal city

'In the Milano Santa Giulia project I wanted to bring together not just my knowledge and experience of the world of architecture but my vision of a city in the twenty-first century and a new lifestyle; an emerging future with strong roots in the past'
Norman Foster

Milano Santa Giulia, the largest urban planning scheme in Europe and the most important post-war urban redevelopment project in Italy, is a new district of Milan that Risanamento SpA, a real estate development company, led by Luigi Zunino, is costructing on the largest disused area in Europe (1.2 million square metres in the city's south-east). The scheme is designed by Norman Foster, one of the leading names in contemporary architecture.

The project focuses on the future quality of life in the new district. Every aspect has been designed to meet the widest expectations of the people who will live there, according to the standards of the new 'ideal city', with a single objective: to make daily life and work a pleasant experience. This will be achieved by combining a modern, elegant aesthetic in residential and office buildings as well as in communal and social areas.

Milano Santa Giulia is intended to be a 'city within a city', self-sufficient but with good connections to the rest of Milan, and it will be equipped with the facilities to transform a group of people into a community, creating an integrated and well-serviced district. This will be a new centre where people can live, work and play in a beautiful setting, immersed in green open spaces and equipped with numerous facilities for sport, recreation and outdoor pursuits.

'An international project for an international city: Milano Santa Giulia represents an overall vision for the future of every city. The concept is applied at a local level to produce a masterplan that presents a global vision, although it was designed exclusively for the topography of Milan. A model for an integrated and sustainable future lifestyle and at the same time a rare opportunity to create a lively and multi-functional district based on the city's unique urban traditions. This is the first large urban redevelopment project to take place in Milan for over 50 years; the project includes shops, restaurants and bars, and also cultural facilities including a Conference Centre and an Exhibition Area that will be developed alongside residential buildings. The basic logic behind the masterplan is the creation of extensive open green spaces and a large central park, a 'green lung' for the city. Thanks to the combination of compact, intense and lively environments with the necessary open green spaces, natural and urban landscapes are balanced, creating a safe and pleasant public oasis. The Milano Santa Giulia development is a unique opportunity to build an entire new urban district in Milan: a city within the city.'
Norman Foster

15

15
Sketch of the interior of the residences.

Milano Santa Giulia is a highly contemporary urban quarter from a structural, architectural and functional perspective. The green areas will be extensive and well-equipped, there will be special routes for cars and people will be able to use generous pedestrianised areas, while the district's social life will be concentrated around a 600 metre long promenade, the real heart of the development.

The area is situated in a strategic location and benefits from a complete and far-reaching infrastructure.

Milano Santa Giulia will feature residential buildings designed to satisfy every need in terms of the most modern and technologically advanced standards. The Crescent Housing has an open curvilinear shape facing south-west. Relating to the landscape, the form of the building optimizes views between internal and external areas and also enhances ventilation through the development, creating a pleasant microclimate. A safe, internal garden is created by the elliptic shape of the architecture, the raised level of the buildings with respect to the park, the controlled access points and the internal paths.

The green area, designed by the Dutch studio WEST 8 urban & design landscape architecture, will not be mere decoration but rather the project's soul: an extensive 350,000 square metre park, bordered by two residential and service areas, represents a 'city gate' that will add quality to communal living and social relations.

The new city will take its name from the church of Santa Giulia, to be built in the new district, which will be the first and only one in Milan. It will be designed by the Swiss architect Peter Zumthor.

The Milano Santa Giulia project as a whole has its own aesthetic dimension, which is conveyed by the project's ability to coexist harmoniously and in proportion with the surrounding environment. Beauty is subjective, but if it can successfully relate to both the environment and the community, it acquires a universal significance that does us a great service: the creation of places that add functionality to ordinary lifestyles, while at the same time pleasing the eye with the aesthetic beauty of its buildings.

Milano Santa Giulia is all of this. Milano Santa Giulia is a great opportunity from both a social and individual perspective. For Milan it represents an extraordinary driver of development and a real alternative for those who have new ideas of a city - the ideal city.

16

17

18

19

16
Sketch of the residences.
17
Model of the residences.
18
View of the promenade.
19
Living-room showflat.

20

21

20
Sketch representative of a typical day at Milan Santa Giulia.
21
Public park.
22
General plan.

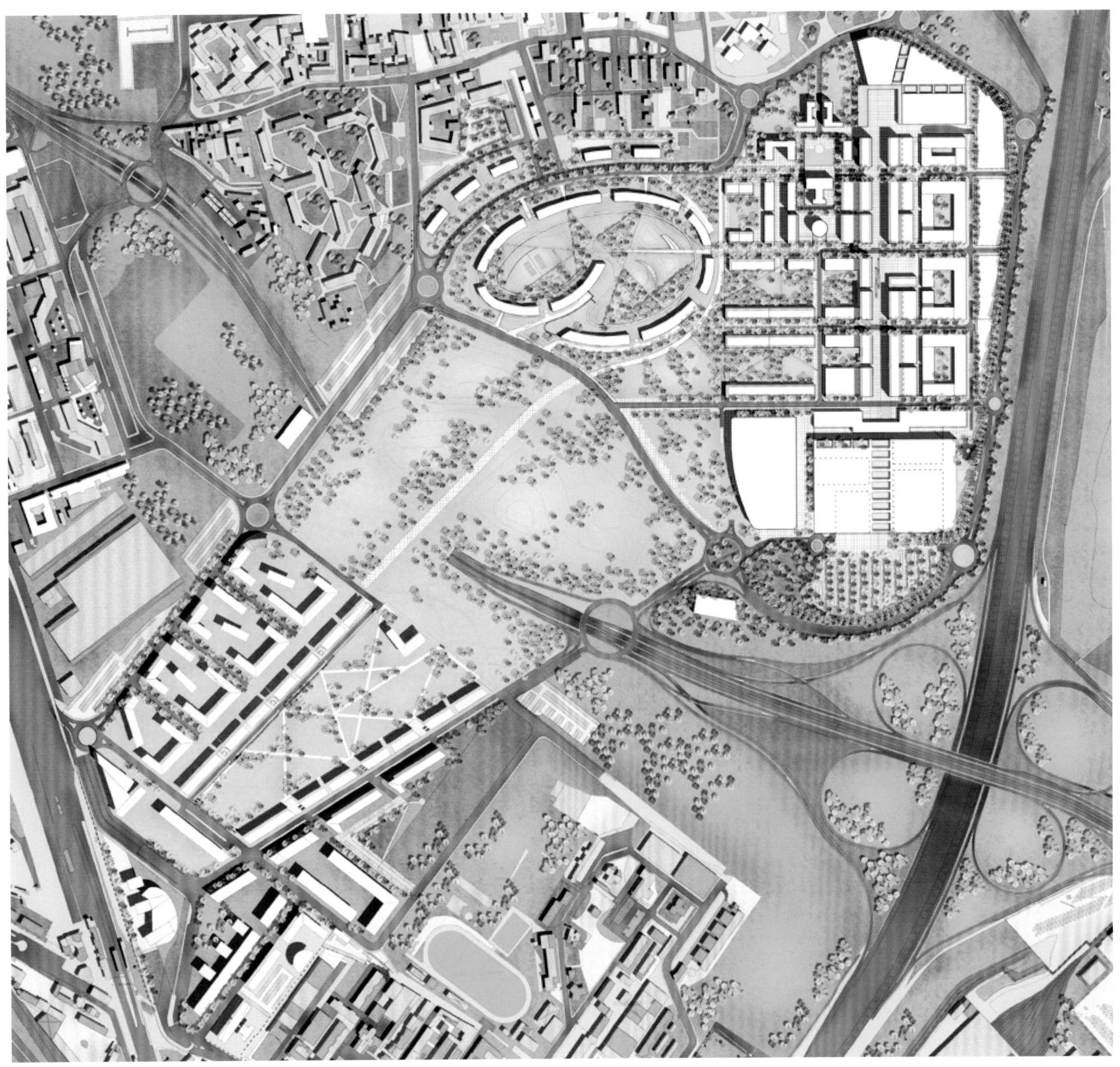

22

Metrò-polis

It is now culturally accepted that the traditional link between 'city' and 'hinterland' has been surpassed. The dissolution of the metropolis into an area with no limits is now quite evident on the international scene. Among the various theoretical writings on this, the essay by François Ascher, *Métapolis, ou l'avenir des villes* (Paris 1995), speaks for all.

Beyond the new interpretative models, the actual condition of the big conurbations confirms this unequivocal condition of the habitat. The metropolitan area of Naples is emblematic for various reasons, marked by a dense and branched building continuum. A population of about 4,000,000 lives in the area gravitating around the city (in a radius of 50 kilometres). A multitude of people use private cars every day (for work, shopping, leisure) causing traffic jams and pollution. So the 'challenge of rail transport' that the Campania regional administration has launched and partly begun is decisive for the future of this 'extended city'. When the planned metro lines are complete, every part of Naples and almost all the small outlying towns will be linked to one another and to the big infrastructures of the airport, the port (with the 'sea metro' branch) and the national rail lines.

The new station for high speed trains, conceived by Zaha Hadid, expresses the aesthetics of rapid movement with iconic immediacy in the architectural form itself, diagonally spanning the rails with an aerodynamic body of steel and glass.

The search for aesthetic seduction is on the other hand the distinctive quality of all the train stations built in Naples and Campania at the dawn of the new century. Indeed, the five stations on line 1 of the Naples metro are now known as the 'art stations'. These first stations (built between 2001 and 2003) were designed by Gae Aulenti, Alessandro Mendini and Domenico Orlacchio, and mark a new way of conceiving railway architecture, in a skilful blend of art and architecture.

The innovation has also reverberated outside, in the squares and urban settings, redesigned in relation to the new works. There is then the notable quantity and quality of the works of art inserted into this 'skilful play' under the farsighted direction of Achille Bonito Oliva, which have converted the stopping places of the metro into a kind of dynamic underground museum.

The main *raison d'être* of such infrastructure remains, however, the rapid connection of urban areas, triggering a

METRÒ-POLIS

The challenge of rail transport for the urban and territorial advancement in Naples and in Campania

INSTITUTIONS
Regione Campania
Ente Autonomo Volturno srl
Comune di Napoli
M.N. Metropolitana di Napoli spa

ORGANIZATIONS REPRESENTED
Contractors for the design and construction of lines 1 and 6 of the Naples Underground
M.N. Metropolitana di Napoli spa
Ansaldo Trasporti Sistemi Ferroviari spa
EAV srl partner companies
Circumvesuviana srl
Sepsa spa
MetroCampania NordEst srl
RFI Rete Ferroviaria Italiana spa Gruppo Ferrovie dello Stato
TAV spa Gruppo Ferrovie dello Stato

CURATORS
Benedetto Gravagnuolo
Alessandro Mendini
Arte contemporanea nelle stazioni
Achille Bonito Oliva

EXHIBITION DESIGN
Dada Saligeri

GRAPHICS
Massimo Caiazzo with Smallfish
Gabriella Grizzuti Zabo

ORGANIZATION TEAM
Marina Habetswallner
Sergio Negro
GianfrancescoPomicino
Francesca Sarnataro
Giovanna Torcia

EXHIBITORS
Le stazioni dell'arte
Gae Aulenti
Michele Capobianco
Alessandro Mendini (Atelier Mendini)
Domenico Orlacchio

New Projects
Mario Botta
Sergio Cappelli (Cappelli e Ranzo) and Karim Rashid
Silvio D'Ascia
Peter Eisenman
Massimiliano Fuksas
Zaha Hadid
Anish Kapoor
Hans Kollhoff
Vittorio Magnago Lampugnani
Benedetta Miralles Tagliabue
Dominique Perrault
Boris Podrecca
Richard Rogers
Alvaro Siza Vieira and Eduardo Souto De Moura
Uberto Siola
Oscar Tusquets Blanca

useful social symbiosis between the areas of oldest historic stratification and the newly built, outlying areas. The Piazza Municipio station, conceived by Alvaro Siza and soon to be built, will in this sense represent the climax of an emotional journey, finding its 'pre-text' for an unrepeatable combination of the ancient and contemporary in the archaeological remains of the Greek-Roman port.

This is precisely the point. The 'transport challenge' is aimed not only at expanding infrastructure, but also (and especially) at introducing a new way of conceiving urban and district planning. According to the new point of view, the places of the city where the crowds of individuals who travel along the intermodal transport networks meet must become more and more attractive and aesthetically exciting. The old functional formula of the station as 'non place' (to say it with Marc Augé), as anonymous technical space (of 'get your ticket and run'), must give way to the manifesto of the new poetics, whose first exemplary expressions are the metro stations of Naples and Campania. But there is more. In the course of time, the entire region will become one big, unique, multi-centred, seductive *Metrò-polis*.

Benedetto Gravagnuolo

The philosophy of the Naples metro

A metro is an invisible channel of communication underground that emerges at its stations in places quite disconnected in terms of their urban characteristics. The engineering and technological uniformity underground is contrasted by an enormous difference in the fabric and bits of city reached by the stations. This is especially true in Naples, a city that is heterogeneous and very closely linked in its geography, history, anthropology and town planning. So the concept is quite valid that each station should have its own architectural characteristics precisely suited to each individual site. In order to accentuate the organic relationship of languages between the various places and buildings of each station, which are often vast, coordinated complexes, a policy was adopted of commissioning individual designers to design not only their own station, but also the surrounding road system and furnishings, with squares, streets, green areas, lighting, signage, urban objects and other important details. So the emergence of each station from the winding path of the tunnel is an opportunity for the social and aesthetic upgrading of entire districts, from the

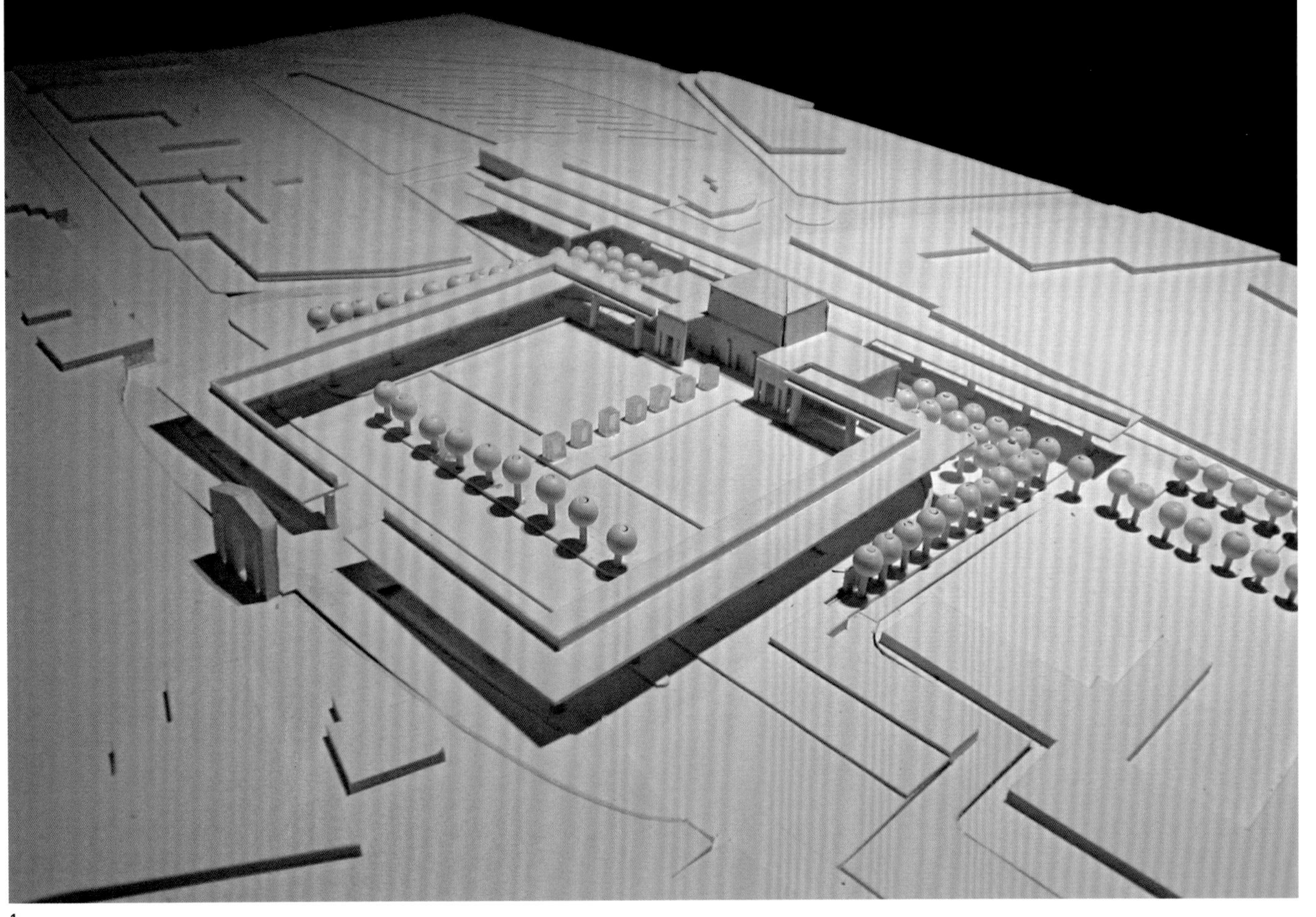

1

1
Mario Botta,
Project for the Tribunale and Poggioreale stations.

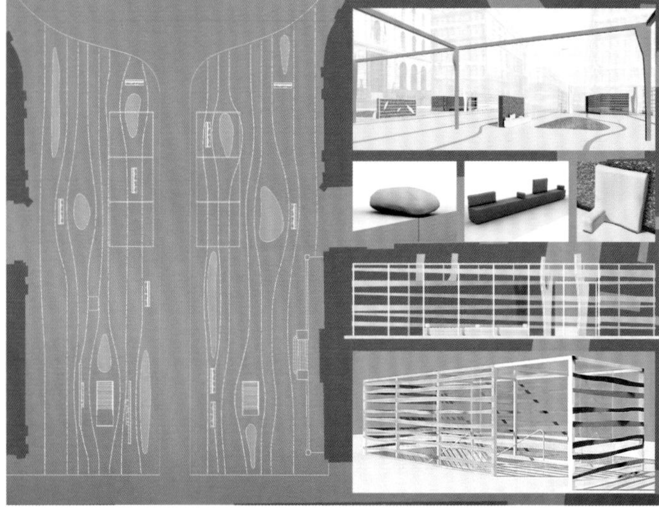
2

3

outlying areas to the hills, the waterfront, the historic zones, the most delicate archaeological sites and the airport: there is total eclecticism and any attempt to force a uniformity of language, a single architectural formula onto it would be chastening, heavy and determinist.

Acknowledging the enormous engineering project it represents, and its technical efficiency, what appears to the public eye is its visibility and aesthetic value, which are intended to gratify the local sites and inhabitants with new attractive urban images. The task is both a new, more dignified liveability, and an informed interpretation of the settings where each station emerges; the creation of new urban stages, of new symbols and proud new utopias; stagings seen as aesthetic works, fragments of external theatre with a high anthropological and emotional meaning.

On the basis of these premisses, the two methods for achieving them are: the involvement of a different architect for each station; the involvement of numerous artists creating works closely connected to the spaces, studied and placed from the outset with the designers.

In the great variety of its fabric, Naples may be defined as a city of generous eclecticism. It has expanded by consistencies, aberrations and additions, often admirable, often in speculative and disorderly contexts. The role of architecture today is to punctuate the banal repetition and degradation of the city with strong signals, with artistic evidence, intended by their presence and aura to infuse positive energy into the local districts concerned.

The formula of a close integration of architecture and public art is a difficult planning operation whose great historic epic has been the synthesis of the arts; the intention with the Naples metro was to accomplish this using the most contemporary approach of assembly. The eclecticism and linguistic dispersal of the various places almost naturally led to this decision: the choice of an appropriate architect or designer for each station; of artists and graphic designers

4

5

for each station who are able to communicate with that site and with that architect. Each choice is based on quality and skills. It was then decided to impartially define colours and ideologies corresponding to contemporary theories and research on the world cultural scene, both for the architects and the artists, so as to obtain a range of languages in the entirety of the works.

The three principles that govern the entire project for Naples' new metro are: first, the stations as an opportunity for urban renewal; second, the eclecticism of the designers; third, the close collaboration of artists with the architecture.

The design philosophy that subtends the work is intended to lead to an entire, vast patchwork image. In its conclusion and synthesis, this is presented as a system of spaces that are both museum of contemporary architecture and urban exhibition of public art.

Alessandro Mendini

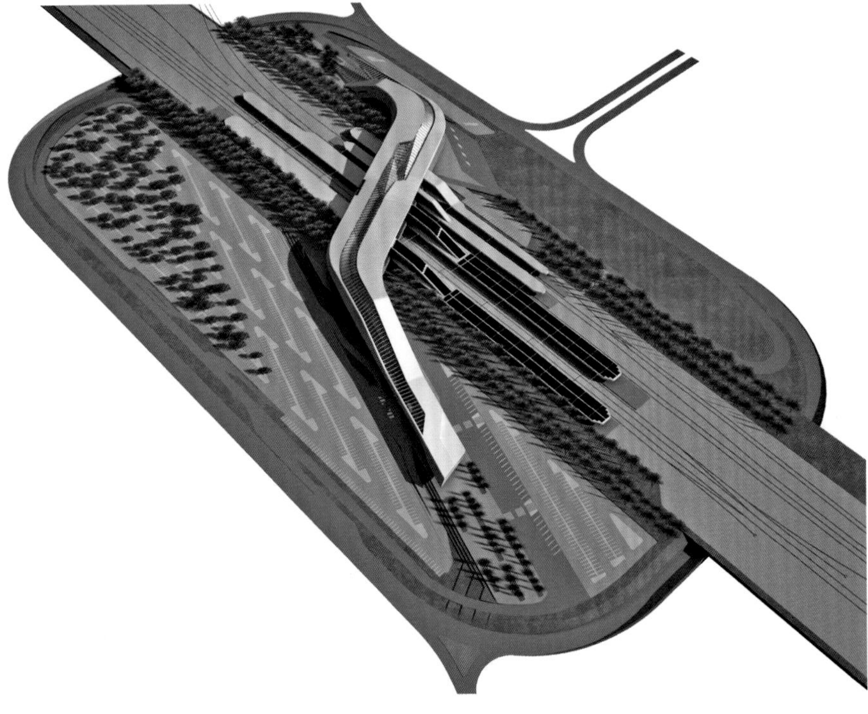

6

2
Cappelli e Ranzo (Sergio Cappelli, Maria Antonietta Sbordone with Alessia Coto, Daniele Pannicelli, Rosanna Veneziano),
Project for the surface setting of the Università station.
3
Karim Rashid,
Project for the Università station.
4
Silvio D'Ascia,
Project for the Montesanto station.
5
Massimiliano Fuksas,
Project for the Duomo station.
6
Zaha Hadid,
Project for the AV/AC station of Afragola.

7

8

9

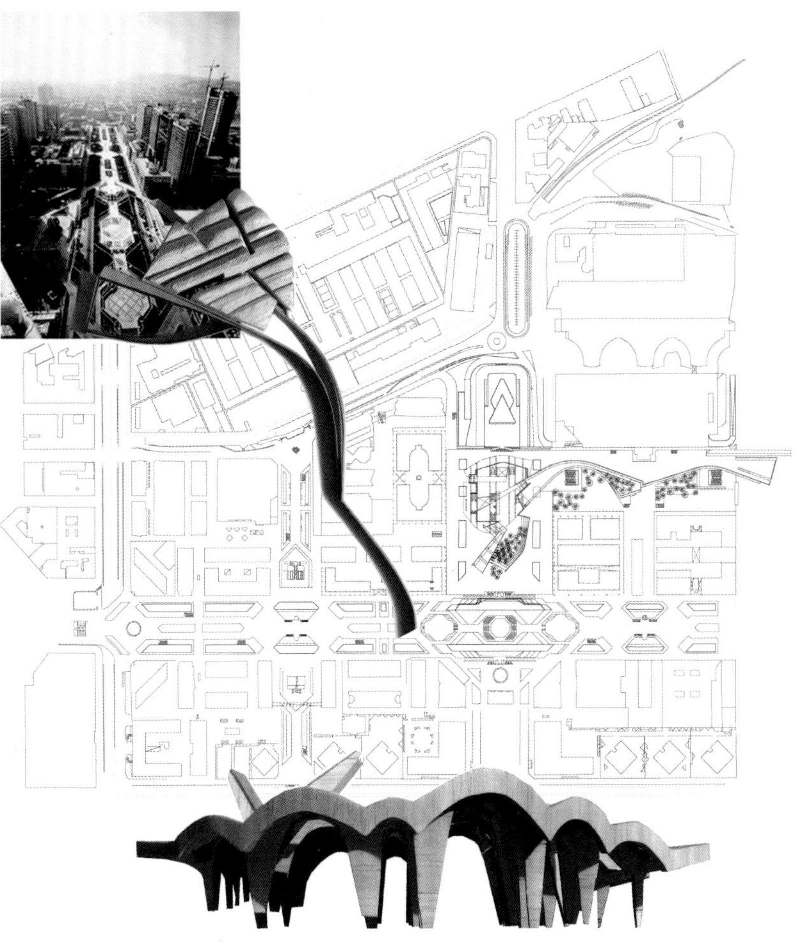

10

11

7
Anish Kapoor,
Artistic conception of the Montesantangelo station.
8
Hans Kollhoff,
Project of the Arco Mirelli station.
9
Vittorio Magnago Lampugnani,
Project of the Mergellina station.
10
Benedetta Miralles Tagliabue,
Project of the Centro Direzionale station.
11
Dominique Perrault,
Project of the Garibaldi station,
Piazza Garibaldi.

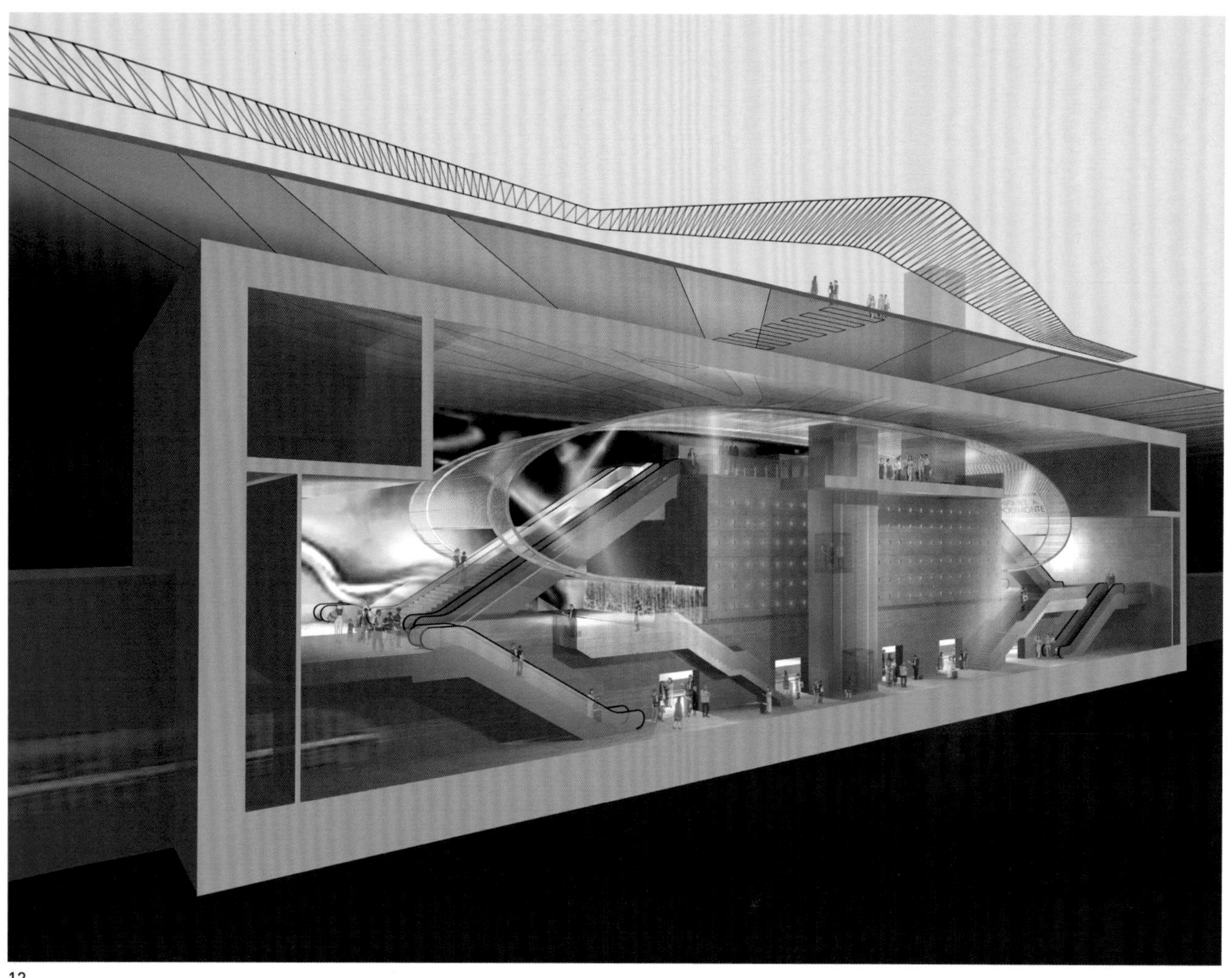

12

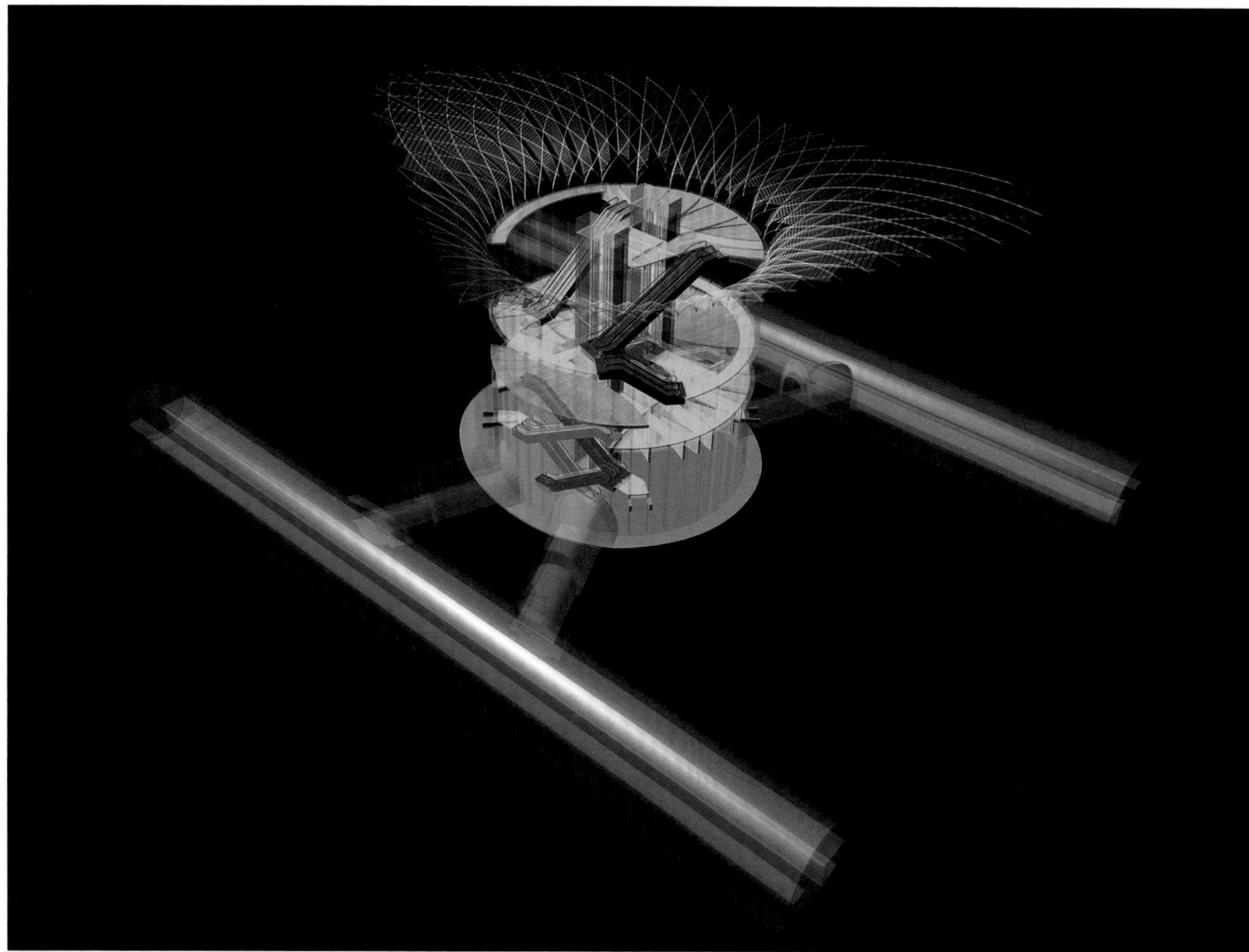

13

14

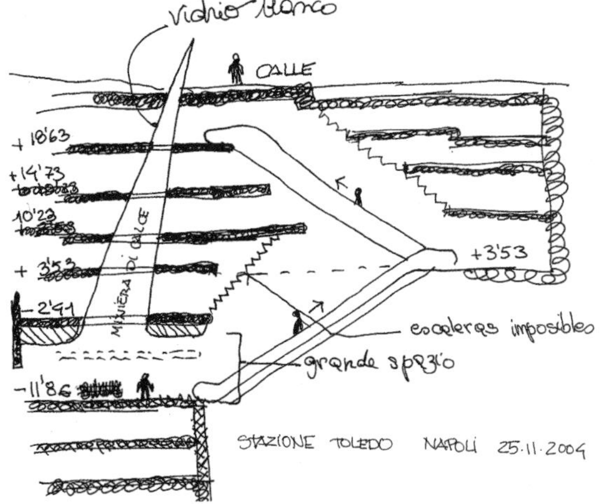

16

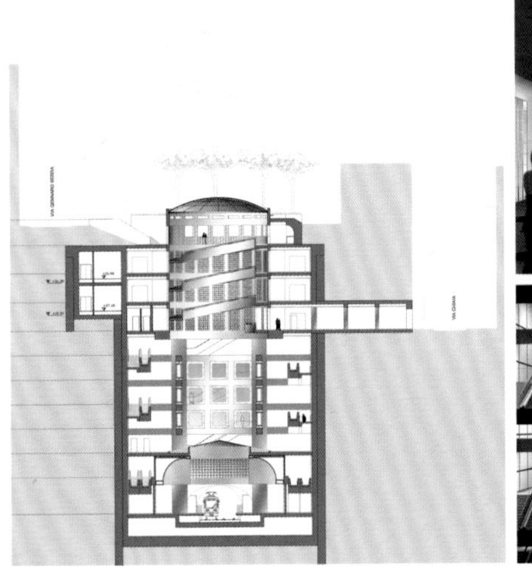

15

12
Boris Podrecca,
Project of the San Pasquale station.

13
Richard Rogers (R. Rogers, A. Kalsi, I. Harbour, L. Grutt, D. Costa, E. Bartolini, J. Stopps, A. King, M. Fairbrass),
Project of the Capodichino station.

14
Alvaro Siza Vieira and Eduardo Souto De Moura,
Project of the Municipio station.

15
Uberto Siola,
Project of the Chiaia station.
Cross section of the station building end interior views.

16
Oscar Tusquets Blanca (with Javier Mariscal, Paolo Carriero and Magda Michelesio, A.I.A. Instal·lacions Arquitectòniques),
Project of the Toledo station.

The ancient city of Tong Li
Situated south-east of the city of Wujang in the province of Jiangsu, 60 kilometres from Shanghai and 18 from Suzhou, Tong Li can be reached by national and provincial roads and the Suzhou-Jiaxing-Hangzhou motorway. It extends over a surface of 133.7 square kilometres and has a population of 55,000. The historic city, however, has a surface area of one square kilometre and a population of 10,000.

Archaeological remains show that Tong Li was already making history five and six thousand years ago: many examples of architecture remain from the last two Ming and Qing dynasties. According to official documents, 47 temples and 38 grand residences and gardens were built between 1271 and 1911. The ancient city of Tong Li is surrounded by water, studded with the five lakes of Tong Li, Jiu Li, Ye Ze, Nan Xing and Pang Shan. The town is divided into seven sections by 15 canals and connected by 49 bridges. Tong Li has been called the 'Village of Rice and Fish' and 'the Granary'. Along with its abundant production of rice, Tong Li also has diverse aquatic fauna.

In 1981 Tong Li was included in the list of tourist areas of national interest; in 1986 it was chosen by China's Ministry of Construction as a candidate to be made part of the world heritage. In 2000 the garden of Tui Su became part of UNESCO's World Heritage. In 2001 Tong Li was classified as one of the AAAA level tourist destinations identified by the Chinese Tourism Board. In the same year the State Council added the Tui Su garden to the list of the most important tourist destinations in China. In 2002 Tong Li became one of the most important natural areas in the country. In December 2003 it was numbered as one of the most important historical and cultural centres in China.

The Tong Li project
In China today, cultural constructs and ways of life are changing significantly and constantly. Different and even contrary cultural elements are randomly mixed in a phenomenon with no historical precedent. A profound reconsideration of what architecture and what development China should have is now the theme of the project.

The aims
To safeguard the continuity between past, present and future. To reflect on the future development of Tong Li from the point of view of historic research, sociology, anthropology, customs, local conventions and economics.

The project may be summarized in three macro-areas:
- the old city: the tourist industry, residential areas, crafts, small business;
- the new urban area: schools and institutes, research and development centres, museums, clubs, sport and leisure, residential areas;
- the ecological district: the system of organic farms, the green production base, the fishing industry, forestry, well-being centres.

The aim of the Tong Li project is to test a new model of development in which a relationship is established between the historic, cultural heritage, the natural environment and the new city, and made sustainable.

Tong Li Project – China

PROMOTING INSTITUTION
Wujiang Municipal Committee
City of Tong Li

ARCHITECTS/PLANNERS
Mi Qiu
Francesco Morena

GRAPHICS AND EXHIBITION DESIGN
Mi Qiu Modern Art Workshop
Studio Morena
Architectural Team
European Architectural Works

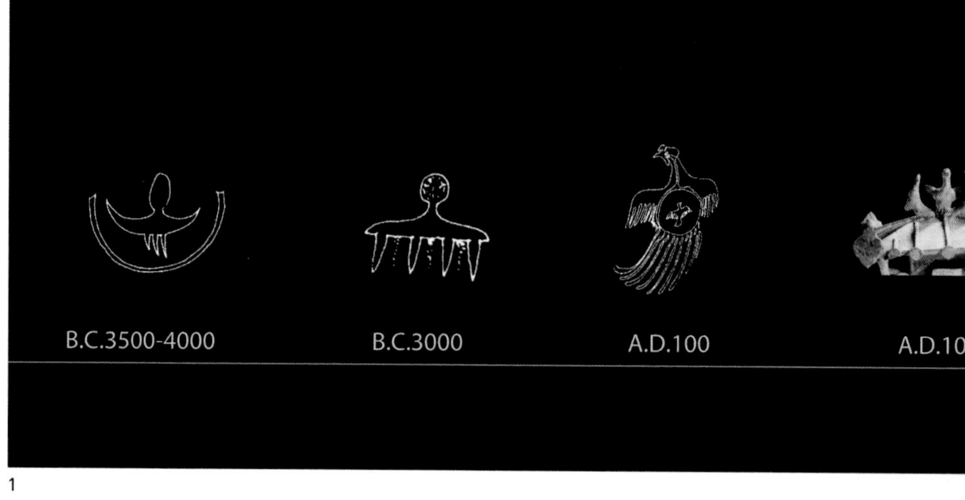

1

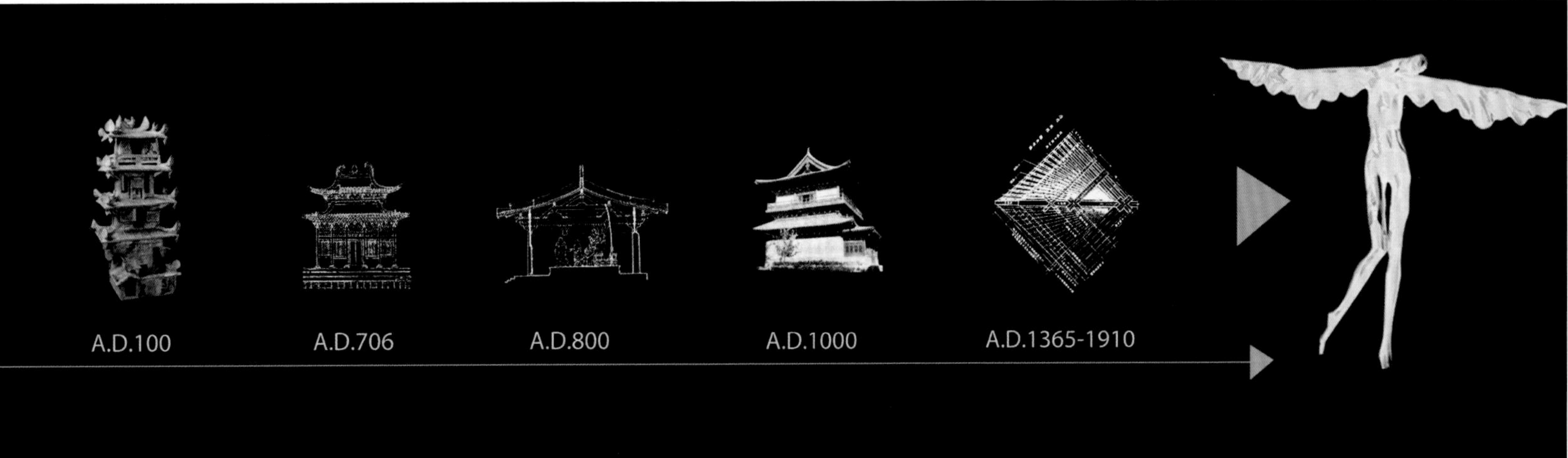

1
The posture of Miaodigou phoenix's wings is at the origin of traditional Chinese architecture.
The man with the wings represents the new mind.

同里四面湖界圖
三都東八斥鎮界
二十四都平望鎮界
二十八都梅墩界
八叉漾
清水漾
西長白蕩
二十五都尚湖
南新湖
葉澤湖
同里鎮界
同里湖
龐山湖
九里湖
二十七都庵村鎮界
吳淞江

2

3

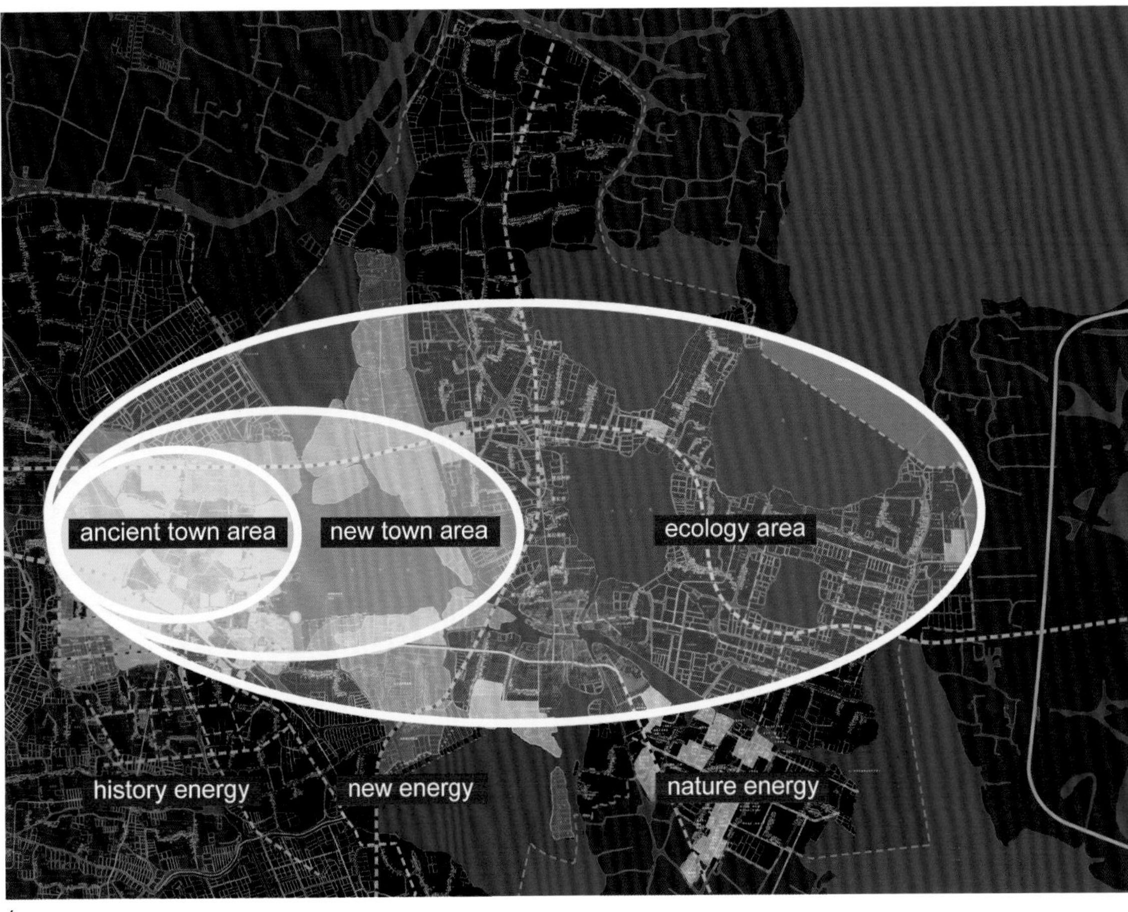

4

2
Old map of Tong Li dating to the Ching dinasty.
3
Meditation.
4
New urban grid of organic development.

5

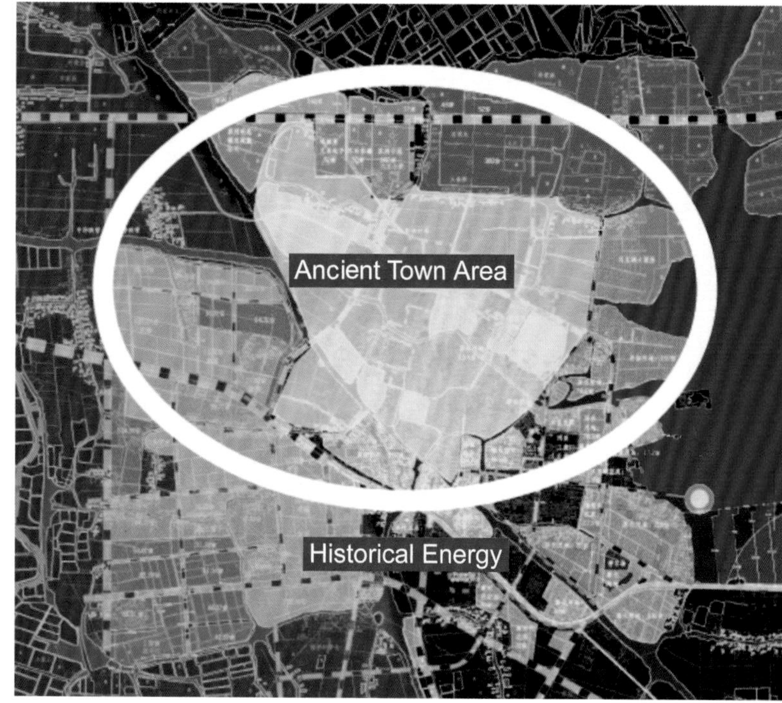

6

7

5
Geographic location.
6
The historical town, restricted general area.
7
Analysis of architectonic restrictions.
Total restrictions are indicated in red and yellow colours, partial restrictions in grey.
8
New edification areas (in blue) related to the historical town.
9
The ecological district (in green): organic relationship with the historical centre and the new town.
10
Relationship between the new edification and the historical area. Cultural areas (museums, theatres, temples), built on water, are indicated in red colour.
11
The ecological farms system.

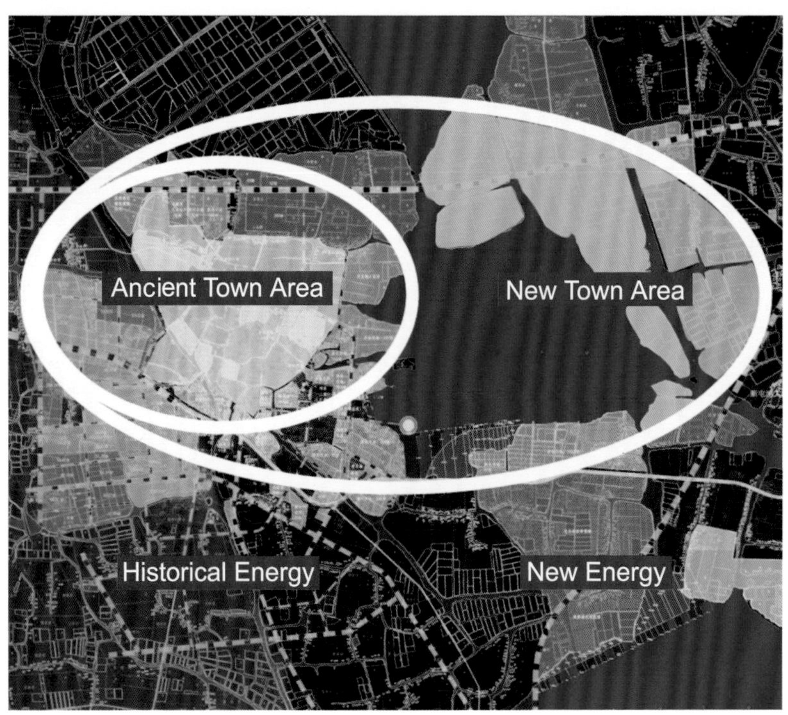
Ancient Town Area
New Town Area
Historical Energy
New Energy
8

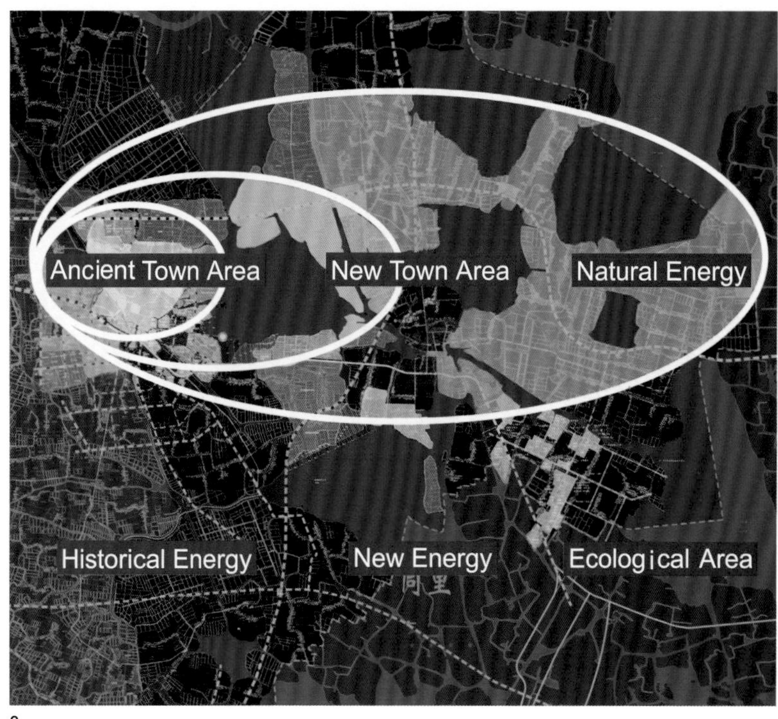
Ancient Town Area
New Town Area
Natural Energy
Historical Energy
New Energy
Ecological Area
9

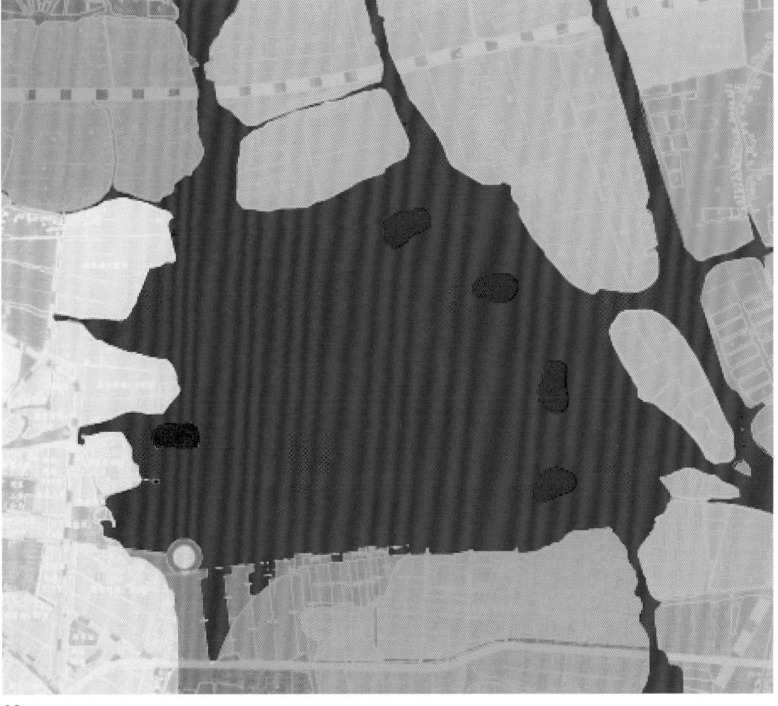
10

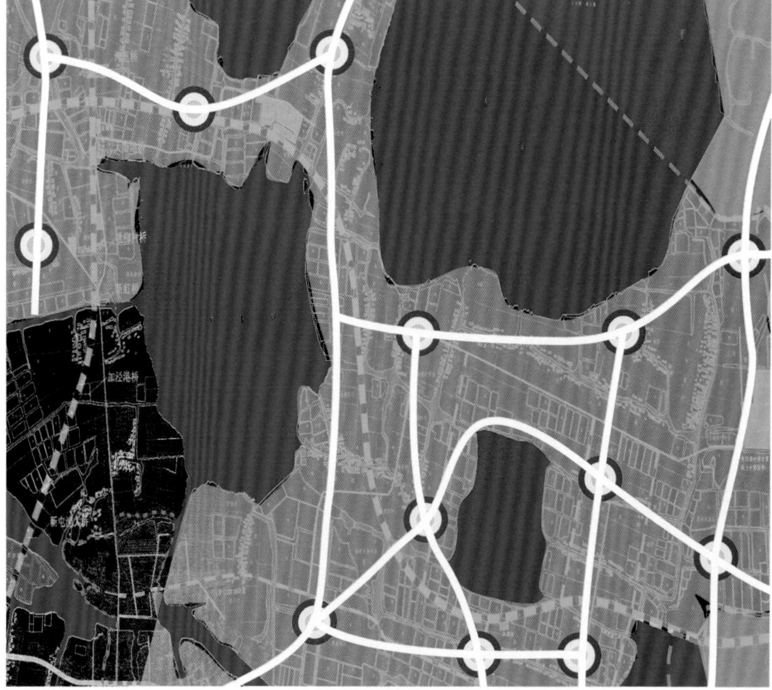
11

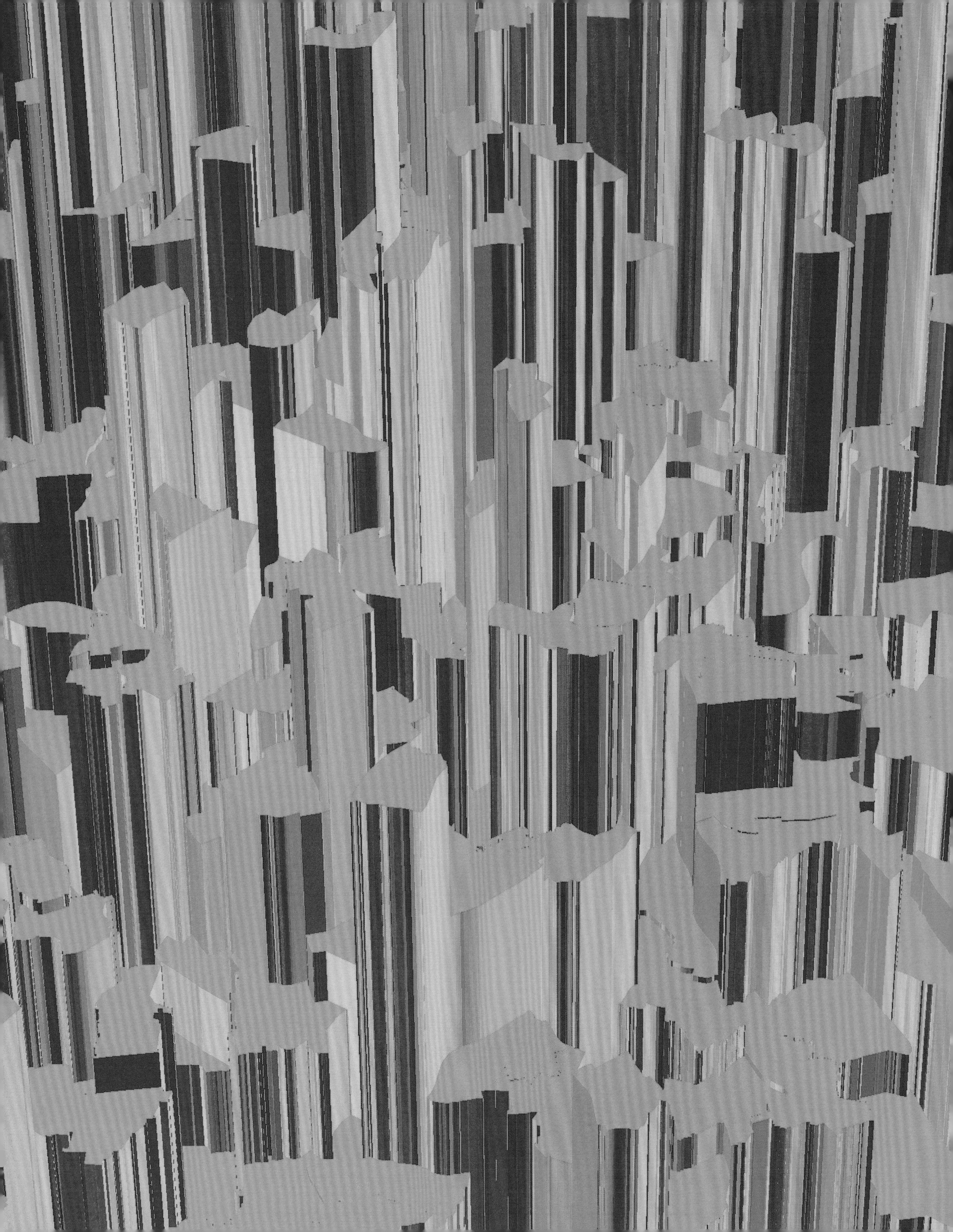

Collateral Events

Church, architecture, society

It is not necessary to refer to far off times to note the importance of the church's role in society and the city. The relationship between city and society in Italy, but not only, and especially after the Second World War, has been powerfully marked by the unifying presence of the churches, both from an urban and social point of view. The ecclesiastical structures attached to the places of worship, or parish centres, have been fundamental in this because of their role offering welcome, assistance, refuge, education, recreation and more besides. Although in the past the places of worship were also cultural centres par excellence, because of their archives, libraries and various historic-artistic assets, the value of these places in a multicultural and rapidly changing world like ours is primarily confirmed by the function they fulfil, often in the absence of other local safeguards. Their presence in the urban fabric is therefore still decisive, both with regard to the buildings of the past and those still to be built or undergoing alterations to meet the needs of their change of use.

What is the role of the church buildings in the city today and what will it be in the near future?

The church building, created within society and therefore a mirror of society, which in time has taken on new forms, has recently absorbed the cultural, artistic and liturgical stimuli of the Vatican II ecumenical council. The route unequivocally drawn out for the religious building ranges from the transcendent dimension to the convivial, from the vertical to the horizontal: is this really the case?

Once again these themes will be considered thanks to the initiative of the CEI's National Office for Ecclesiastical Cultural assets and the Patriarchate of Venice. They are promoting the fourth edition of the international conference within the context of the 10th International Architecture Exhibition, continuing the dialogue begun at previous events. Austria, Belgium, Portugal and the Czech Republic have been invited to participate.

A confluence of ideas, involving art, architecture and society, will be presented during the conference to underline the characteristics of places of worship as developing buildings with regard to history, styles and liturgy. A Venetian church will be proposed for a project of adaptation according to the indications of the current liturgy. This work is intended to emphasize that the churches are not museums of historic art, nor architectural objects to be conserved, but living buildings within the city and society, brought to life by them and in constant dialogue with them.

Gianmatteo Caputo, Giorgio Della Longa, Antonio Marchesi, Massimiliano Valdinoci

Architecture and Liturgy in the 20th Century European experiences compared

Ufficio Nazionale per i Beni Culturali Ecclesiastici della Conferenza Episcopale Italiana

Patriarcato di Venezia

IN COLLABORATION WITH
MART, Museo d'Arte Moderna e Contemporanea di Trento e Rovereto

TECHNICAL-SCIENTIFIC COORDINATION
Estèban Fernandez Cobiàn
Frédéric Debuyst
Giorgio Della Longa
Antonio Marchesi
Massimiliano Valdinoci
Walter Zahner

ORGANIZING COORDINATION
Gianmatteo Caputo with the collaboration of Ufficio Promozione Beni Culturali - Venezia Culturart srl

WITH THE SUPPORT OF
Pontificia Commissione per i Beni Culturali della Chiesa
Ministero per i Beni e le Attività Culturali
Regione del Veneto
Provincia di Venezia
Comune di Venezia

WEBSITE
www.chiesacattolica.it/beniculturali

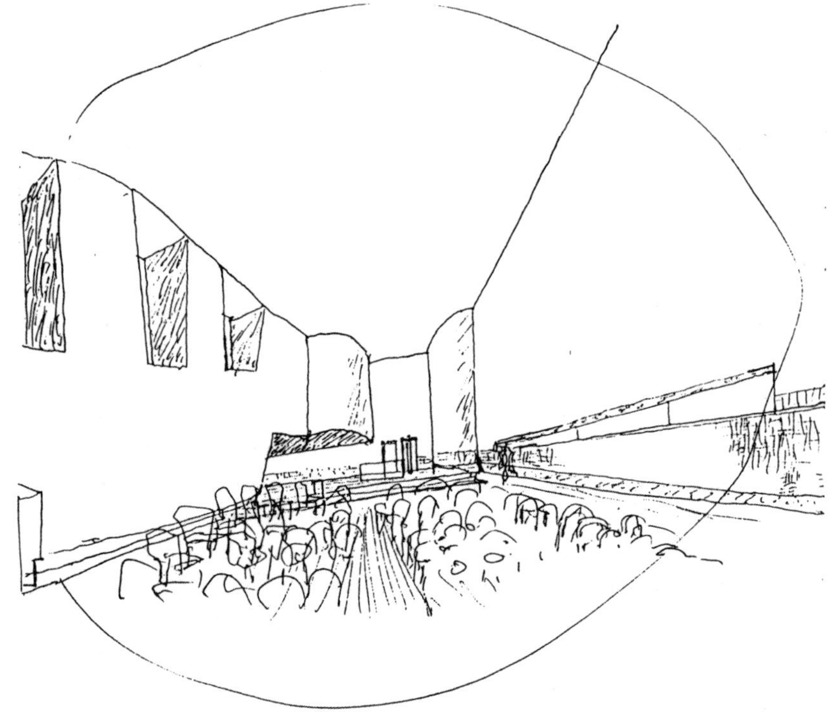

1

2

1
Álvaro Siza Vieira,
Sketch of the hall of the Church of Saint Mary,
Marco de Caneveses (Porto), 1990-1997.

2
Heinz Tesar,
The Church of Christus Öffnung der Welt,
between the building of ONU Office District in Donaucity, Vienna, 1997-2000.
PHOTO BY CHRISTIAN RICHTERS

Is there such a thing as contemporary Ticino architecture? In what sense can it be spoken of? What distinguishes it? And what is meant by Ticino architecture? A geographical, cultural, political or marketing determination? Is it what is done by Ticino architects, or simply what is done in Ticino? How is the definition of belonging decided? Who decides?

Starting from the work of six architecture studios, chosen for the knowingly rooted and culturally international nature of their work, the aim is to offer a reflection on the new trends that are emerging in the panorama of architecture of and from Ticino, a border region where things, places and lifestyles are changing form, and where the architectural elaboration is open to a study of forms and contents suited to the characteristics of today's mobile and contradictory society. It is a region that is increasingly a place of transit and the formulation of different ideas, that are also increasingly found beyond their planning application.

Focusing on the architectural, urban, landscape and cultural development of Ticino, on the architecture of a 'diffuse city' that now stretches from Milan to the St Gotthard, and on the experiences of the society and the architects that create such architecture, *Architecture of Passage* contributes to the more general thinking on the relationship – real, imaginary or often reduced to mere cliché – between architecture and identity: personal, cultural, local, global.

Although architecture does not have juvenile or senile values, only those of good or bad quality, architects and society cannot avoid their own time and place. And now, at this time of apparent widespread interconnection and knowledge, it is becoming fundamental to create new meeting opportunities that go beyond the increasingly stereotyped definitions and identifications lodged around a few key words and creative new expressions, which seem to take in everything and everyone everywhere, but actually cover a persistent simultaneity that is negated or forgotten, but always ready to emerge.

The title of the exhibition *Architecture of Passage* reveals the open nature of all contemporary discourse on architecture.

The transit is primarily Ticino itself as perceived by others: a corridor for going from the north to the south of the Alps; a place that is sometimes seen as the antechamber of the Mediterranean, or the first sign of the North.

The transit is cultural and local. It is the alteration of the social fabric of a powerful place, which has a powerful impact on architecture and on the city being built today.

Finally, the transit is cultural and general. It is that which makes architecture everywhere less easily assimilated directly to clearly local or general ideas, and increasingly the result of personal or group positions.

The aim of *Architecture of Passage* is to stimulate ongoing reflection on the specific nature and similarities of designing and doing architecture by means of a constantly updated display of architecture videos and project-related posters, direct confrontation of targeted dialogue and a composite, open publication.

Alberto Alessi

Architecture of Passage. Perspectives on architecture from Ticino

ISR - Spazio Culturale Svizzero di Venezia

CURATOR
Alberto Alessi

SCIENTIFIC CONTRIBUTIONS
Alberto Dell'Antonio
Gian Paolo Torricelli
Roman Hollenstein

WEBSITE
www.istitutosvizzero.it

EXHIBITORS
Arassociati, Milan
Andrea Bassi, Geneve
Buzzi e Buzzi, Locarno
Durisch+Nolli, Lugano
Luca Gazzaniga, Lugano
Giraudi – Wettstein, Lugano

1

2

3

4

5

6

1
Andrea Bassi,
School complex in Ouches,
Geneve.
PHOTO BY LAURENCE BONVIN, GENEVE.

2
Buzzi e Buzzi,
Cubic landscape n. 2,
Tegna.

3
Arassociati,
Villa in Cagliari.
PHOTO BY DESSÌ&MUNARI, CAGLIARI.

4
Luca Gazzaniga,
Casino of Lugano.

5
Durisch+Nolli,
maxMuseum,
Chiasso.
PHOTO BY GIANPAOLO MINELLI.

6
Giraudi-Wettstein,
"Terraces" house,
Lugano.
PHOTO BY GASTON WICKY.

The first *Celebration of cities* international consultation, launched in 2004 by the President of the International Union of Architects (UPA), Jaime Lerner, invited architects and students of architecture to imagine 'urban acupuncture' operations that would remedy the imbalances and fractures from which all the cities of the world suffer and that would, at the same time, have a positive effect on their development.

This consultation met with such success that the International Union of Architects decided to renew the experience. Once again, architects and students of architecture were invited to participate in an urban democracy process to improve living conditions in cities by inventing the humanism of the third millennium: knowledge, awareness, sharing and solidarity. This initiative received the patronage of UNESCO and is part of the co-operation programme between the UIA and the United Nations Human Settlements Programme, UN-HABITAT.

Attractive, Welcoming, Mobility

The aim of this competition is to develop three orientations that can engender positive transformations in the city:

- Make the city attractive and welcoming:

Attractive for everyone by multiplying the opportunities to increase the citizens' well-being; Welcoming for both inhabitants and visitors: entertaining, pleasant, healthy, accessible and convivial.

- Highlight mobility by inventing efficient and harmonious solutions for urban and suburban transport that fully respect the environment.

The procedure was entirely organized on the Internet, at the national and then international level, fully respecting competitors' anonymity and UIA-UNESCO regulations for international competitions in architecture and town planning.

The competition was organized by the CNAPPC (Consiglio Nazionale Architetti, Planificatori, Paesaggisti e Conservatori), UIA Italian Section, in association with the Italian magazine l'ARCA.

The International Union of Architects

The UIA is a federation of professional architectural organizations in 117 countries and represents more than 1,400,000 architects around the world – an unrivalled professional network. Amongst its many missions in favour of professionals and the quality of the architectural environment, the UIA guarantees the exemplary nature of international competitions, such as those that preceded the construction of such landmark buildings as: the Sydney Opera House, the Georges Pompidou Centre in Paris, the Tokyo International Forum and the Alexandria Library, Egypt.

Periodically, the UIA associates students of architecture and professionals by launching vast consultations on themes of major international interest, such as the *Celebration of Cities*.

Gaétan Siew

Celebration of cities 2: an idea for the city

UIA - International Union of Architects

CURATORS
Gaetan Siew
Giancarlo Ius

TELECOMMUNICATION AND ORGANIZATIONAL SUPPORT
Consiglio Nazionale degli Architetti, Pianificatori, Paesaggisti e Conservatori - CNAPPC
Istituto di cultura architettonica - ICAR

WITH THE SUPPORT OF
Coordinamento degli Ordini degli Architetti delle Province del Veneto, Friuli Venezia Giulia, Trento e Bolzano

SPONSOR
Kos
Illuminazione Lucifero's
Crassevig

EXHIBITION DESIGN
Roberto Palomba

WEBMASTER
Mario Caruso

WEBSITES
www.uiatv.org
www.uia-architectes.org

EXHIBITORS
This competition, Celebration of cities 2: *an idea for the city*, has adjudicated anonymously the prices and mentions in Vancouver chosen between the projects selected by 37 National Juries.
The first best 40 projects are exposed.

1

2

3

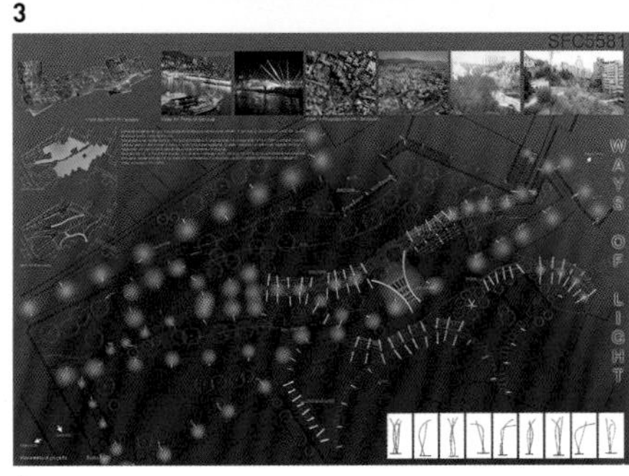

4

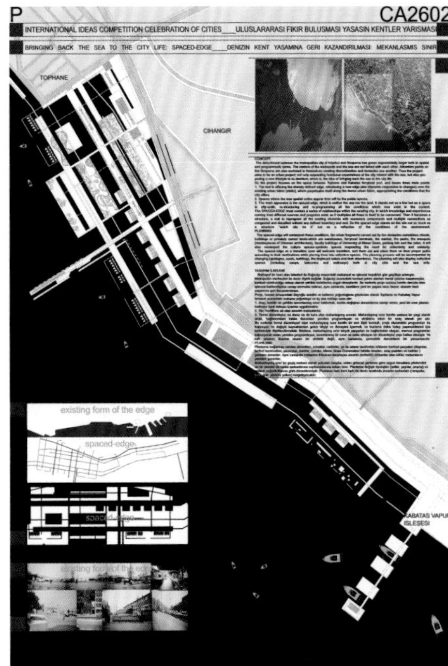

5

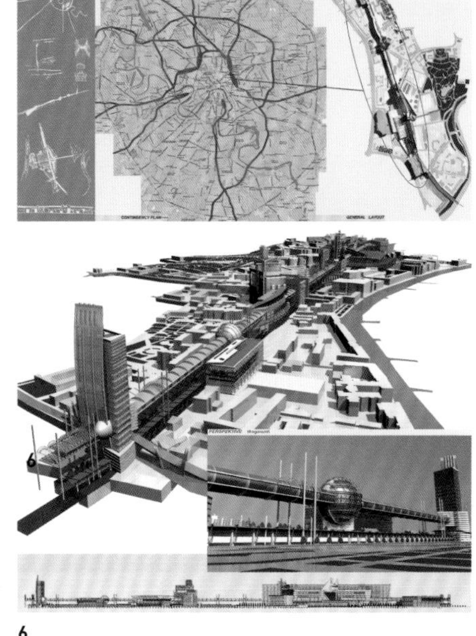

6

7

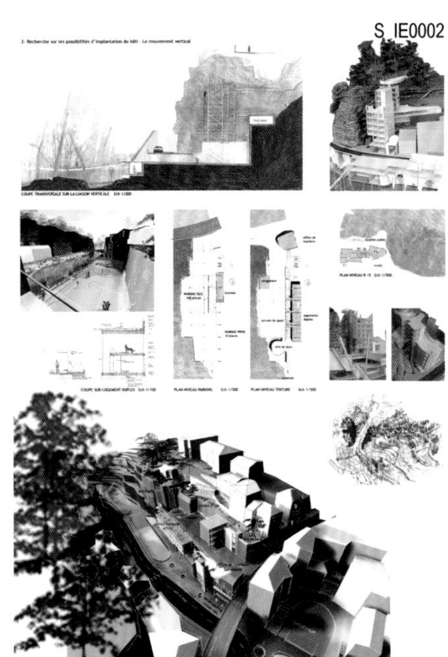

8

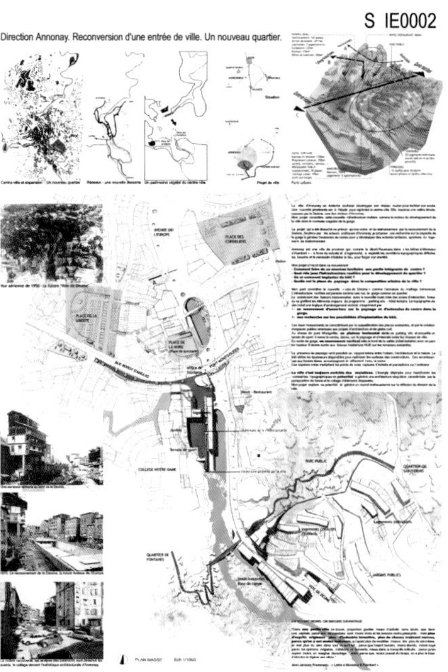

9

1-2
International Grandprix, Category architects, Maurizio Marzi and others,
Reuniting Milan.

3
Regional Grandprix, Category architects, Joe Verons and others,
A line of urban handwriting.

4
Mention, Categoria architects, Ali Ozer,
Sea and shore.

5
Mention, Category architects, Victor Zoubkov and others,
A central metropolitan axis.

6
International Grandprix, Category students, Francesca Puddu, Cinzia Pucciarelli and others,
The paths of light.

7
Regional Grandprix, Category students, Gerard Lynch and others,
Mobsta mobile station.

8-9
Mention, Category students, Julien Rouby and others,
Reconversion of the city's entrance new community.

The *CZ_VPI2006* project is a multi-intentional exhibition event with three dimensions:
- a *communicative-associative dimension*: performances, concerts, multimedia and interactive events encouraging rich reflection, a chance to meet and share the main social, town planning and cultural themes of city living;
- an *installation dimension*: of powerful environmental-urban impact through the reconfiguration and upgrading of the covered spaces at CZ (outside, terrace, garden, access);
- a *cultural-interactive dimension*: interactive illustration of themes and projects on the urban environment, city art, the environmental and ecosystemic impact of urban society; promotion of forums and virtual debates to raise public awareness on themes of urban community, the local body and the shared city space.

CZ_VPI2006 is divided into four sections developing the following themes: 'metacity', town planning, sustainability and recycling. The CZ cultural centre aims to draw visitors closer to the concrete themes of creating architecture and creating the 'landscape' in an urban context – not easy in some respects – such as the Giudecca in Venice, ideally by speaking directly with the populace. It is presented as the initial generator of courageous, open, creative discourse between the various parties involved (inhabitants, artists, academic institutes, local bodies), offering possibly permanent urban upgrading solutions.

Cultural-interactive section organized by Massimo Caiazzo with Gruppo Valpadana Costruzioni. Coordinator of BBAA Verona students' works: Sebastiano Zanetti. Video production: Peppe Bellucci, Salvatore Giannone, Peppe Pillone.
This section will illustrate some urban upgrading works in Verona and Naples using photographic panels, rendering and computer images. It features in particular *The new perception of colour*, a synaesthetic installation conceived to also become an original stage set for concerts, performances and seminars.

Outdoor video and installation section organized by Luigi Viola
The show presents ten installations in the CZ's outdoor spaces by young artists invited to consider the theme of the 'metacity': a fractal, atomized, accelerated city.

Communicative-associative section organized by Mauro Arrighi
The exhibition proposal is on two levels:
1. a series of performances (audio/video production in real time);

CZ_VPI2006 Centro Zitelle: Video Performances & Interactive Street Art

ESU di Venezia

IN COLLABORATION WITH
Accademia di Belle Arti di Venezia
Accademia di Belle Arti di Verona

CURATORS
Luigi Viola
Mauro Arrighi
Maurizio Zennaro
Massimo Caiazzo
Guglielmo Di Mauro

CONCEIVING AND ARTISTIC DIRECTION
Carlo Damiani
Monica Maschio
Alessandra Guida
Massimo Caiazzo

WORKSHOP SCIENTIFIC COORDINATOR
Pierluigi Sacco
(with the collaboration of Eclettica and Gruppo A12)

CULTURAL CONSULTANT OF THE "LA NUOVA PERCEZIONE DEL COLORE"
Raffaele Cardone

LIGHT PROJECT
Marco Rizzuto

SPONSOR
Valpadana Costruzioni srl

WITH THE CONTRIBUTION OF
Urban Italia "Apriamo i Muri", Venezia
Assicurazioni Generali spa – Generali Vita spa
Vesta spa, Venezia
AMT Verona
Pasqua Vigneti e Cantine
Galerie Drytone Moretti, Parigi
Italcopy S.a.s., Trieste
Galleria "Spazio Arte dei Mori", Venezia
Nono Risorto, Venezia
Grafiche Nava, Milano
Weingut Prinz von Hessen
Claus Ungelenk
Paolo Casti

EXHIBITORS
Outdoor video and installation section
Michele Bazzana
Primoz Bizjak
Marilia Dimopoulou
Minerva Dominguez
Giorgia Fincato
Paola Ganz
Mario Tomè
Angeliki Tsotsoni
Mei Yuan Chen
Repetitive Strain Injury
Aggregating communicative section
Mauro Arrighi
Mario Tomè
Marco Donnarumma
Andrea Gastaldi
Leonardo Boldrin
Serena Borgatello
Riccardo Zuliani
Marco Buziol
Martin Emilian Balint
Adriano Nasuti Wood
Art & Environment section
Barbara Grossato
Simona Granziero
Gianluca Sanvido
Project Cantine Pasqua
Ludovico Bomben
Stefano Buro
Tommaso Carozzi
Matia Chincarini
Alessandro Lorenzini
Lucia Amalia Maggio
Gabriele Soave
Chiara Zizioli
Multimedia synaesthesias section
Gruppo Proxima
Andrea Penzo
Riccardo Venturi
Gruppo Sinestetico
Enzo Pituello
Emiliano Bazzanella
Fabio Fornasier
Emilio e Franca Morandi

1

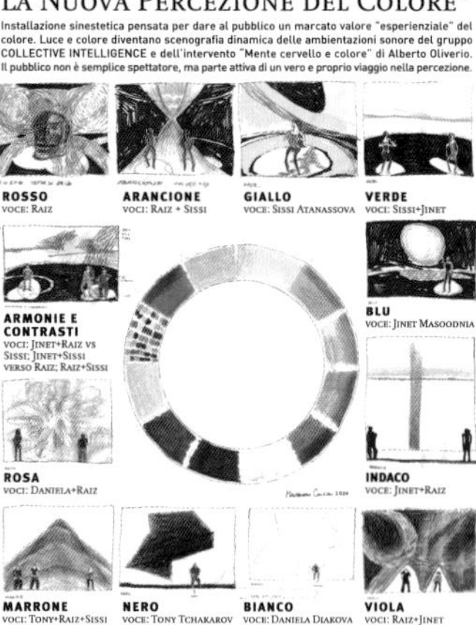

2

2. interactive installation and video-installation works.
The city appears as a sentient, self-conscious organism in all the works presented.
The sounds, colours and the 'biological' clock of this simil-organism become the raw material for the works.

Art & Environment section organized by Maurizio Zennaro
This section intends investigating/illustrating the eco-systemic impact of a new creative approach to reclamation and environmental respect, aimed at a creative review of the concept of recycling, or the search for new, original ways to conceive of home furnishings.

Multimedia-installation synaesthesias
by Guglielmo Di Mauro
A production of performance techniques and installations with a high sensory impact intended to highlight aspects related to our daily life lead the user to sensory participation in a game, at times ironic, allowing the surrounding reality to be seen through different eyes. Some parts of the multimedia section reveal the aspect related to use of the real where the virtual is placed in symbiosis with daily urban spaces.
Monica Maschio, Alessandra Guida, Carlo Damiani, Massimo Caiazzo

3

4

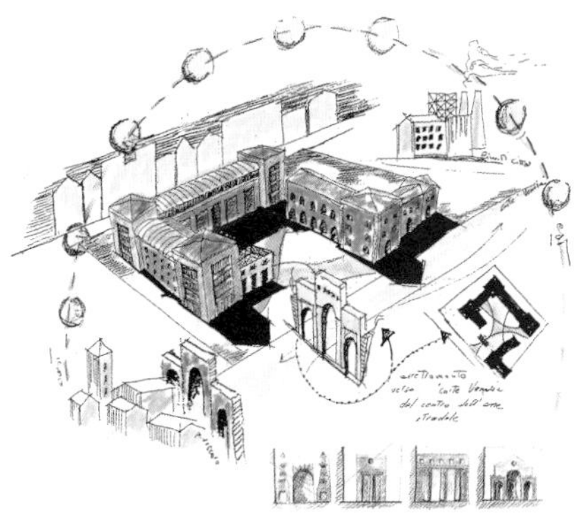
5

6

7

8

1
Campo Venezia,
Accademia Cignaroli of Verona, artistic interventions curated by Sebastiano Zanetti and old part of the ex-convent Cantine Pasqua. Work "Il Piano Alfa" by Stefano Buro.

2
The new perception of colour.
Synestethic installation made by Gruppo Collective Intelligence. Coproduction: Paolo Giulini. Sound: Paolo Coggiola Triggerz

3
Mitochondria.
Audio/video performance by Mauro Arrighi and Andrea Gastaldi.

4
Time turtle.
Interactive video installation by Mauro Arrighi and Emilian Balint with Mario Tomè, Riccardo Zuliani, Marco Buziol.

5
Campo Venezia,
Verona, Ex Cantine Pasqua, sketch of the project.
Project: Massimo Caiazzo, Amelia Scutellaro, Valeriano Benetti, Barbara Migliorini, Alessandro Delle Molle. (Clients: Valpadana Costruzioni - Gruppo Zampini).

6
Mei Yuan Chen,
CZ Garden Project,
2006

7
Primoz Bizjak,
Venice,
2006

8
Sebastiano Zanetti,
The meta city,
2006. Red ink on wall-window. Variable dimensions.

The phenomenon of *favela* – in the multitude of forms in which it presents itself in different parts of the world – is an event that involves, today, a billion people and that will affect two billion in the short span of a couple of decades.
The exhibition aims to offer the viewer an approach to understanding this expanding universe of *favelas* – leaving aside any humanitarian or sociological considerations – by following the model suggested by traditional scientific research which combines practical experience with theoretical analysis.

This practical phase of research, conducted by the architect Giulia Foscari, who visited and studied Brazilian *favelas*, was essential to comprehend that the actual nature of *favela* does not allow any possibility of synthesis. The reality of a *favela* is essentially a collection of fragments – assembled through the challenges of daily life with a high level of unpredictability – that are loosely connected only by reciprocal local interactions.

As a result of this inherent difficulty of reducing the phenomenon of a *favela* to a single vision, Giulia Foscari's report concentrated at this first stage on offering the reader multiple approaches as well as observations of behavioural and architectural detail.

However, the study of these fragments led to research a broader architectural theme: that the methods of construction within a *favela* are founded on principles of assemblage that are similar to procedures of composition proposed by some contemporary architects, as an alternative – if not even in opposition – to the rational procedures of modern architecture.

One could say that certain contemporary architects – whether consciously or not – have adopted from *favela* particular techniques, which would suggests that the *favela* could be seen as prophecies of contemporary society or, vice versa, that contemporary society is a metaphor for *favela*.

That is to say, that the reality of dense urban settlements such as *favelas* presents greater proximity to contemporary architecture's bottom-up approach – spanning complexity theory, emergent systems, parametric design – than to modern architecture's linear top-down design.

The above realization formed the starting point for the second – or theoretical – phase of research conducted by Giulia Foscari in collaboration with three other architects Arturo Lyon, Kristof Crolla and Marc Boles, in the context of the Master programme *Design Research Laboratory* at the Architectural Association of London, under the critical supervision of the architect Patrik Schumacher.

This phase focused on the analysis of underlying rules of natural emergent systems (which one could argue are similar to the assembly of human beings within a *favela*) as a starting point for developing new urban growth strategies able to address population densification in metropolitan settlements.

The design proposal, presented by the four architects (Sugar Inc.) in this exhibition, consists of a high-rise, three dimensional urban mesh that offers a counter model to urban sprawl, by allowing the absorption over time of population growth in London through a radical ground to volume relationship.

The project is based on the development of digital technologies that create a parametrically driven, smart environment in which, as the population increases, a spatially differentiated model grows over time by adapting and responding to local conditions.

From Favelas to Parametric Cities
Ikona Photo Gallery

CURATOR
Živa Kraus

WEBSITE
www.ikonavenezia.com

EXHIBITORS
Giulia Foscari W.R.
with Sugar Inc.

1

2

3

4

1
Giulia Foscari W.R.,
Vende-Se,
Sao Paulo, 2004.
2
Giulia Foscari W.R.,
Rocinha,
Rio de Janeiro, 2004.

3
Giulia Foscari W.R.,
Barraco,
Sao Paulo, 2004.
4
Sugar Inc,
Diagram of extreme density for London,
2006. Rendering.

Habitar Portugal is a selection of works by Portuguese architects built between 2003 and 2005. The architecture is seen as a way of inhabiting a town, living in the collective space, creating the conditions for daily life. The exhibition offers a portrait of Portugal based on its architecture: objects scattered around a land where the same architecture may be done by non-architects and the price of land drives an imperfect and opaque economy; where these works become anchors of improvement and self-esteem, and at the same time starting points for a sustainable and distinctive land.

The *Habitar Portugal* project is an initiative of the Ordem dos Arquitectos that is repeated every three years with the aim of selecting a sample of 80 works. It may be considered an observatory of architecture that provides a picture of what is built, when, how and by whom. It is a demonstration of the potential and importance of architecture, of what it represents in different geographical, cultural, economic, social and functional contexts; it is a process of approaching architecture itself, which reveals what is closest to each member of the public, from Lisbon to Porto, from Faro to Vila Real de Trás-os-Montes. It is a family album, page by page, portrait by portrait.

The presentation conceived specifically for the Biennale di Venezia is a selection made from this group of works reproducing part of the world of Portuguese architecture – from the small to the grand project, from the single family home to the public space: a geo-referential map, a vision obtained from a first approach to continental Portugal and its islands. It is selective but global, a single image made up of different identities.

Habitar Portugal 2003-2005

Ordem dos Arquitectos

Instituto das Artes

COMMISSIONER
José António Bandeirinha

COORDINATORS
Ana Vaz Milheiro
João Afonso
Manuel Henriques

EXHIBITION DESIGN
ReD|Research+Design – Marta Malé-Alemany, José Pedro Sousa

COORDINATION IN VENICE
Arte Communications

SPONSOR
MAPEI, LusoMapei sa

WEBSITES
www.arquitectos.pt
www.iartes.pt/bienalveneza2006

1

2

3

4

5

6

7

8

9

1
Álvaro Siza Vieira,
"Terraços de Bragança" residential complex,
Lisbon.
PHOTO BY JOSÉ MANUEL RODRIGUES.

2
Fernando Távora and José Bernardo Távora,
Restoration of Freixo Palace,
Porto.
PHOTO BY LUÍS FERREIRA ALVES.

3
Gonçalo Byrne and João Pedro Falcão de Campos,
Area surrounding the Monastery of Saint Mary of Alcobaça,
Alcobaça.
PHOTO BY JOSÉ MANUEL RODRIGUES.

4
Manuel Graça Dias + Egas José Vieira and Gonçalo Afonso Dias,
Almada Town Theatre (Teatro Azul).
PHOTO BY ANTÓNIO PEDRO FERREIRA.

5
Manuel Graça Dias + Egas José Vieira and Gonçalo Afonso Dias,
Almada Town Theatre (Teatro Azul).
PHOTO BY FRANCISCO COSTA.

6
Paulo David,
"Casa das Mudas" - Art Center,
Madeira.

7
Paulo David,
"Casa das Mudas" - Art Center,
Madeira.

8
Eduardo Souto Moura,
City Stadium,
Braga.
PHOTO BY LUÍS FERREIRA ALVES.

9
Eduardo Souto Moura,
City Stadium,
Braga.
PHOTO BY CHRISTIAN RICHTERS.

Any perception of space and society requires some kind of embodiment in the environment. Given the human body as a sensual organism, we are creating instruments that define our immediately given territories of perception through feedback loops with society in general and with specific sites. Through the experience of these complex territories spaces are established by contemporary meaning, always shifted by moments of consciousness in a constant redefinition of space from sensual inputs.

This embodiment is highly affected by means of technological influence and the experiences of the human body, which are increasingly affected by digital networks and unforeseen influences. The project rises from the ambiguity of meaning and the multiple dynamics of a current society of change, generating a sensual environment as a basis for a livable point in space extending the territories of perception.

The NoRA-project by Architecture & Design, Aalborg University, Denmark, for Food College Denmark explores the soft spaces occurring by people moving through an architecture affected by sensual inputs as in constant feedback with society.

The Venice Biennale is a symptom of a potential cultural dynamism where innovative aspects of the Biennale theme will be enlightened by staging human behaviour and by dynamic multiplicity reaching above finite totality. Therefore the visitors of the Biennale are invited to exploit the pavilion and to engage in the exhibited projects presenting future city developments, design and food from Northern Denmark and Skagen. The projects should be seen as an experimental basis emphasizing the relation between cities, architecture, design and society.

The territorial basis focuses on establishing a personal experience of these relations in an attractive event setting. The project sets out directions for the urban condition, not to evolve from pre-conditions of function and aesthetics, but to evolve from the interactions between inhabitants and activities, hence involving dynamic generative fields between local site constraints, cultural dynamics and cross-spatial events.

The pavilion involves cultural input from the visitors to direct future design processes for architecture and urban design, and through the experimental environment it redefines the territories of urban reality.

Specifically, the urban systems of culinary cultural productions inject space as direct sensual phenomena to engage visitors in social urban settings, as well as

NoRA - Nordic Research Application

Department of Architecture & Design, Aalborg University, Denmark

PROJECT CURATOR
Anna Marie Fisker

PROJECT ARCHITECT
Claus Bonderup

PROJECT MANAGER
Bo Stjerne Hansen

PAVILION PROJECT TEAM
Allan Nørregaard Pedersen
Anders Dam
Anders Deleuran
Anja Humljan
Erinch Malkondu
Esben Poulsen
Henrik Rubek Mortensen
Jeffrey David Serio
Joseph Tornabell
Kristian Bjerre Kistorp
Mads B. Jensen
Mads Dines Petersen
Marie Frier
Søren Alfang
Tenna Doktor Olsen
Food College Denmark

PROJECT CONSULTANTS
Per Mandrup, Culinary Institute of Denmark
Hans Kiib, Aalborg University
Poul Henning Kirkegaard, Aalborg University
Rasmus Lund Jensen, Aalborg University

COORDINATION IN VENICE
M+B Studio
Daniela Murgia
Troels Bruun
Luca Delise
Ines Tolic
Francesco Steffinlongo

SPONSORS
Vækstforum
Food College Denmark
Department of Architecture & Design, Aalborg University
Aalborg University

WEBSITE
www.aod.aau.dk/arkitekturbiennale

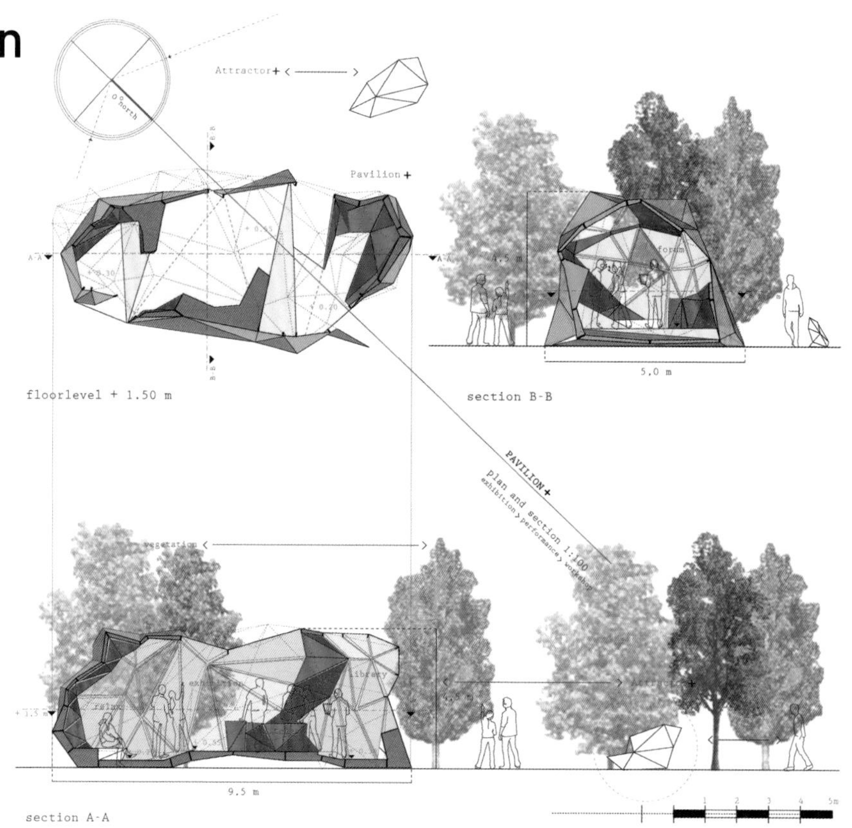

1

staging the process of a common approach to sustainable architecture, urban development and experimental performative environments.

The university and students engage in the Biennale by developing concepts for design, architecture and urban design with current projects, research programmes and food experiments from Northern Denmark and Skagen in a continuous interaction with the visitors.

The research and educational sections of the department of Architecture & Design, Aalborg University, Denmark, work within the fields of Architecture, Urban Design, Digital Design and Industrial Design, emphasizing the implementation of technical competences. The project is developed and built using modern design technologies and kept always vibrant and lively through real-time sensor-technology. The students are carrying out projects in group work emphasizing problem based learning and creative organizations, participating in interdisciplinary design scenarios in close collaboration with professional corporations and organizations.

A University department of Architecture and Design raises issues of creating vibrant open-minded design experiments, which pose questions for the cultural diversity of the biennale visitors and reflect current urban challenges.

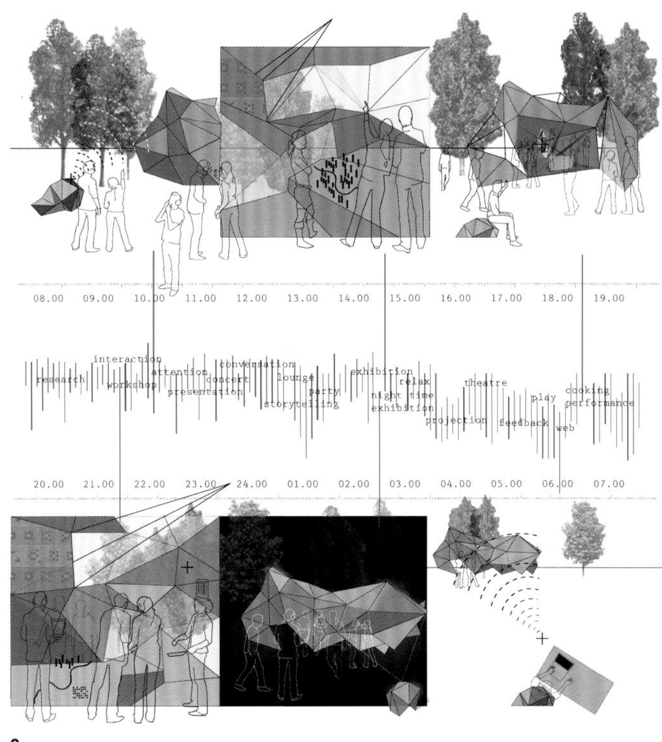

2

3

1
Plan and section.
2
Activity diagram.
3
NoRa perspective.

Taiwan's modern cities show the contrast between the large metropolises and small townships that were formed during the industrialization of the last century. Traditions, beliefs and social systems that people relied on in agricultural societies collapsed with industrial growth: farming villages were evacuated and cities swelled. Imbalance has become the destiny of modern civilization; high-rise buildings symbolise not only our worship of technology but also the consequence of large systems annexing small systems.

The magnetism of metropolises and desertion of rural villages are the results of the relationship between capital and labour in the industrial age. A self-sufficient country with a complete cycle of production-consumption-decomposition in communities with a population in the thousands no longer exists. Instead, the new hyper cities are universalizing diversity.

A small, self-sufficient city with a complete cycle of food, energy, waste and information would be able to face the individual needs of its people, and develop an autonomous organic entity with a sustainable metabolism. Such a city would be able to co-exist inside or outside any Meta-city.

We call such a city a MicroCity.

A MicroCity is also an adapted city. While many developing countries are blindly pursuing huge cities, we should rethink the connotations of city life, the inequality between upper and lower structures and how disadvantageous, exploited cities can break away from their destiny. Furthermore, how can a city find its real position given the difficult ecological, social and ethical situation?

The aim of our exhibition is to reflect on the price our environment has paid for our comfort and convenience; on what the conventional cultural, social, moral and religious structures are losing to the emergence of a giant, singular, universal, global system.

Roan Ching-yueh

Paradise Revisited: Micro Cities & Non-Meta Architecture in Taiwan

National Taiwan Museum of Fine Arts

COMMISSIONER
Lin Jeng-yi

ASSISTANT COMMISSIONERS
Paolo De Grandis
Wang Wan-ju
Shih Shu ping

CURATOR
Roan Ching-yueh

ASSISTANT CURATOR
Enta Yang

COORDINATION IN VENICE
Arte Communications

WEBSITE
www.tmoa.gov.tw

EXHIBITORS
Hsieh Ying-chun
Huang Sheng-yuan
Liu Kuo-chang and Casagrande Laboratory
3RW Architects

1

2

3

4

5

6

7

8

1
Liu Kuo-chang,
Blue Print,
Tainan, Taiwan, 2002.
2
Liu Kuo-chang,
Fishing Tools Warehouse,
Tainan, Taiwan, 2005

3
Huang Sheng-yuan,
I-Lan Rail Station Plaza,
I-Lan, Taiwan, 2002.
4
Huang Sheng-yuan,
Social Welfare Building,
I-Lan,Taiwan, 2000.

5
Huang Sheng-yuan,
Jiaosi Household Registration Office,
I-Lan, Taiwan, 2001.
6
Huang Sheng-yuan,
Sanshing Performance Pavilion,
I-Lan, Taiwan 2003.

7
Hsieh Ying-chun,
Lan Cow Village Farmers' Housing,
Henan Province, China.
8
Hsieh Ying-chun,
Lan Cow Village Farmers' Housing,
Henan Province, China.

The city of Belgrade must once more define its role in the macro Balkan-European sphere of interests and in a global world market, an emporium. Today it is a potential, tomorrow an input; a field of investment that is the reason for considering its matrix provisionally, as a transition process. Its main merit is its discontinuity. Formed on a border of different cultures and influences, its matrix has been erased and revived for centuries. That is the nature of high-potential cities: to be able to transform structural bias into multiple reflections so they seem open to each input. Our focus is on the practically unused and intact resource of Belgrade rivers and central island, and on developing the circulation and reorganization of the city matrix: connections over the rivers and the redevelopment of new areas. Overlapping in one future centre is designed to overcome the temporary eccentric and disarranged city core. Finally, this multidisciplinary project is intended to rationalize growth, with great emphasis on economics.

Three regions that are naturally shaped by the Danube and Sava river extensions are formally called 'Belgrade', but each develops separately. In the formal play of rivers there is a big island with its own identity that reflects the complexity of the city as its geographical centre. It brings together all the external influences that make the island an empty space of the city and give it its identity. It is the main focus of this project: its implosion and the process of growth.
Aleksandar Janković

Project Belgrade: Transition-ism

Project Belgrade

COMMISSIONER
Aleksandar Janković

CO-CURATOR
Vladimir Jovanović

COLLABORATORS
Project Belgrade
Multidisciplinary Team

COORDINATORS
Zlatan Jusufović
Milos Milovanović

COORDINATION IN VENICE
Arte Communications

SPONSORS
The City Council
of Belgrade
Belgrade Land
Development Public
Agency

WEBSITE
www.projekatbeograd.com

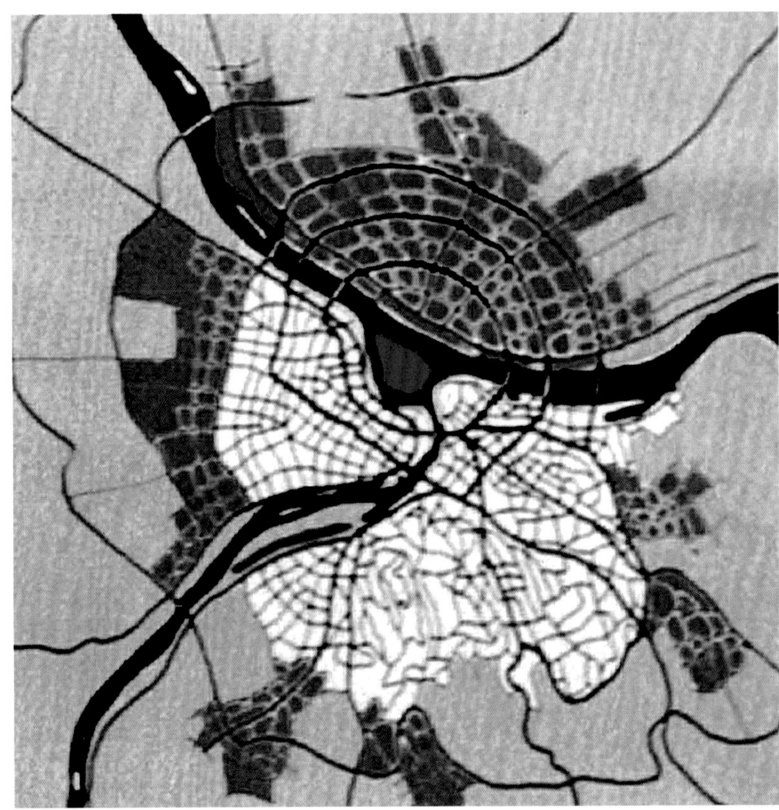

P:BG
STD
V:06

.. the **city of belgrade** is our motive .. it is a future **brand** .. a symbol of change .
. a dynamic emporium .... an enormous potential that inspires our work ....
. .

.. we claim that **multi-culturality/multi-identity** produced chaos is an adventage of our city in the future and we use that as an important parameter in creating our visions ..
.. therefore as it's medium we aim to represent **a new age** of belgrade's architecture that is yet to come .. in this manner **p:bg** grows into a certain **movement/**a system of young people who wish to rebuild the standards and the level of residence culture ..
.... we bring **tendencies** and we propose **new program of global city development** ....
. we are creating **new bg:id** . new definition ..
. our main goal is a system of new values/a doctrine/**standards** ..
.. we form term **transition.ism** as a factor of common aesthetic formulation and as a symbol of what belgrade is today ..

. . . .

.... main focus of our project is on upgrowth **strategy of evolution** into the form of future centre of **grand city island** and it's extension on **waterfront** ....
. we use this impuls . this intact resource in our **multi-disciplinary flavoured research** and we strive to speed up the process/rhythm of city's ineer-translation ....
.. **this island is it's heart** . an absorb of energy from where it's next de-materialised matrix/shape comes out ..
.. it is mental/physical connection of three city's fragments ..
. **point of intersections** that reflects total complexity of our city .

. . . .

.... the time has come that belgrade reveals into it's final form . **metazoan** ..
.. to generate it's **future centre** and to achieve it's **final spatial distribution** ..
.. it will become a multi-dimensional conglomerate amenably to a **mechanism of flexible market** ..
. .
.. city of belgrade is a project now .. **www.projekatbeograd.com** ..

Urbanpromo is an urban and district marketing event intended to promote awareness of the town planning, economic and environmental feasibility of transformation projects, improving the quality of the planning and design processes, and making urban markets more open and competitive.

Urbanpromo was launched in 2004, directed mainly at transformation projects on an urban scale. The 2005 event built on these aims, organizing 32 conferences and seminars at the Palazzo Franchetti over four days, with the participation of 62 companies and organizations, which presented more than 100 projects.

The 2006 version is intended to further reinforce and develop this vital network of relations. The main themes to be looked at are those of most interest to people working in urban transformation and local development:
- strategic planning and district marketing;
- the relationship between infrastructure and locale in plans and policies;
- innovative tools for collaboration between public and private: town planning equalization and compensation, project financing, urban transformation companies;
- programmes for the upgrading and divestment of real estate;
- efficient management of property holdings;
- the relationship between town planning and architectural design;
- energy savings in town planning and building;
- social housing and specialized housing for special categories of user;
- the critical nature of town plans: from reclamations to parking, from social sharing to financing;
- revival of commercial activities in urban transformation projects.

Numerous conferences organized by the INU (Italian town planning institute) and other associations and research institutions are concentrated over five days, along with case presentation seminars, discussions and debates on relevant topical matters.

The main projects for Italian cities, the investment opportunities that are opening up and prominent examples of urban transformation and local development will be displayed in an exhibition featuring panels, models, video screenings, video presentations and personalized environments.

Urbanpromo is organized in association with the specialist magazine *Edilizia e Territorio* (published by "Il Sole 24 Ore"), and includes publication of a dossier sent to 20,000 subscribers explaining the projects and responsibilities of the organizations and companies taking part in the project.

Files on the organizations and companies included in the dossier are available on the website www.urbanpromo.it, along with the press release and other materials useful for participation. Year after year, the site is accumulating an important archive on projects, investments and those involved in urban transformation in Italy.

One of *Urbanpromo's* missions is publication of the results of studies and research carried out on urban transformation and local development. The Urbit technical committee for *Urbanpromo* identifies the projects received that are worthy of promotion and organizes their presentation in agreement with those involved.

Urbanpromo 2006

Città trasformazioni investimenti

INU - Istituto Nazionale di Urbanistica

ORGANIZATIVE COORDINATION
URBIT - Urbanistica Italiana Srl

TECHNICAL COMMITTEE
Stefano Stanghellini
Manuela Ricci
Gastone Ave
Agostino Cappelli
Emilio Erario
Fabio Fiocco
Massimo Giuliani
Sauro Moglie
Simone Ombuen
Marco Pompilio
Iginio Rossi
Francesco Sbetti
Stefano Storchi
Michele Talia

EXHIBITION PROJECT AND GRAPHICS
Carlo Bassetti

COLLABORATORS
Elisa Alfonsi
Valentina Cosmi
Elena Marcat
Francesca Minelli
Marianna Nociforo
Valeria Ruaro

SPONSORS
"Edilizia e Territorio"
Ance - Associazione Nazionale Costruttori Edili
Camera di Commercio, Industria, Artigianato, Agricoltura di Venezia
Fondazione di Venezia

WEBSITES
www.inu.it
www.urbanpromo.it

EXHIBITORS
Many projects, both town planning and infrastructural, will be shown at Urbanpromo2006, made by: Municipalities, Provinces and Regions, agencies and participating societies of public institutions, banks' foundations, real estate promoters, contractors, planners and engineering societies.

saba
35percentro

INU
10 -20 novembre 2004

Displacement relates two contexts with a singular move, possibly architectural

From the Torre dell'Orologio, to the gilded quadriga for the translation of the evangelist, Venice once gained its prosperity by continual displacements. A virtual reflection in late urban history, Hong Kong is confined to being a vigorous laboratory for magnifying this urban tactic, formerly as a colonial state between 1843-1997 and now by the multiple restraints of hyper density, soaring land values and economic competition with other Asian cities. We have continued to challenge slow boundaries, to narrate arguments and to generate values and transactions by alienation, while the city could be read as a fragmented palimpsest being continuously transcribed, transformed, transferred and even transported. There have been the extreme cases of the historic Murray House being displaced stone by stone from our city centre to a beach, a massive airport was displaced overnight in 1997, and we have 'borrowed' Disneyland: a displaced excursion built away from Mainland China but to attract and cater to Mainland Chinese. There is then the infamous Kowloon Walled City, a displaced garrison turned urban village and finally a park of remembrance. We also imported Karaoke in the '80s, a displaced gathering from a friend's living room. But, above all, Hong Kong is a displaced city-state and urban test-bed for China, for instance in our estranged practice of common law and driving on the left-hand side.

Displacement incites resistance and redundancy at times, a synergy of two contexts asks for imagination and calculation. At VICE VERSA, exhibiting parties from plural positions are invited to create displacements and each articulate a thesis in parallel:
- *Double Displacement*, understanding duality and a move back-and-forth. Installation of a dialogue;
- *Formulated Displacement*, restructuring of building element(s) for high-density living;
- *Displacing Identity*, exploration of urban typology through programmatic news;
- *Displacement / Misplacement*, an urban vernacular found and unfolded;
- *Displaced Ground, Displaced (E)motions*, infrastructure superimposes and rejuvenates an aging neighbourhood;
- *Value-added Displacements*, mapping of built ventures and catalysts of displacement;
- *Displacement of Community*, displacing visions, energy and memory via participation;
- *Intertwining Displacements*, displaced common objects for body-engagement and body-direction.

Hostelling hot cash and volatile desires, Hong Kong encompasses displacements of unprecedented scales and different kinds. The presentation at the 10th International Architecture Exhibition is instrumental in imagining new town planning paradigms, tactics and identities for Chinese cities in a global age.

At VICE VERSA, each extrapolates two contexts with a singular move.

Billy Tam, Joshua Lau, Alvin Yip

"VICE VERSA: displacing Acts, Lives & Thresholds of a Hyper City" from Hong Kong, China

Hong Kong Arts Development Council
Hong Kong Institute of Architects

COMMISSIONERS
Fung-kwok Ma
Bernard Wan-fung
V. Lim

ASSISTANT COMMISSIONERS
Peter King-keung Wong
Carolin Suet-yuen Fong

CURATORS
Joshua Lau
Billy Tam
Alvin Yip

WITH THE SUPPORT OF
Home Affairs Bureau, the Hong Kong Special Administrative Region

THANKS TO
Venice Biennale Steering Committee of Hong Kong Institute of Architects

COORDINATION IN VENICE
Arte Communications

WEBSITES
www.hkadc.org.hk
www.hkia.net

EXHIBITORS
CL3 Architects Ltd
Andrew Lee King Fun & Associates Architects Ltd
Rocco Design Ltd
Vito Bertin, Pui-leng Leng Woo, Daqing Gu
Lawrence Liauw Architecture Design and Research Group Ltd
Wallace Chang
The Hong Kong Housing Authority

KVÆRNER
JOINT VENTURE

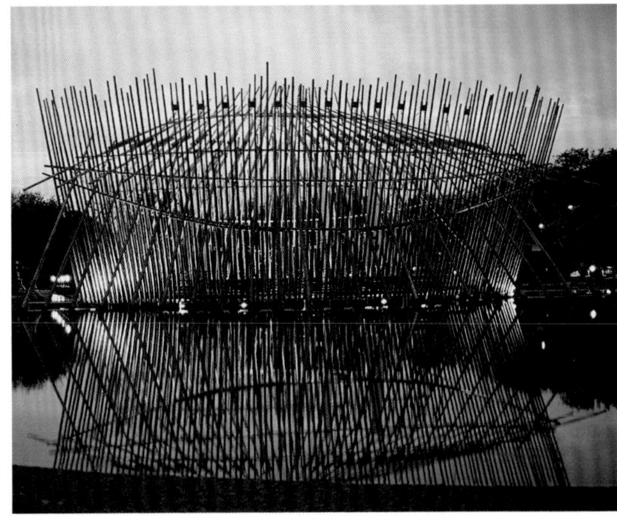

Light on the city

It is said that light is the nervous system of contemporary civilization. A Biennale dedicated to the city and the close links between architecture and society could not but welcome its visitors with a luminous sign. The Info Light Box by Targetti was conceived for this purpose: to welcome them and guide them through the event. Images, videos and performances of chromatic and dynamic light and information relating to the main content of the 10th International Architecture Exhibition will scroll across the sides of this big cube of light, consisting of more than 80,000 leds.

The iridescent structure of the Info Light Box metaphorically takes up the central theme of this Biennale dedicated to the *City. Architecture and Society* by recognizing the indefinable nature and constant mutation of the contemporary metropolis, within which architecture and new technologies play an essential role, especially in terms of relations and communications.

Designed by Pino Brugellis as a highly distinctive architectural element and, at the same time, an innovative vector of multimedia communication, the Info Light Box is a modular structure in steel supporting a translucent external coating in alveolar polycarbonate. The technological innovation of the product lies mainly in the use of hexel™ (hexagonal pixel) technology. This ensures excellent perception of the images at considerable distances and high luminosity compared to traditional screens, despite using a smaller number of pixels. Its main design feature is that it can be connected without any visible join to a potentially unlimited number of modular panels controlled by the same software. This is compatible with all the most widely used graphic programmes and configured in self-supporting structures, highlighting new possibilities in a specifically architectural and multimedia use of light.

The Florentine company, Targetti, has become a synonym for the 'architectural culture of light' around the world thanks to its almost 80 years' experience in the field of architectural lighting. As a partner of the 10th International Architecture Exhibition, it has also installed the lighting for the Italian Pavilion, the Corderie, the Artiglierie, the Tese and the exhibitions in the Palermo section, putting its most innovative products at the disposal of the Biennale. These are the result of constant investments in research and development, for years the highest of any company in the sector.

The partnership with the Biennale di Venezia is part of a policy of investment in the promotion and appreciation of the most innovative expressions of design culture pursued by Targetti for more than a decade through the work of the Fondazione Targetti. This is expressed in a programme of advanced specialization for professionals interested in using light as an architectural building tool (the Lighting Academy) and in a cycle of meetings with the leading exponents of contemporary architectural thinking and procedures (the Osservatorio sull'architettura).

Targetti Info Light Box

PROJECT
Pino Brugellis

ENGINEERING
UT Targetti
(supervision Pio Nahum)

TECHNOLOGY
SmartsLab (design:
Tom Barker, Royal
College of Art, Londra)

VIDEO EDITING
Emiliano Morgia

CONTACTS
Stella Targetti and
Consuelo de Gara

Exhibitors Index

CAPPELLI E RANZO, 150

SERGIO CAPPELLI, 150
Naples, Italy 1948.
Lives and works in Naples, Italy.

TOMMASO CAROZZI, 172
Villafranca, Italy 1977.
Lives and works in Verona, Italy.

LUCIANA CARVALHO PINTO, 52

CASAGRANDE LABORATORY, 180
Marco Casagrande
Purku, Finland 1971.
Lives and works in Taipei, Taiwan and Helsinki, Finland.

CEBRA, 62
Mikkel Frost, Kolja Nielsen, Carsten Primdahl, Anders Lonka, Jacob Ulvsrod Sørensen, Kim Bangsgaard Olesen, Nikolaj Harving, Peter Jørgensen, Peter Neckelmann, Rasmus Andersen
www.cebra.info

WALLACE CHANG, 186

MARIA CHARALAMBIDOU, 110
Kerynia, Cyprus 1969.
Lives and works in Nicosia, Cyprus.

GIOVANNI CHIARAMONTE, 90
Varese, Italy 1948.
Lives and works in Milan, Italy.

MATIA CHINCARINI, 172
Valdagno, Italy 1975.
Lives and works in Verona, Italy.

IZASKUN CHINCHILLA, 126

DAVID CHIPPERFIELD ARCHITECTS, 76
www.davidchipperfield.com

DAVID CHIQOVANI, 74

WOOK CHOI, 112
Lives and works in Seoul, Korea.

CHONGQING UNIVERSITYV, 62
Zhao Wanmin, Wang Jiwu, Zhou Xuehong, Huang Ling, Liu Jianmin, Dai Yan, Li Jin, Huang Yong, Yangqinchuan, Wangjian, Menjiaorong, Fangyu, Zuoxiaojian, Pengweiyin
www.cqu.edu.cn/html/default.htm

MARIOS CHRISTODOULIDES, 110
Nicosia, Cyprus 1970.
Lives and works in Nicosia, Cyprus.

CHRISTOS CHRISTODOULOU, 110
Nicosia, Cyprus 1973.
Lives and works in Nicosia, Cyprus.

CHRYSANTHOS CHRYSANTHOU, 110
Nicosia, Cyprus 1956.
Lives and works in Nicosia, Cyprus.

CL3 ARCHITECTS LTD, 186

GILLES CLÉMENT, 72

COBE, 62
Dan Stubbergaard, Vanessa Miriam Carlow, Caroline Nagel, Kristian Elleby Sundquist, Mads Rudi Lassen, Jakob Nørbjerg Madsen, Mikkel Olsen, Kristine Annabell Torp, Rong Bin, Manon Fantini
www.cobe.dk

MARTÍN CORULLON, 52

SILVIO D'ASCIA, 150
Naples, Italy 1969.
Lives and works in Paris, France.

MARGARITA DANOU, 110
Nicosia, Cyprus 1965.
Lives and works in Nicosia, Cyprus.

FERNANDO DE MELLO FRANCO, 52

DE PAOR ARCHITECTS, 84
www.depaor.com

PAOLA DE PIETRI, 90
Reggio Emilia, Italy 1960.
Lives and works in Reggio Emilia, Italy.

PATRICK DEGEORGES, 72

DELUGAN MEISSL ASSOCIATED ARCHITECTS, 48

IRWIN DICKON, 110
Glasgow, Scotland, UK 1966.
Lives and works in Nicosia, Cyprus.

MARILIA DIMOPOULOU, 172
Born Larissa, Greece 1978.

NIKOLA DOBROVIĆ, 122

DOGMA|OFFICE, 28
Pier Vittorio Aureli
Kersten Geers
Martino Tattara
Sabina Tattara
David Van Severen

MINERVA DOMINGUEZ, 172
Born Guadalajara Jalisco, Mexico 1978.

DOMINIC STEVENS ARCHITECTS, 84

MARCO DONNARUMMA, 172
Naples, Italy 1984.
Lives and works in Milan and Venice, Italy.

ALEKSANDAR ĐORĐEVIĆ, 122

IGOR DROMESKO, 72

JAN DUBOVY, 122

DURISCH+NOLLI, 168
Pia Durisch
Lugano, Switzerland 1964.
Lives and works in Lugano, Switzerland.
Aldo Nolli
Milan, Italy 1959.
Lives and works in Lugano, Switzerland.

STEFAN EBERSTADT, 76

DEJAN EĆIMOVIĆ, 122

EFFEKT, 62
Kristoffer Lindhart Weiss, Sinus Lynge, Tue Foged, Kevin Hviid Nielsen, Maria Ahn Walther, Anders Bergmann, Ditte Bendix Lanng
www.effektdata.dk

CHRISTOPHE EGRET, 80
Paris, France 1959.
Lives and works in London, UK.
www.egretwest.com

GREGOR EICHINGER, 46
Wels, Austria 1956.
Lives and works in Wien, Austria.

PETER EISENMAN, 150
Newark, USA 1932.
Lives and works in New York, USA.

HATEM EL SAID, 64
Il Cairo, Egitto 1973.
Lives and works in Tokyo, Giappone.
www.geocities.com/hatemelsaid

ELASTICO 3, 28
Alberto Del Maschio

ELASTICO SPA, 28
Stefano Pujatti Architetti

ÓLAFUR ELÍASSON, 76, 86
www.olafureliasson.net

EMBT, 126
Enric Miralles
Benedetta Tagliabue

ENCOUNTERS, 80
www.sharrowencounters.org.uk

EPI TESSERA ARCHITECTS, 110

ESTUDIO ENTRESITIO, 126
María Hurtado de Mendoza Wahrolén
César Jiménez de Tejada Benavides

TIM ETCHELLS & HUGO GLENDINNING, 80
www.forcedentertainment.co.uk

EXYZT ARCHITECTURE, 72

FACULTAD DE ARQUITECTURA - UNIVERSIDAD DE LA REPÚBLICA MONTEVIDEO, 134
www.farq.edu.uy

GIUSEPPE FALLACARA, 28

RAMAK FAZEL, 90
Abadan, Iran 1965.
Lives and works in Milan, Italy.

MASSIMO FERRARI, 28

GIORGIA FINCATO, 172
Born Marostica, Italy 1982

FKL ARCHITECTS, 84
www.fklarchitects.com

FLOSUNDK, 76
www.flosundk.de

FABIO FORNASIER, 172

GIULIA FOSCARI, 172
Venezia, Italia, 1980.
Lives and works in London, UK.

VITTORE FOSSATI, 90
Alessandria, Italy 1954.
Lives and works in Alessandria, Italy.

FOSTER AND PARTNERS, 144
Norman Foster
Manchester, UK 1935.
Lives and works in London, UK.

ARKKITEHTISTUDIO KIMMO FRIMAN, 70
Kimmo Friman

TERUNOBU FUJIMORI, 78
Nagano, Japan 1946.
Lives and works in Tokyo, Japan.

MASSIMILIANO FUKSAS, 150
Rome, Italy 1944.
Lives and works in London, UK, and Rome, Italy.

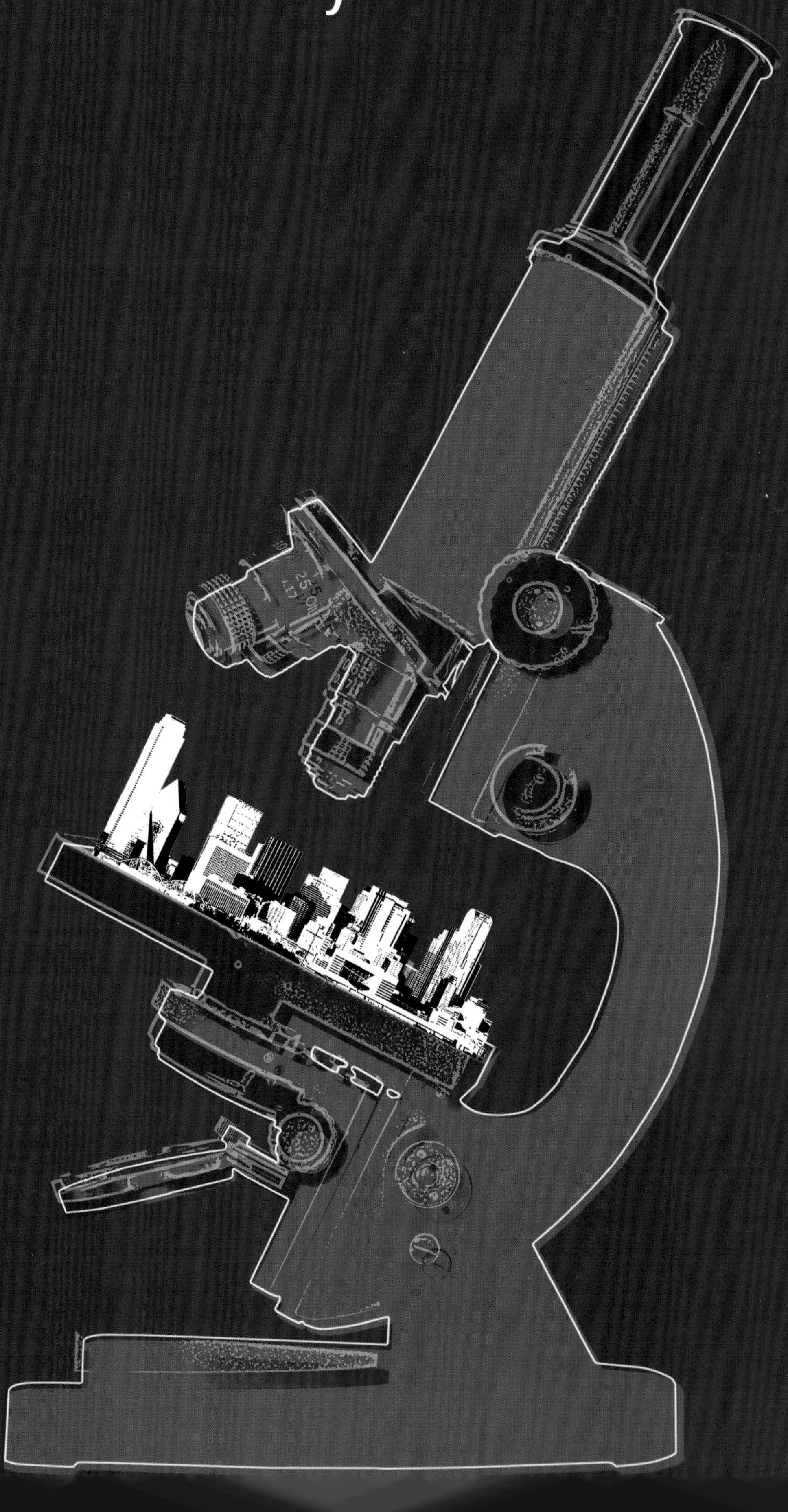

Printed by
Offset Print Veneta - Verona
for Marsilio Editori® s.p.a. in Venice

edizione	year
10 9 8 7 6 5 4 3 2 1	2006 2007 2008 2009 2010